PARIS NIGHTS

And other
Impressions of Places and People

With an Essay from
Arnold Bennett
By F. J. Harvey Darton

By

ARNOLD BENNETT

With Illustrations By

E. A. RICKARDS

First published in 1913

British Library Cataloguing-in-Publication Data
A catalogue record for this book is available
from the British Library

CONTENTS

3

THE RIVIERA
1907

FONTAINEBLEAU
1904-1909

SWITZERLAND
1909-1911

ENGLAND AGAIN
1907

THE MIDLANDS
1910-1911

THE BRITISH HOME
1908

STREETS, ROADS AND TRAINS
1907-1909

ILLUSTRATIONS

THE INDUSTRIOUS APPRENTICE

An Excerpt From
Arnold Bennett
By F. J. Harvey Darton

By a custom not unusual among authors, Arnold Bennett has re- nounced one gift of his godparents. It may be a mere perversion of modesty; or it may be one of those practical, insidious attacks on the pubic memory which lead to the stereotyping of such labels as Henry Irving or Hall Caine: whatever the cause, the novelist of the Five Towns has sloughed a name. He was christened Enoch Arnold Bennett. Which noted, the first name may be left to resemble its first holder, of whom we are told that he " was not."

Arnold Bennett came into the world on 27th May 1867. On the same day of the same year was born the Card, Edward Henry Machin, and in the same year the nuptials of the Bursley old wives, Constance Povey and Sophia Scales (nèes Baines), were celebrated. This exact chronological parallel between creator and created is hardly of profound significance, but it is one of a number of minor coincidences of the kind.

"The town which had the foresight to bear me, and which is going to be famous on that score"—a cheerful piece of mock egotism from *The Truth about an Author*— was, more strictly, the district of Shelton, north-east of Hanley, in "The Five Towns" or Potteries. It is obvious that that whole region made an indelible impression on the young Arnold Bennett. He was evidently very sensitive to early impressions, and the minuteness of the local descriptions in the Five Towns novels reflects his extraordinary boyish receptivity. He says of the Baines' s shop,

9

for instance—the scene of much of *The Old Wive's Tale*—*that* "in the seventies, I had lived in the actual draper's shop, and knew it as only a child could know it." He remembered also the sound of rattling saucepans when he was about two or three, and "a very long and mysterious passage that led to a pawnshop all full of black bundles." These are unexciting details, but they suggest that strange process of unconscious assimilation of environment during youth which so many authors transmute in later days into the fabric of life.

Arnold Bennett clearly discovered the solace of literature, in any real sense, after his school days were over, and it may perhaps be concluded that on the whole he received in youth little vital encouragement towards letters. It was not intended that the polite profession of writing was to furnish him with the bread and butter of life, much less the cakes and ale. Like Edwin Clayhanger, he was educated at Newcastle- under- Lyme, at the Endowed Middle School. He matriculated at London University ("that august negation of the very idea of a University") about 1885, and thenceforth devoted himself to the study of the law, in the office of his father, a solicitor.

He left the Five Towns in 1889, and went to London, where he entered a solicitor's office, and "combined cunning in the preparation of costs with a hundred and thirty words a minute at shorthand." He received £200 a year for these services, and it was some time before he realised that he was one of Nature's journalists, and could earn greater sums by more congenial work.

Yet the realisation might have come to him even earlier. Before he left Hanley he had been an unpaid contributor to a prominent local paper. It may have been the well-known *Staffordshire Sentinel* (the *Signal* of the novels) ; or it may have been an evanescent rival, like those connected with "Denry" Machin and George Cannon, the bigamous husband of Hilda Lessways. For some such journal, at any rate, he acted as local correspondent, and turned out, unfailingly, half-a-column a week of facetious and satirical comments upon the town's public and semi-public life. He tried also, during this early period, to write a short story and a serial: both failures. These experiences, no doubt, helped to give him facility, while they could hardly have afforded him room for useless vanity. If the solicitor's office did not drive him into literature, it at any rate permitted the study of it. Arnold Bennett collected books—as a collector, not as a reader—and " simply gorged on English and French literature for the amusement I could extract from such gluttony." A chance observation by a friend, according to his own account, revealed to him that there might be an aesthetic side to art and letters: an equally fortuitous remark, a little later, suggested to him that he himself (*soi-disant*, till then, the most callous and immobile of philosophers) might possess the artistic temperament. He won a prize of twenty guineas in a journal which it is hard not to identify as *Tit- Bits*. He had a story accepted by *The Yellow Book*. The thing was done, both psychologically and in the facts of the market: he was an author, a man of letters. The date of this new birth may be put approximately at 1893.

The *Tit-Bits* prize was awarded for a compact humorous compression of that famous one-thousand-pound competition serial, Grant Allen's *What's Bred in the Bone*. The *Yellow Book* story (*A Letter Home*) now appears as the last of *Tales of the Five Towns*, with the footnote " written in 1893 " ; it appeared in print in 1895. That same year, 1893, saw the appearance of a work at once less ambitious and less loudly proclaimed—a serial story in the children's magazine. *Chatterbox*, called *Sidney Yorke's Friend*.

His activity soon became multifarious and incessant. Arnold Bennett turned free-lance journalist, contributing all manner of articles to all manner of magazines. He attained very soon a position of some security and responsibility, as sub- editor and subsequently editor of the woman's journal, *Woman* (now defunct). Before long he was a regular contributor to *The Academy*, then passing through a St Martin's summer of literary excellence under the editorship of Mr Lewis Hind (inspirer also of H. G. Wells). The mark of *The Academy* of those days was extreme clearness and flexibility of expression, wide knowledge, and a well-balanced alertness of judgment: there is to-day no literary journal quite of the type.

Arnold Bennett also acted, during this period, as a fluent and omniscient reviewer, a dramatic critic, a playwright and a publisher's reader. An amusing account of these diversions appears in *The Truth about an Author.*

These were the outward signs of the apprentice author. The inward grace was a very deliberate and conscious study of what writing meant. In 1896 Arnold Bennett resolved to keep a journal.

"Already he had decided to be a successful author, and, as he viewed it, the keeping of a journal was a most valuable part of the apprenticeship to that career. . . . The peril he most dreaded was idleness, and the sin of thinking without writing."

The quotation is from a privately printed volume of selections from this journal (*Things that Interested me.* Burslem, 1906); some extracts also appeared in *Methuen's Annual* (1914). The diary- keeper resolved to write in the journal so many words a day, to improve his powers of observation ; and he kept his word. The outcome of such discipline, joined to industry, may be judged from an entry made three years later :

" Sunday, 31st Dec. 1899. This year I have written 335,340 words, grand total. 224 articles and stories, and four instalments of a serial called *The Gates of Wrath* have actually been published ; also my book of plays, *Polite Farces.* My work included six or eight short stories not yet published, also the greater part of a 55,000 word serial —*Love and Life*—for Tillotsons, and the whole draft, 80,000 words, of my Staffordshire novel, *Anna Tellwright.* "

The end of the century, more or less, closes this period. The books actually produced during it, apart from minor or anonymous works, and those already recorded, were *The Truth about an Author, Fame and Fiction* (both of which appeared in *The Academy*), *A Man from the North* (1898), *Journalism for Women* (1898 : the fruit of experiences on Woman), and doubtless the substance of *How to become an Author* (published in 1903). In 1900 Arnold Bennett went to live in France, remaining there nearly eight years. Many of his books were written there, at a cottage in Fontainebleau.

Artistic Evening

PARIS NIGHTS

1910

I

ARTISTIC EVENING

The first invitation I ever received into a purely Parisian interior might have been copied out of a novel by Paul Bourget. Its lure was thus phrased: *"Un peu de musique et d'agréables femmes."* It answered to my inward vision of Paris. My experiences in London, which fifteen years earlier I had entered with my mouth open as I might have entered some city of Oriental romance, had, of course, done little to destroy my illusions about Paris, for the ingenuousness of the artist is happily indestructible. Hence, my inward vision of Paris was romantic, based on the belief that Paris was essentially "different." Nothing more banal in London than a "little music," or even "some agreeable women"! But what a difference between a little music and *un peu de musique!* What an exciting difference between agreeable women and *agréables femmes!* After all, this difference remains nearly intact to this day. Nobody who has not lived intimately in and with Paris can appreciate the unique savour of that word *femmes.* "Women" is a fine word, a word which, breathed in a certain tone, will make all

15

men—even bishops, misogynists, and political propagandists— fall to dreaming! But *femmes* is yet more potent. There cling to it the associations of a thousand years of dalliance in a land where dalliance is passionately understood.

The usual Paris flat, high up, like the top drawer of a chest of drawers! No passages, but multitudinous doors. In order to arrive at any given room it is necessary to pass through all the others. I passed through the dining-room, where a servant with a marked geometrical gift had arranged a number of very small plates round the rim of a vast circular table. In the drawing-room my host was seated at a grand piano with a couple of candles in front of him and a couple of women behind him. See the light glinting on bits of the ebon piano, and on his face, and on their chins and jewels, and on the corner of a distant picture frame; and all the rest of the room obscure! He wore a jacket, negligently; the interest of his attire was dramatically centred in his large, limp necktie; necktie such as none hut a hero could unfurl in London. A man with a very intelligent face, eager, melancholy (with a sadness acquired in the Divorce Court), wistful, appealing. An idealist! He called himself a publicist. One of the women, a musical composer, had a black skirt and a white blouse; she was ugly but provocative. The other, all in white, was pretty and sprightly, but her charm lacked the perverseness which is expected and usually found in Paris; she painted, she versified, she recited. With the eye of a man who had sat for years in the editorial chair of a ladies' paper, I looked instinctively at the hang of the skirts. It was not good. Those vague frocks were such as had previously been something else, and would soon he transformed by discreet modifications into something still else. Candlelight was best for them. But what grace of demeanour, what naturalness, what candid ease and appositeness of greeting, what absence of self-consciousness! Paris is the self-unconscious.

I was presented as *le romancier anglais*. It sounded romantic. I thought: "What a false impression they are getting, as of some vocation exotic and delightful! If only they knew the prose of it!" I thought of their conception of England, a mysterious isle. When Balzac desired to make a woman exquisitely strange, he caused her to be born in Lancashire.

My host begged permission to go on playing. In the intervals of being a publicist, he composed music, and he was now deciphering a manuscript freshly written. I bent over between the two women, and read the title:

"Ygdrasil: reverie."

When there were a dozen or fifteen people in the room, and as many candles irregularly disposed like lighthouses over a complex archipelago, I formed one of, a group consisting of those two women and another, a young dramatist who concealed his expressive hands in a pair of bright yellow gloves, and a middle-aged man whose constitution was obviously ruined. This last was librarian of some public library—I forget which—and was stated to be monstrously erudite in all literatures. I asked him whether he had of late encountered anything new and good in English.

"I have read nothing later than Swinburne," he replied in a thin, pinched voice—like his features, like his wary and suffering eyes. Speaking with an icy, glittering pessimism, he quoted Stendhal to the effect that a man does not change after twenty-five. He supported the theory bitterly and joyously, and seemed to taste the notion of his own intellectual rigidity, of his perfect inability to receive new ideas and sensations, as one tastes an olive. The young dramatist, in a beautifully curved phrase, began to argue that certain emotional and purely intellectual experiences did not come under the axiom, but the librarian would have none of such a reservation. Then the women joined in, and it was just as if they had all five learnt off by heart one of Landor's lighter imaginary conversations, and were performing it. Well convinced that they were all five absurdly wrong, fanciful, and sentimental either in optimism or pessimism, I nevertheless stood silent and barbaric. Could I cut across that lacework of shapely elegant sentences and apposite gestures with the jagged edge of what in England passes for a remark? The librarian was serious in his eternal frost. The dramatist had the air of being genuinely concerned about the matter; he spoke with deference to the librarian, with chivalrous respect to the women, and to me with glances of appeal for help; possibly the reason was that he was himself approaching the dreadful limit of twenty-five. But the women's eyes were always contradicting the polite seriousness of their tones. Their eyes seemed to be always mysteriously talking about something else; to be always saying: "All this that you are discussing is trivial, but I am brooding for ever on what alone is important." This, while true of nearly all women, is disturbingly true of Parisians. The ageing librarian, by dint of freezing harder, won the altercation: it was as though he stabbed them one by one with a dagger of ice. And presently he was lecturing them. The women were now admiring him. There was something in his face worn by maladies, in his frail physical unpleasantness, and in his frigid and total disgust with life, that responded to their secret dream. Their gaze caressed him, and he felt it falling on him like snow. That he intensely enjoyed his existence was certain.

They began talking low among themselves, the women, and there was an outburst of laughter; pretty giggling laughter. The two who had been at the piano stood aside and whispered and laughed with a more intimate intimacy, struggling to suppress the laughter, and yet every now and then letting it escape from sheer naughtiness. They cried. It was the *fou rire.* Impossible to believe that a moment before they had been performing in one of Landor's imaginary conversations, and that they were passionately serious about art and life and so on. They might have been schoolgirls.

"*Farceuses, toutes les deux!*" said the host, coming up, delightfully indulgent, but shocked that women to whom he had just played *Ygdrasil*, should be able so soon to throw off the spell of it.

18

The pretty and sprightly woman, all in white, despairing, whisked impulsively out of the room, in order to recall to herself amid darkness and cloaks and hats that she was not a giddy child, but an experienced creature of thirty if she was a day. She came back demure, her eyes liquid, brooding.

"By the way," said the young dramatist to the host, "Your People's Concert scheme—doesn't it move?"

"By the way," said the host, suddenly excited, "Shall we hold a meeting of the committee now?"

He had a project for giving performances of the finest music to the populace at a charge of five sous per head. It was the latest activity of the publicist in him. The committee appeared to consist of everybody who was standing near. He drew me into it, because, coming from London, I was of course assumed to be a complete encyclopædia of London and to be capable of furnishing detailed statistics about all twopence-halfpenny enterprises in London for placing the finest music before the people. The women, especially the late laughers, were touched by the beauty of the idea underlying the enterprise, and their eyes showed that at instants they were thinking sympathetically of the far-off "people." The librarian remained somewhat apart, as it were with a rifle, and maintained a desolating fire of questions: "Was the scheme meant to improve the people or to divert them? Would they come? Would they like the finest music? Why five sous? Why not seven, or three? Was the enterprise to be self-supporting?" The host, with his glance fixed in appeal on me (it seemed to me that he was entreating me to accept him as a serious publicist, warning me not to be misled by appearances)—the host replied to all these questions with the sweetest, politest, wistful patience, as well as he could. Certainly the people would like the finest music! The people had a taste naturally distinguished and correct. It was *we* who were the degenerates. The enterprise must be and would be self-supporting. No charity! No, he had learnt the folly of charity! But naturally the artists would give their services. They would be paid in terms of pleasure. The financial difficulty was that, whereas he would not charge more than five sous a head for admission, he could not hire a hall at a rent which worked out to less than a franc a head. Such was the problem before the committee meeting! Dufayel, the great shopkeeper, had offered to assist him.... The librarian frigidly exposed the anti-social nature of Dufayel's business methods, and the host hurriedly made him a present of Dufayel. Dufayel's help could not be conscientiously accepted. The problem then remained!. . . London? London, so practical? As an encyclopaedia of London I was not a success. Politeness hid a general astonishment that, freshly arrived from London, I could not suggest a solution, could not say what London would do in a like quandary, nor even what London had done!

"We will adjourn it to our next meeting," said the host, and named day, hour, and place. And the committee smoothed business out of its brow and dissolved itself, while at the host's request a girl performed some Japanese music on the Pleyel.

When it was finished, the librarian, who had listened to Japanese music at an embassy, said that this was not Japanese music. "And thou knowest it well," he added. The host admitted that it was not really Japanese music, but he insisted with his plaintive smile that the whole subject of Japanese music was very interesting and enigmatic.

Then the pretty sprightly woman, all in white, went and stood behind an arm-chair and recited a poem, admirably, and with every sign of emotion. Difficult to believe that she had ever laughed, that she did not exist continually at these heights! She bowed modestly, a priestess of the poet, and came out from behind the chair.

"By whom?" demanded the librarian.

And a voice answered, throbbing: "Henri de Régnier."

"Indeed," said the librarian with cold, careless approval, "it is pretty enough."

Some Japanese music on the Pleyel

But I knew, from the tone alone of the answering voice, that the name of Henri de Régnier was a sacred name, and that when it had been uttered the proper thing was to bow the head mutely, as before a Botticelli.

"I have something here," said the host, producing one of these portfolios which hurried men of affairs carry under their arms in the streets of Paris, and which are called *serviettes*; this one, however, was of red morocco. The pretty, sprightly woman sprang

21

forward blushing to obstruct his purpose, but other hands led her gently away. The host, using the back of the arm-chair for a lectern, read alternately poems of hers and poems of his own. And he, too, spoke with every sign of emotion. I had to conquer my instinctive British scorn for these people because they would not at any rate pretend that they were ashamed of the emotion of poetry. Their candour appeared to me, then, weak, if not actually indecent. The librarian admitted occasionally that something was pretty enough. The rest of the company maintained a steady fervency of enthusiasm. The reader himself forgot all else in his increasing ardour, and thus we heard about a score of poems—all, as we were told, unpublished—together with the discussion of a score of poems.

We all sat around the rim of an immense circle of white tablecloth. Each on a little plate had a portion of pineapple ice and in a little glass a draught of Asti. Far away, in the centre of the diaper desert, withdrawn and beyond reach, lay a dish containing the remains of the ice. Except fans and cigarette-cases, there was nothing else on the table whatever. Some one across the table asked me what I had recently finished, and I said a play. Everybody agreed that it must be translated into French. The Paris theatres simply could not get good plays. In a few moments it was as if the entire company was beseeching me to allow my comedy to be translated and produced with dazzling success at one of the principal theatres on the boulevard. But I would not. I said my play was unsuitable for the French stage.

"Because?"

"Because it is too pure."

I had meant to be mildly jocular. But this joke excited mirth that surpassed mildness. "Thou hearest that? He says his play is too pure for us!" My belief is that they had never heard one of these strange, naïve, puzzling barbarians make a joke before, and that they regarded the thing in its novelty as really too immensely and exotically funny, in some manner which they could not explain to themselves. Beneath their politeness I could detect them watching me, after that, in expectation of another outbreak of insular humour. I might have been tempted to commit follies, had not a new guest arrived.

A new guest arrived

This was a tall, large-boned, ugly, coquettish woman, with a strong physical attractiveness and a voice that caused vibrations in your soul. She was in white, with a powerful leather waistband which suited her. She was intimate with everybody except me, and by a natural gift and force she held the attention of everybody from the moment of her entrance. You could see she was used to that. The time was a quarter to midnight, and she explained that she had been trying to arrive for hours, but could not have succeeded a second sooner. She said she must recount her *journée*, and she recounted her *journée*, which, after being a vague prehistoric nebulosity up to midday seemed to begin to take a definite shape about that hour. It was the *journée* of a Parisienne who is also an amateur actress and a dog-fancier. And undoubtedly all her days were the same: battles waged against clocks and destiny. She had no sense of order or of time. She had no exact knowledge of anything; she had no purpose in life; she was perfectly futile and useless. But she was acquainted with the secret nature of men and women; she could judge them shrewdly; she was the very opposite of the *ingénue*; and by her physical attractiveness, and that deep, thrilling voice, and her distinction of gesture and tone, she created in you the illusion that she was a capable and efficient woman, absorbed in the most important ends. She sat down negligently behind the host, waving away all ice and Asti, and busily fanning both him and herself. She flattered him by laying her ringed and fluffy arm along the back of his chair.

"Do you know," she said, smiling at him mysteriously. "I have made a strange discovery to-day. Paris gives more towards the saving of lost dogs than towards the saving of lost women. Very curious, is it not?"

The host seemed to be thunderstruck by this piece of information. The whole table was agitated by it, and a tremendous discussion was set on foot. I then witnessed for the first time the spectacle of a fairly large mixed company talking freely about scabrous facts. Then for the first time was I eased from the strain of pretending in a mixed company that things are not what they in fact are. To listen to those women, and to watch them listening, was as staggering as it would have been to see them pick up red-hot irons in their feverish, delicate hands. Their admission that they knew everything, that no corner of existence was dark enough to frighten them into speechlessness, was the chief of their charms, then. It intensified their acute femininity. And while they were thus gravely talking, ironical, sympathetic, amused, or indignant, they even yet had the air of secretly thinking about something else.

Discussions of such subjects never formally end, for the talkers never tire of them. This subject was discussed in knots all the way down six flights of stairs by the light of tapers and matches. I left the last, because I wanted to get some general information from my host about one of his guests.

"She is divorcing her husband," he said, with the simple sad pride of a man who had been a petitioner in the matrimonial courts. "For the rest, you never meet any but divorced women at my place. It saves complications. So have no fear."

We shook hands warmly.

"*Au revoir, mon ami.*"

"*Au revoir, mon cher.*"

II

THE VARIÉTIÉS

The filth and the paltry shabbiness of the entrance to the theatre amounted to cynicism. Instead of uplifting by a foretaste of light and magnificence, as the entrance to a theatre should, it depressed by its neglected squalour. Twenty years earlier it might have cried urgently for cleansing and redecoration, but now it was long past crying. It had become vile. In the centre at the back sat a row of three or four officials in evening dress, prosperous clubmen with glittering rakish hats, at a distance of twenty feet, but changing as we approached them to indigent, fustian-clad ticket-clerks penned in a rickety rostrum and condemned like sandwich-men to be ridiculous in order to live. (Their appearance recalled to my mind the fact that a "front-of-the-house" inspector at the principal music-hall in France and in Europe is paid thirty sous a night.) They regarded our tickets with gestures of scorn, weariness, and cupidity. None knew better than they that these coloured scraps represented a large lovely gold coin, rare and yet plentiful, reassuring and yet transient, the price of coals, boots, nectar, and love.

We came to a very narrow, low, foul, semi-circular tunnel which was occupied by hags and harpies with pink bows in their hair, and by marauding men, and by hats and cloaks and overcoats, and by a double odour of dirt and disinfectants. Along the convex side of the tunnel were a number of little doors like the doors of cells. We bought a programme from a man, yielded our wraps to two harpies, and were led away by another man. All these beings looked hungrily apprehensive, like dogs nosing along a gutter. The auditorium which was nearly full, had the same characteristics as the porch and the *couloir*. It was filthy, fetid, uncomfortable, and dangerous. It had the carpets of a lodging-house of the 'seventies, the seats of an old omnibus, the gilt and the decorated sculpture of a circus at a fair. And it was dingy! It was encrusted with dinginess!

Something seemed to be afoot on the stage: from the embittered resignation of the audience and the perfunctory nonchalance of the players, we knew that this could only be the curtain-raiser. The hour was ten minutes past nine. The principal piece was advertised to commence at nine o'clock. But the curtain-raiser was not yet finished, and after it was finished there would be the *entr'acte*—one of the renowned, interminable *entr'actes* of the Théâtre des Variétés.

The Variétés is still one of the most "truly Parisian" of theatres, and has been so since long before Zola described it fully in *Nana*. The young bloods of Buenos Ayres and St. Petersburg still have visions of an evening at the Variétés as the superlative of intense living. Every theatre with a reputation has its "note," and the note of the Variétés is to make a fool of its public. Its attitude to the public is that of an English provincial hotel or an English bank: "Come, and be d——d to you! Above all, do not imagine that I exist for your convenience. You exist for mine." At the Variétés had management is good management; slackness is a virtuous *coquetterie*. It would never do, there, to be prompt, clean, or honest. To make the theatre passably habitable would be ruin. Its *chic* would be lost if it ceased to be a Hades of discomfort and a menace to health. There is a small troupe of notorious artistes, some of whom show great talent when it occurs to them to show it; the vogue of the rest is one of the innumerable mysteries which abound in theatrical life. It is axiomatic that they are all witty, and that whatever lines they enunciate thereby become witty. They are simply side-splitting as Sydney Smith was simply side-splitting when he asked for the potatoes to be passed. Also the manager of the theatre always wears an old straw hat, summer and winter. He is the wearer of an eternal battered straw hat, who incidentally manages a theatre. You go along the boulevard, and you happen to see that straw hat emerging from the theatre. And by the strange potency of the hat you will be obliged to say to the next acquaintance you meet: "I've just seen Samuel in his straw hat." And the thought in your mind and in the mind of your acquaintance will be that you are getting very near the heart of Paris.

Beyond question the troupe of favourites considers itself to be the real centre of Paris, and, therefore, of civilisation. Practically the entire Press, either by good nature, stupidity, snobbishness, or simple cash transactions, takes part in the vast make-believe that the troupe is conferring a favour on civilisation by consenting to be alive. And the troupe of course behaves accordingly. It puts its back into the evening when it thinks it will, and when it thinks it won't, it doesn't. "*Aux Variétés on travaille quand on a le temps.*" The rise of the curtain awaits the caprice of a convivial green-room. "Don't hurry—the public is getting impatient." Naturally, the underlings are not included in the benefits of the make-believe. "At rehearsals we may wait two hours for the principals," a chorus-girl said to me. "But if *we* are five minutes late, one flings us a fine. A hundred francs a month I touch, and it has happened to me to pay thirty in fines. Some one gets all that, you know!" She went off into an impassioned description of scenes at rehearsals of a ballet, how the ballet-master, after epical outbursts, would always throw up his arms in inexpressible disgust and retire to his room, and how the women would follow him and kiss and cajole and hug him, and how then, after a majestic pause, his step could be heard slowly descending the stairs, and at last the rehearsal would resume....

The human interest, no doubt!

The Variétés has another *rôle* and justification. It is what the French call a women's theatre. When I asked a well-known actress why the *entr'-actes* at the Variétés were so long, she replied with her air of finding even the most bizarre phenomena quite natural: "There are several reasons. One is, so that the gentlemen may have time to write notes and to receive answers." I did not conceal my sense of the oddness of this method of conducting a theatre, whereupon she reminded me that it was the Variétés we were talking about. She said that little by little I should understand all sorts of things.

As the principal piece progressed—it was an *opérette*—the apathy of the public grew more and more noticeable. They seemed to have forgotten that they were in one of the most truly Parisian of theatres, watching players whose names were household words and synonyms of wit and allurement. There was no applause, save from a claque which had carried discipline to the extreme. The favourites were evidently in one of their moods of casualness. Either the piece had run too long or it was not going to run long enough. It was a piece brightly and jinglingly vulgar, ministering, of course, in the main, to the secret concupiscence which drives humanity forward; titillating, like most stage-spectacles, all that is base, inept, and gross in a crowd whose units are perhaps, not quite odious. A few of the performers had moments of real brilliance. But even these flashes did not stir the public, whose characteristic was stolidity. A public which, having regard to the conditions of the particular theatre, necessarily consisted of simple snobbish gulls whose creed is whatever they read or hear, with an admixture of foreigners, provincials, adventurers, and persons who, having no illusions, go to the Variétés because they have been to everything else and must go somewhere! The first half-dozen rows of the stalls were reserved for males: a custom which at the Variétés has survived from a more barbaric age, as the custom of the finger-bowl has survived in the repasts of the polite. The self-satisfied and self-conscious occupants of these rows seemed to summarise and illustrate all the various masculine stupidity of a great and proud city. To counterbalance this preponderance of the male, I could glimpse, behind the lath grilles of the cages called *baignoires*, the forms of women (each guarded) who I hope were incomparable. The sight of these grilles at once sent the mind to the seraglio, and the House of Commons, and other fastnesses of Orientalism.

The evening was interminable, not for me alone, but obviously for the majority of the audience. Impossible to describe the dull fortitude of the audience without being accused of wilful exaggeration! Only in the *entr'actes*, in the amplitude and dubious mystery of the *entr'actes*, did the audience arouse itself into the semblance of vivacity. There was but little complaining. Were we not at the Variétés? At the Variétés, to suffer was part of the entertainment. The French public is a public which accepts all in Christian meekness—all! It knows that it exists for the convenience of the bureaucracy and the theatres. It covers its cowardice under a mantle of philosophy and politeness. Its fierce protest is a shrug. *"Que voulez-vous? C'est comme ça."*

At last, at nearly half after midnight, we came forth, bitterly depressed, as usual, by the deep consciousness of futile waste. I could see, in my preoccupation, the whole organism of the Variétés, which is only the essence of the French theatre. A few artistes and a financier or so at the core, wilful, corrupt, self-indulgent, spoiled, venal, enormously unbusinesslike, incredibly cynical, luxurious in the midst of a crowd of miserable parasites and menials; creating for themselves, out of electric globes, and newspapers, and posters, and photographs, and the inexhaustible simplicity and sexuality of the public, a legend of artistic greatness. They make a frame, and hang a curtain in front of it, and put footlights beneath; and lo! the capricious manouvres of these mortals become the sacred, authoritative functioning of an institution!

It was raining. The boulevard was a mirror. And along the reflecting surface of this mirror cab after cab, hundreds of cabs, rolled swiftly. Dozens and dozens were empty, and had no goal; but none would stop. They all went ruthlessly by with offensive gestures of disdain. Strangers cannot believe that when a Paris cabman without a fare refuses to stop on a wet night, it is not because he is hoping for a client in richer furs, or because he is going to the stables, or because he has earned enough that night, or because he has an urgent appointment with his enchantress— but simply from malice. Nevertheless this is a psychological fact which any experienced Parisian will confirm. On a wet night the cabman revenges himself upon the *bourgeoisie* though the base satisfaction may cost him money. As we waited, with many other princes of the earth who could afford to throw away a whole louis for a few hours' relaxation, as we waited vainly in the wet for a cabman who would condescend, I could savour only one sensation—that of exasperating tedium completely achieved.

III

EVENING WITH EXILES

I lived up at the top of the house, absolutely alone. After eleven o'clock in the morning, when my servant left, I was my own doorkeeper. Like most solitaries in strange places, whenever I heard a ring I had a feeling that perhaps after all it might be the ring of romance. This time it was the telegraph-boy. I gave him a penny, because in France, much more than in England, every one must live, and the notion still survives that a telegram has sufficient unusualness to demand a tip; the same with a registered letter. I read the telegram, and my evening lay suddenly in fragments at my feet. The customary accident, the accident dreaded by every solitary, had happened. "Sorry, prevented from coming to-night," etc. It was not yet six o'clock. I had in front of me a wilderness of six hours to traverse. In my warm disgust I went at once out in the streets. My flat had become mysteriously uninhabitable, and my work repugnant. The streets of Paris, by reason of their hospitality, are a refuge.

The last sun of September was setting across the circular Place Blanche. I sat down at the terrace of the smallest *café* and drank tea. Exactly opposite were the crimson wings of the Moulin Rouge, and to the right was the establishment which then held first place among nocturnal restaurants in Montmartre. It had the strange charm of a resort which is never closed, night or day, and where money and time are squandered with infantile fatuity. Somehow it inspired respect, if not awe. Its terrace was seldom empty, and at that hour it was always full. Under the striped and valanced awning sat perhaps a hundred people, all slowly and deliberately administering to themselves poisons of various beautiful colours. A crowd to give pause to the divination of even the most conceited student of human nature, a crowd in which the simplest bourgeois or artist or thief sat next to men and women exercising the oldest and most disreputable professions—and it was impossible surely to distinguish which from which!

Opposite The Moulin Rouge

Out of the medley of trams, omnibuses, carts, automobiles, and cabs that continually rattled over the cobbles, an open *fiacre* would detach itself every minute or so, and set down or take up in front of the terrace. Among these was one carrying two young dandies, an elegantly dressed girl, and another young girl in a servant's cap and apron. They were all laughing and talking together. The dandies and the elegancy got out and took a vacant table amid the welcoming eager bows of a *maître d'hotel*, *a chasseur,* and a waiter. She was freshly and meticulously and triumphantly got up, like an elaborate confection of starched linen fresh from the laundress. Her lips were impeccably rouged. She delighted the eye by her health and her youth and her pretty insolence. A single touch would have soiled her, but she had not yet been touched. Her day had just begun. Probably, her bed was not yet made. The black-robed, scissored girls of the drapery store at the next angle of the *place* were finishing their tenth hour of vigil over goods displayed on the footpath. And next to that was a creamery where black-robed girls could obtain a whole day's sustenance for the price of one glass of poison. Evidently the young creature had only just arrived at the dignity of a fashionable dressmaker, and a servant of her own. Her ingenuous vanity obliged her to show her servant to the *place*, and the ingenuous vanity of the servant was content to be shown off; for the servant might have a servant to-morrow—who could tell? The cabman and the servant began to converse, and presently the cabman in his long fawn coat and white hat descended and entered the vehicle and sat down by the servant, and pulled out an illustrated comic paper, and they bent their heads over it and giggled enormously in unison; he was piling up money at the rate of at least a sou a minute. Occasionally the young mistress threw a loud sisterly remark to the servant, who replied gaily. And the two young dandies bore nobly the difficult *rôle* of world-worn men who still count not the cost of smiles. Say what you like, it was charming. It was one of the reasons why Paris is the city which is always forgiven. Could one reasonably expect that the bright face of the vapid little siren should be solemnised by the thought: "To-day I am a day nearer forty than I was yesterday"?

The wings of the Moulin Rouge, jewelled now with crimson lamps, began to revolve slowly. The upper chambers of the restaurant showed lights behind their mysteriously-curtained windows. The terrace was suddenly bathed in the calm blue of electricity. No austere realism of the philosopher could argue away the romance of the scene.

Montmartre

I turned down the steep Rue Blanche, and at the foot of it passed by the shadow of the Trinité, the great church of illicit assignations, at whose clock scores of frightened and expectant hearts gaze anxiously every afternoon; and through the Rue de la Chaussée d'Antin, where corsets are masterpieces beyond price and flowers may be sold for a sovereign apiece, and then into the full fever of the grand boulevard with its maddening restlessness of illuminated signs. The shops and *cafés* were all on fire, making two embankments of fire, above which rose high and mysterious *façades* masked by trees that looked like the impossible verdure of an opera. And between the summits of the trees a ribbon of rich, dark, soothing purple—the sky! This was the city. This was what the race had accomplished, after eighteen Louises and nearly as many revolutions, and when all was said that could be said it remained a prodigious and a comforting spectacle. Every doorway shone with invitation; every satisfaction and delight was offered, on terms ridiculously reasonable. And binding everything together were the refined, neighbourly, and graceful cynical gestures of the race; so different from the harsh and awkward timidity, the self-centred egotism and artistocratic hypocrisy of Piccadilly. It seemed difficult to be lonely amid multitudes that so candidly accepted human nature as human nature is. It seemed a splendid and an uplifting thing to be there. I continued southwards, down the narrow, swarming Rue Richelieu, past the immeasurable National Library on the left and Jean Goujon's sculptures of the rivers of France on the right, and past the Theatre Français, where nice plain people were waiting to see *L'Aventurière*, and across the arcaded Rue de Rivoli. And then I was in the dark desert of the Place du Carrousel, where the omnibuses are diminished to toy-omnibuses. The town was shut off by the vast arms of the Louvre. The purple had faded out the sky. The wind, heralding October, blew coldly across the spaces. The artfully arranged vista of the Champs Elysées, rising in flame against the silhouette of Cleopatra's needle, struck me as a meretricious device, designed to impress tourists and monarchs. Everything was meretricious. I could not even strike a match without being reminded that a contented and corrupt inefficiency was corroding this race like a disease. I could not light my cigarette because somebody, somewhere, had not done his job like an honest man. And thus it was throughout.

I wanted to dine, and there were a thousand restaurants within a mile; but they had all ceased to invite me. I was beaten down by the overwhelming sadness of one who for the time being has no definite arranged claim to any friendly attention in a huge city—crowded with pre-occupied human beings. I might have been George Gissing. I re-wrote all his novels for him in an instant. I persisted southwards. The tiny walled river, reflecting with industrious precision all its lights, had no attraction.

The quays, where all the book shops were closed and all the bookstalls locked down, and where there was never a *café*, were as inhospitable and chill as Riga. Mist seemed to heave over the river, and the pavements were oozing damp.

I went up an entry and rang a bell, thinking to myself: "If he isn't in, I am done for!" But at the same moment I caught the sound of a violoncello, and I knew I was saved, and by a miracle Paris was herself again.

"Not engaged for dinner, are you?" I asked, as soon as I was in the studio.

"No. I was just thinking of going out."

"Well, let's go, then."

"I was scraping some bits of Gluck."

The studio was fairly large, but it was bare, unkempt, dirty, and comfortless. Except an old sofa, two hard imperfect chairs, and an untrustworthy table, it had no furniture. Of course, it was littered with the apparatus of painting. Its sole ornamentation was pictures, and the pictures were very fine, for they were the painter's own. He and his pictures are well known among the painters of Europe and America. Successful artistically, and with an adequate private income, he was a full member of the Champ de Mars Salon, and he sold his pictures upon occasion to Governments. Although a British subject, he had spent nearly all his life in Paris; he knew the streets and resorts of Paris like a Frenchman; he spoke French like a Frenchman. I never heard of him going to England. I never heard him express a desire to go to England. His age was perhaps fifty, and I dare say that he had lived in that studio for a quarter of a century, with his violoncello. It was plain, as he stood there, well dressed, and with a vivacious and yet dreamy eye, that the zest of life had not waned in him. He was a man who, now as much as ever, took his pleasure in seeing and painting beautiful, suave, harmonious things. And yet he stood there unapologetic amid that ugly and narrow discomfort, with the sheet of music pinned carelessly to an easel, and lighted by a small ill-regulated lamp with a truncated, dirty chimney—

sole illumination of the chamber! His vivacious and dreamy eye simply did not see all that, never had seen it, never saw anything that it did not care to see. Nobody ever heard him multiply words about a bad picture, for example,—he would ignore it.

With a gesture of habit that must have taken years to acquire he took a common rose-coloured packet of caporal cigarettes from the table by the lamp and offered it to me, pushing one of the cigarettes out beyond its fellows from behind; you knew that he was always handling cigarettes.

"It's not really arranged for 'cello," he murmured, gazing at the music, which was an air from *Alceste*, arranged for violin. "You see it's in the treble clef."

"I wish you'd play it," I said.

He sat down and played it, because he was interested in it. With his greying hair and his fashionable grey suit, and his oldest friend, the brown 'cello, gleaming between his knees, he was the centre of a small region of light in the gloomy studio, and the sound of the 'cello filled the studio. He had no home; but if he had had a home this would have been his home, and this his home-life. As a private individual, as distinguished from a public artist, this was what he had arrived at. He had secured this refuge, and invented this relaxation, in the middle of Paris. By their aid he could defy Paris. There was something wistful about the scene, but it was also impressive, at any rate to me, who am otherwise constituted. He was an exile in the city of exiles; a characteristic item in it, though of a variety exceedingly rare. But he would have been equally an exile in any other city. He had no consciousness of being an exile, of being homeless. He was above patriotisms and homes. Why, when he wanted even a book he only borrowed it!

"Well, shall we go out and eat?" I suggested, after listening to several lovely airs.

"Yes," he said, "I was just going. I don't think you've seen my last etching. Care to?"

I did care to see it, but I also desired my dinner.

"This is a pretty good print, but I shall get better," he said, holding the sheet of paper under the lamp.

"How many shall you print?" I asked.

"Thirty."

"You might put me down for one."

"All right. I think it will give you pleasure," he said with impartial and dignified conviction.

After another ten minutes, we were put on the quay.

"Grand autumn night?" he said appreciatively. "Where shall we have the *apéritif?*

"*Apéritif!* It's after eight o'clock, man!"

"I think we shall have time for an *apéritif*" he insisted, mildly shocked.

Drawing-rooms have their ritual. His life, too, had its ritual.

At nearly midnight we were sitting, three of us, in a *café* of the Montparnasse quarter, possibly the principal *café* of the Montparnasse quarter. Neither notorious nor secretly eccentric; but an honest *café*, in the sense of "honest" applied to certain women. Being situated close to a large railway terminus, it had a broad and an indulgent attitude towards life. It would have received a frivolous *habitué* of the Place Blanche, or a nun, or a clergyman, with the same placidity. And although the district was modified, and whole streets, indeed, de-Parisianised by wandering cohorts of American and English art-amateurs of both sexes, this *café* remained, while accepting them, characteristically French. The cohorts thought they were seeing French life when they entered it; and they in fact were.

This *café* was the chief club of the district, with a multitudinous and regular *clientèle* of billiard-players, card-players, draught-players, newspapers readers, chatterers, and simple imbibers of bock. Its doors were continually a-swing, and one or the other of the two high-enthroned caissières was continually lifting her watchful head from the desk to observe who entered. Its interior seemed to penetrate indefinitely into the hinterland of the street, and the effect of unendingness was intensified by means of mirrors, which reflected the shirt-sleeved arms and the cues of a score of billiard-players. Everywhere the same lively and expressive and never ungraceful gestures, between the marble table-tops below and the light-studded ceiling above! Everywhere the same murmur of confusing pleasant voices broken by the loud chant of waiters intoning orders at the service-bar, and by the setting down of heavy glass mugs and saucers upon marble! Over the *café*, unperceived, unthought of, were the six storeys of a large house comprising perhaps twenty-five separate and complete homes.

La Dame Du Comptoir

The third man at our table was another exile, also a painter, but a Scotchman. He had lived in Paris since everlasting, but before that rumour said that he had lived for several years immovable at the little inn of a Norman village. Now, he never left Paris, even in summer. He exhibited, with marked discretion, only at the Indépendants. Beyond these facts, and the obvious fact that he enjoyed independent means, nobody knew anything about him save his opinions. Even his age was exceedingly uncertain. He looked forty, but there were acquaintances who said that he had looked forty for twenty years. He was one of those extremely reserved men who talk freely. Of his hopes, ambitions, ideals, disappointments, connections, he never said a word, but he did not refuse his opinion upon any subject, and on every subject he had a definite opinion which he would express very clearly, with a sort of polite curtness. His tendency was to cynicism—too cynical to be bitter. He did not complain of human nature, but he thoroughly believed the worst of it. These two men, the 'cellist and the Scotchman, were fast friends; or rather—as it might be argued in the strict sense neither of them had a friend—they were very familiar acquaintances, each with a profound respect for the other's judgment and artistic probity. Further, the Scotchman admired his companion for a genius, as everybody did.

They talked together for ever and ever, but not about politics. They were impatient on politics. Both were apparently convinced that politics are an artificiality imposed upon society by adventurers and interferes, and that if such people could be exterminated politics would disappear. Certainly neither had any interest in the organic aspect of society. Their political desire was to be let alone. Nor did they often or for long "talk bawdy"; after opinions had been given which no sensible man ever confides to more than two reliable others at a time, the Scotchman would sweep all that away as secondary. Nor did they talk of the events of the day, unless it might be some titillating crime or mystery such as will fill whole pages of the newspaper for a week together. They talked of the arts, all the arts. And although they seemed

41

to be always either in that *café*, or in their studios, or in bed, they had the air of being mysteriously but genuinely abreast of every manifestation of art. And since all the arts are one, and in respect to art they had a real attitude and real views, all that they said was valuable suggestively, and their ideas could not by any prodigality be exhausted. As a patron of the arts even the State interested them, and herein they showed glimmerings of a social sense. In the intervals of this eternal and absorbing "art," they would discuss with admirable restrained gusto the exacerbating ridiculousness of the cohorts of American and English art-amateurs who infested and infected the quarter.

Little bands of these came into the *café* from time to time, and drifting along the aisles of chairs would sit down where they could see as much as possible with their candid eyes. The girls, inelegant and blousy; the men, inept in their narrow shrewdness: both equally naïve, conceited, uncorrupted, and incorruptible, they were absolutely incapable of appreciating the refined and corrupt decadence, the stylistic charm, the exquisite tradition of the civilisation at which they foolishly stared, as at a peep-show. Not a thousand years would teach them the human hourly art of life as it was subtly practised by the people whose very language they disdained to learn. When loud fragments of French phrases, massacred by Americans who had floated on but not mingled with Paris for years, reached us from an Anglo-Saxon table, my friends would seem to shudder secretly, ashamed of being Anglo-Saxon. And if they were obliged to salute some uncouth Anglo-Saxon acquaintance, and thus admit their own unlatin origin, their eyes would say: "Why cannot these people be imprisoned at home? Why are not we alone of Anglo-Saxons permitted to inhabit Paris?"

Occasionally a bore would complacently present himself for sufferance. Among these the chief was certainly the man whose existence was an endless shuttle-work between the various cities where art is or has been practised, from Munich to Naples. He knew everything about painting, but he ought to have been a bookmaker. He was notorious everywhere as the friend of Strutt, Strutt being the very famous and wealthy English portrait-painter of girls. All his remarks were *àpropos* of Tommy Strutt, Tommy Strutt—Tommy. He was invariably full of Tommy. And this evening he was full of Tommy's new German model, whose portrait had been in that year's Salon.. . . How Tommy had picked her up in the streets of Berlin; how she was nineteen, and the rage of Berlin, and was asked to lunch at the embassies, and had received five proposals in three months: how she refused to sit for any one but Tommy, and even for him would only sit two hours a day: how Tommy looked after her, and sent her to bed at nine-thirty of a night, and hired a woman to play with her; and how Tommy had once telegraphed to her that he was coming to Berlin, and how she had hired a studio and got it painted and furnished exactly to his fastidious taste all on her own, and met him at the station and driven him to the studio, and tea was all ready, etc.; and how pretty she was.. . .

"What's her figure like?" the Scotchman inquired gruffly.

"The fact is," said Tommy's friend, dashed, "I haven't seen her posing for the nude. I've seen her posing to Tommy in a bathing-costume on the seashore, but I haven't yet seen her posing for the nude..." He became reflective. "My boy, do you know what my old uncle used to say to me down at the old place in Kildare, when I was a youngster? My old uncle used to say to me—and he was dying—'My boy, I've always made a rule of making love to every pretty woman I met. It's a sound rule. But let me warn you—you mustn't expect to get more than five per cent, on your outlay!'"

"'The old place in Kildare!'" murmured the Scotchman, in a peculiarly significant tone, after Tommy Strutt's friend had gone; and this was the only comment on Tommy Strutt's friend.

The talk on art was resumed, the renowned Tommy Strutt being reduced to his proper level of the third-rate and abruptly dismissed. One o'clock! A quarter past one! The *café* was now nearly empty. But these men had no regard for time. Time did not exist for them, any more than the structure of society. They were not bored, nor tired. They conversed with ease, and with mild pleasure in their own irony and in the disillusioned surety of their judgments. Then I noticed that the waiters had dwindled to two, and that only one cashier was left enthroned behind the bar; somewhat later, she too had actually gone! Both had at length rejoined their families, if any. The idea was startling that these prim and neat and mechanically smiling women were human, had private relations, a private life, a bed, a wardrobe. All over Paris, all day, every day, they sit and estimate the contents of trays, which waiters present to their practised gaze for an instant only, and receive the value of the drinks in bone discs, and write down columns of figures in long ledgers. They never take exercise, nor see the sun; they even eat in the *café*. Mystic careers!... A quarter to two. Now the chairs had been brought in from the terrace, and there was only one waiter, and no other customer that I could see. The waiter, his face nearly as pale as his apron, eyed us with patient and bland resignation, sure from his deep knowledge of human habits that sooner or later we should in fact depart, and well inured to the great Parisian principle that a *café* exists for the convenience of its *habitués*. I was uneasy: I was even aware of guiltiness; but not my friends.

Then a face looked in at the doorway, as if reconnoitring, and hesitated.

"By Jove!" said the violoncellist. "There's the Mahatma back again! Oh! He's seen us!"

The peering face preceded a sloping body into the *café*, and I was introduced to a man whose excellent poems I had read in a limited edition. He was wearing a heavily jewelled red waistcoat, and the largest ring I ever saw on a human hand. He sat down. The waiter took his order and intoned it in front of the service-bar, proving that another fellow-creature was hidden there awaiting our pleasure. When the Mahatma's glass was brought, the Scotchman suddenly demanded from the waiter the total of our modest consumption, and paid it. The Mahatma said that he had arrived that evening direct from the Himalayas, and that he had been made or ordained a "khan" in the East. Without any preface he began to talk supernaturally. As he had known Aubrey Beardsley, I referred to the rumour that Beardsley had several times been seen abroad in London after his alleged death.

"That's nothing," he said quickly. "I know a man who saw and spoke to Oscar Wilde in the Pyrenees at the very time when Oscar was in prison in England."

"Who was the man?" I inquired.

He paused. "Myself," he said, in a low tone.

"Shall we go?" The Scotchman, faintly smiling, embraced his friend and me in the question.

We went, leaving the Mahatma bent in solitude over his glass. The waiter was obviously saying to himself: "It was inevitable that they should ultimately go, and they have gone." We had sat for four hours.

Outside, cabs were still rolling to and fro. After cheerful casual good-nights, we got indolently into three separate cabs, and went our easy ways. I saw in my imagination the vista of the thousands of similar nights which my friends had spent, and the vista of the thousands of similar nights which they would yet spend. And the sight was majestic, tremendous.

IV

BOURGEOIS

You could smell money long before you arrived at the double portals of the flat on the second floor. The public staircase was heated; it mounted broadly upwards and upwards in a very easy slope, and at each spacious landing was the statue of some draped woman holding aloft a lamp which threw light on an endless carpet, and on marble mosaics. There was, indeed, a lift; but who could refuse the majestic invitation of the staircase, deserted, silent, and mysterious? The bell would give but one *ting*, and always the same *ting*; it was not an electric device by which the temperament and mood of the intruder on the mat are accurately and instantly signalled to the interior.

The door was opened by the Tante herself—perhaps she had been crossing from one room to another—and I came into the large entrance-hall, which even on the brightest summer day was as obscure as a crypt, and which the architect had apparently meant to be appreciated only after nightfall. A vast *armoire* and a vast hat-and-coat stand were features of it.

"My niece occupies herself with the children," the Tante half-whispered, as she took me into the drawing-room. And in her voice were mingled pride, affection, and also a certain conspiratorial quality, as though the mysteries of putting a little boy and a little girl to bed were at once religious and delicious, and must not be disturbed by loud tones even afar off.

She was a stout woman of seventy, dressed in black with a ruching of white at the neck and the wrists; very erect and active; her hair not yet entirely grey; an aquiline eye. The soft,

46

fresh white frill at the wrist made a charming contrast with the experienced and aged hand. She had been a widow for very many years, and during all those years she had matched herself against the world, her weapons being a considerable and secure income, and a quite exceptional natural shrewdness. The result had left her handsomely the victor. She had an immense but justifiable confidence in her own judgment and sagacity; her interest in the spectacle of existence was unabated, and a long and passionate study of human nature had not embittered her. She was a realist, and a caustic realist, but she could excuse; she could accept man as she knew him in his turpitude. Her chief joys were to arrange and rearrange her "reserves" of domestic goods, to discuss character, and to indicate to a later generation, out of her terrific experience of Parisian life, the best methods of defence against the average tradesman and the average menial. So seldom did anybody get the better of her that, when the unusual did occur, she could afford to admit the fact with a liberal laugh: "*Il m'a roulée, celui-là! Il a roulé la vieille!*"

In a corner of the drawing-room she resumed the topic, always interesting to her, of my adventures among charwomen, generously instructing me the whole time in a hundred ways. And when the conversation dropped she would sigh and go back to something previously said, and repeat it. "So she polishes the door-knobs every day! Well, that is a quality, at least." Then my hostess (her niece-inlaw) came blandly in: a woman of thirty-five, also in mourning, with a pale, powdered face and golden hair; benevolent and calm, elegant, but with the elegance of a confessed mother.

"*Ça y est?*" asked the Tante, meaning—were the infants at last couched?

"*Ça y est*" said the mother, with triumph, with relief, and yet also with a little regret.

There was a nurse, but in practice she was only an under-nurse; the head-nurse was the mother.

"*Eh bien, mon petit Bennett,*" the mother began, in a new tone,

47

as if to indicate that she was no longer a mother, but a Parisienne, frivolous and challenging, "what there that is new?"

"He is there," said the Tante, interrupting.

We heard the noise of the front-door, and by a common instinct we all rose and went into the hall.

The master of the home arrived. He entered like a gust of wind, and Marthe, the thin old parlourmaid, who had evidently been lying in wait for him, started back in alarm, but alarm half-simulated. My host, about the same age as his wife, was a doctor, specialising in the diseases of women and children, and he had his cabinet on the ground-floor of the same house. He was late, he was impatient to regain his hearth, he was proud of his industry; and the simple, instinctive joy of life sparkled in his eye.

"Marie," he cried to his wife. "I love thee!" And kissed her furiously on both cheeks.

"It is well," she responded, calmly smiling, with a sort of flirtatious condescension.

"I tell thee I love thee!" he insisted, with his hands on her shoulders. "Tell me that thou lovest me!"

"I love thee," she said calmly.

"It is very well!" he said, and swinging round to Marthe, giving her his hat. "Marthe, I love you." And he caught her a smack on the shoulder.

"Monsieur hurts me," the spinster protested.

"Go then! Go then!" said the Tante, as the beloved nephew directed his assault upon her in turn. She was grimly proud of him. He flattered her eye, for, even at his loosest, he had a professional distinction of deportment which her long-deceased husband, a wholesale tradesman, had probably lacked.

"Well, my old one," the host grasped my hand once more, "you cannot figure to yourself how it gives me pleasure to have you here!" His voice was rich with emotion.

This man had the genius of friendship in a very high degree. His delight in the society of his friends was so intense and so candid that only the most inordinately conceited among them could have failed to be aware of an uncomfortable grave sense of unworthiness, could have failed to say to themselves fearfully: "He will find me out one day!"

A by-product of Russian politics

The dining-room was large, and massively furnished, and lighted by one immense shaded lamp that hung low over the table. Among the heavily framed pictures was a magnificent Jules Dupré, belonging to the Tante. She had picked it up long ago at a sale for something like ten thousand francs, apparently while the dealers were looking the other way. It was a known picture, and one of the Tante's satisfactions was that some dealer or other was always trying to relieve her of it, without the slightest success. She had a story, too, that on the day after the sale a Duchesse

who affected Duprés had sent her footman offering to take
the picture off her at a ten per cent, increase because it would
make a pair with another magnificent Dupré already owned by
the Duchesse. "Eh, well," the widow of the tradesman had said
to the footman, "you will tell Madame la Duchesse that if she
wants my picture she had better come herself and inquire about
it." In the flat, the Dupré was one of the great pictures of the
world. Safer to sneeze at the Venus de Milo than at that picture!
Another favourite picture, also the property of Tante, was one by
a living and super-modern painter, an acquaintance of another
nephew of hers. I do not think she much cared for it, or that she
cared much for any pictures. She had bought it by a benevolent
caprice. "What would you? He had not the sou. *C'est un très
gentil garçon*, of a great talent, but he was eating all his money
with women—with those birds that you know. And one day it
may be worth its price."

What always interested me most in the furniture of that
dining-room was not the pictures, nor the ample plate, nor the
edifices called sideboards, etc., but the apron of Marthe, who
served. A plain, unstarched, white apron, without a bib—an
apron that no English parlourmaid would have deigned to wear;
but of such fine linen, and all the exactly geometric creases of
its folding visible to the eye as Marthe passed round and round
our four chairs! Whenever I saw that apron I could see linen-
chests, and endless supplies of linen, and Tante and Marthe
fussing over them on quiet afternoons. And it went so well with
her dark-blue shiny frock! When Tante had joined her nephew's
household she had brought with her Marthe, already old in her
service. These two women were devoted to each other, each in
her own way. "Arrive then, with that sauce, *vieille folle!*" Tante
would command; and Marthe, pursing her lips, would defend
herself with a "*Mais madame—!*" There was no high invisible
wall between Marthe and her employers. One was not worried,
as one would have been in England, by the operation of the
detestable and barbaric theory that Marthe was an automaton,

50

inaccessible to human emotions. I remember seeing in the work-basket of the wife of a wealthy English socialist a little manual of advice to domestic servants upon their deportment, and I remember this: "Learn to control your voice, and always speak in a low voice. Never show by your demeanour that you have heard any remark which is not addressed to you." I wonder what Marthe, who had never worn a cap, nor perhaps seen one, would have thought of the manual, which possibly was written by a distressed gentlewoman in order to earn a few shillings. Martha could smile. She could even laugh and answer back—but within limits. We had not to pretend that Marthe consisted merely of two ministering hands animated by a brain, but without a soul. In France a servant works longer and harder than in England, but she is permitted the constant use of a soul.

A simple but an expensive dinner, for these people were the kind of people that, desiring only the best, were in a position to see that they had it, and accepted the cost as a matter of course. Moreover, they knew what the best was, especially the Tante. They knew how to buy. The chief dish was just steak. But what steak! What a thickness of steak and what tenderness! A whole cow had lived under the most approved conditions, and died a violent death, and the very essence of the excuse for it all lay on a blue and white dish in front of the hostess. Cost according! Steak; but better steak could not be had in the world! And the consciousness of this fact was on the calm benignant face of the hostess and on the vivacious ironic face of the Tante. So with the fruits of the earth, so with the wine. And the simple, straightforward distribution of the viands seemed to suit well their character. Into that flat there had not yet penetrated the grand modern principle that the act of carving is an obscene act, an act to be done shamefully in secret, behind the backs of the delicate impressionable. No! The dish of steak was planted directly in front of the hostess, under her very nose, and beyond the dish a pile of four plates; and, brazenly brandishing her implements, the Parisienne herself cut the titbits out of the titbit, and deposited them on plate after plate, which either Marthe took or we took ourselves, at hazard. Further, there was no embarrassment of multitudinous assorted knives and forks and spoons. With each course the diner received the tools necessary for that course. Between courses, if he wanted a toy for his fingers, he had to be content with a crust.

During the meal the conversation constantly reverted with pleasure to the question of food; it was diversified by expressions of the host's joy in his home, and the beings therein; and for the rest it did not ascend higher than heterogeneous personal gossip,—"unstitched," as the French say.

Instead of going into the drawing-room, we went through a bed-chamber, into a small room at the back. By taking a circuitous service-passage, and infringing on the kitchen, we might ultimately have arrived at that room without passing through the bedchamber; but the proper, the ceremonious way to it was through the bedchamber. This trifling detail illuminates the methods of the French architect even when he is building expensively—methods which persist to the present hour. Admirable at façades, he is an execrable planner, wasteful and maladroit, as may be seen even in the most important public buildings in Paris—such as the Town Hall. In arranging the "disposition" of flats, he exhausts himself on the principal apartments, and then, fatigued, lets the others struggle as best they may for light and air and access in the odd corners of space which remain. Of course, he is strong in the sympathy of his clients. It is a wide question of manners, stretching from the finest palaces of France down to the labyrinthine coverts of industrialism. Up to twenty-five years ago, architects simply did not consider the factors of either light or ventilation. I have myself lived in a flat, in one of the best streets of central Paris, of which none of the eight windows could possibly at any period of the year receive a single direct gleam of sunlight. Up to twenty-five years ago, nobody had discovered a reason why, in a domestic interior, a bedroom should not be a highroad.. . .

Visualise the magnificent straight boulevard, full of the beautiful horizontal glidings of trams and automobiles; the lofty and stylistic frontages; the great carved doors of the house; the quasi-Oriental entrance and courtyard, shut in from the fracas of the street; the monumental staircase; the spacious and even splendid dining-room; and then the bedroom opening directly off it; and then the still smaller sitting-room opening directly off that; and us there—the ebullient doctor, his elegant and calm wife, the Tante (on a small chair), and myself—sitting round a lamp amid a miscellany of bookcases and oddments. This was the room that the doctor preferred of an evening. He would say, joyously: "*C'est le décor home!*"

A cousin of the host was announced; and his relatives and I smiled archly, with affectionate malice, before he came in; for it was notorious that this cousin, an architect by profession, and a bachelor of forty years standing, had a few days earlier solemnly and definitely "broken" with his *petite amie*. I knew it. Everybody knew it within the wide family-radius. It was one of those things that "knew themselves." This call was itself a proof that the cousin had dragged his anchor. Moreover, he embraced his aunt with a certain self-consciousness. He was a tall, dark-bearded man, well dressed in a dark-grey suit—a good specimen of French tailoring, but a French tailor cannot use an iron and he cannot "roll" a collar. A rather melancholy and secretive and flaccid man, but somewhat hardened and strengthened by the lifelong use of a private fortune. They all had money—money of their own, independently of earned money; the wife had money—and I do not think that it occurred to any of them to live up to his or her income; their resources were always increasing, and the reserves that the united family could have brought up to face a calamity must have been formidable. None of them had ever been worried about money, and by reason of their financial ideals they were far more solid than a London family receiving, but spending, thrice their income.

Marthe came with another coffee cup, and the cousin,

when the hostess had filled it, set it down to go cold, after the French manner.

"Well, my boy," said Tante, whose ancient eyes were sparkling with eagerness. "By what appears, thou art a widower since several days."

"How a widower?"

"Yes," said the host, "it appears that thou art a widower." And added enthusiastically: "I am pretty content to see thee, my old one."

The hostess smiled at the widower with sympathetic indulgence.

"Who has told you?"

"What! Who has told us? All Paris knows it!"

"Well," said the cousin, looking at the carpet and apparently communing with himself—he always had an air of self-communing, "I suppose it's true!" He drank the tenth of a teaspoonful of coffee.

"Eh, well, my friend," the Tante commented. "I do not know if thou hast done well. That did not cost thee too dear, and she had a good-hearted face." Tante spoke with an air of special intimacy, because she and the cousin had kept house together for some years at one period.

"Thou hast seen her, Tante?" the hostess asked, surprised a little out of the calm in which she was crocheting.

"Have I seen her? I believe it well! I caught them together once when I was driving in the Bois."

"That was Antoinette," said the cousin.

"It was not Antoinette," said the Tante. "And thou hast no need to say it. Thou quittedst Antoinette in '96, before I had begun to hire that carriage. I recall it to myself perfectly."

"I suppose now it will be the grand spree," said the hostess, "during several months."

"The grand spree!" Tante broke in caustically. "Have no fear. The grand spree—that is not his kind. It is not he who will scatter his money with those birds. He is not so stupid as that." She laughed drily.

"Is she *rosse*, the Tante, all the same!" the host, flowing over with good nature, comforted his cousin.

Then Marthe entered again:

"The children demand monsieur."

The host bounded up from his chair.

"What! The children demand monsieur!" he exploded. "At nine o'clock! It is not possible that they are not asleep!"

"They say that monsieur promised to return to them after dinner."

"It is true!" he admitted, with a gesture of discovery. "It is true!"

"I pray thee," said the mother. "Go at once. And do not excite them."

"I think I'll go with you," I said.

"My little Bennett," the mother leaned towards me, "I supplicate you—at this hour—"

"But naturally he will come with me!" the host cried obstreperously.

We went, down a long narrow passage. There they were in their beds, the children, in a small bedroom divided into two by a low screen of ribbed glass, the boy on one side and the girl on the other. The window gave on to a small subsidiary courtyard. Through the half-drawn curtains the lighted windows of rooms opposite could be discerned, rising, storey after storey, up out of sight. A night-light burned on a table. The nurse stood apart, at the door. The children were lively, but pale. They had begun to go to school, and, except the journey to and from school, they seemed to have almost no outdoor exercise. No garden was theirs. The hall and the passages were their sole playground. And all the best part of their lives was passed between walls in a habitation twenty-five or thirty feet above ground, in the middle of Paris. Yet they were very well. The doctor did not romp with them. No! He simply and candidly caressed them, girl and boy, in turn, calling them passionately by the most beautiful names, burying his head in the bedclothes, and fondling their wild hair. He then entreated them, with genuine humility, to compose themselves for sleep, and parted last from the girl.

"She is exquisite—exquisite!" he murmured to me ecstatically, as we returned up the passage from this excursion.

She was.

In the small sitting-room the cousin was offering to the Tante some information of a political nature. The Tante kept a judicious eye on everything in Paris. .

"What!" The host protested vociferously. "He is again in his politics! Cousin, I supplicate thee—"

A good deal of supplication went on there. The host did succeed in stopping politics. With all the weight of his vivacious good-nature he bore politics down. The fact was, he had a real objection to politics, having convinced himself that they were permanently unclean in France. It was not the measures that he objected to, but the men—all of them with scarcely an exception—as cynical adventurers. On this point he was passionate. Politics were incurably futile, horribly *assommant*. He would not willingly allow them to soil his hearth.

"What hast thou done lately?" he asked of the cousin, changing the subject.

And the talk veered to public amusements. The cousin had been "distracting himself" amid his sentimental misadventures, by much theatre-going. They all, except the Tante, went very regularly to the theatres and to the operas. And not only that, but to concerts, exhibitions, picture-shows, services in the big churches, and every kind of diversion frequented by people in easy circumstances and by artists. There was little that they missed. They exhibited no special taste or knowledge in any art, but leaned generally to the best among that which was merely fashionable. They took seriously nearly every craftsman who, while succeeding, kept his dignity and refrained from being a mountebank. Thus, they were convinced that dramatists like Edmond Rostand and Henri Lavedan, actors and actresses like Le Bargy and Cécile Sorel, painters like Edouard Détaille and La Gandara, composers like Massenet and Charpentier, critics like Adolphe Brisson and Francis Chevassu, novelists like René Bazin and Daniel Lesueur, poets like Jean Riche-pin and Abel Bonnard, were original and first-class, and genuinely important in the history of their respective arts. On the other hand their attitude towards the real innovators and shapers of the future was timidly, but honestly, antipathetic. And they could not, despite any theorising to the contrary, bring themselves to take quite seriously any artist who had not been consecrated by public approval. With the most charming grace they would submit to be teased about this, but it would have been impossible to tease them out of it. And there was always a slight uneasiness in the air when they and I came to grips in the discussion of art. I could almost hear the shrewd Tante saying to herself: "What a pity this otherwise sane and safe young man is an artist!"

"Figure to yourself," the host would answer me with an adorable, affectionate mien of apology, when I asked his opinion of a new work by Maurice Ravel, heard on a Sunday afternoon, "Figure to yourself that we scarcely liked it."

And with the same mien, of a very fashionable comedy in which Lavedan, Le Bargy, and Julia Bartet had combined to create a terrific success at the Théâtre Français:

"Figure to yourself, it was truly very nice, after all! Of course one might say.. . ."

The truth was, it had carried them off their feet.

Upon my soul I think I liked them the better for it all. And, in talking to them, I understood a little better the real and solid basis upon which rests all that overwhelming, complex, expensive apparatus of artistic diversions laid out for the public within a mile radius of the Place de l'Opéra. There is a public, a genuine public, which desires ardently to be amused and which will handsomely put down the money for its amusement. And it is never tired, never satiated. The artist, who seldom pays, is apt to wonder if any considerable body of persons pay, is apt to regard the commercial continuance of art as a sort of inexplicable miracle. But these people paid. They always paid, and richly. And there were whole streets of large houses full of other people who shared their tastes and their habits, if not their extreme attractiveness.

I wondered where we should be without them, we artists, as I took leave of them at something after midnight. My good friend, the melancholy cousin, had departed. Tante had gone to bed, though she protested she never slept. We had been drinking weak tea as we wandered about the dining-room. And now I, obdurate against the host's supplications not to desert them so early, was departing too. At the door the hostess lighted a little taper, and gave it to me. And when the door was opened they moderated their caressing voices; for a dozen other domestic interiors, each intricate and complete, gave on the resounding staircase. And with my little taper I descended through the silence and the darkness of the staircase. And at the bottom I halted in the black entrance way, and summoned the concierge out of his sleep to release the catch of the small door within the great portals. There was a responsive click immediately, and in the blackness a sudden gleam from the boulevard. The concierge and his wife, living for ever sunless in a room and a half beneath all those other interiors, were throughout the night at the mercy of a call, mine or another's. "Curious existence!" I thought, as my shutting of the door echoed about the building, and I stepped into the illumination of the boulevard. "The concierge is necessary to them. And without the equivalent of such as they, such as I could not possess even a decent overcoat!" On the *façade* of the house every outer casement was shut. Not a sign of life in it.

V

CAUSE CÉLÈBRE

Quite early in the winter evening, before the light had died out of the sky, central Paris was beginning to be pleasurably excited. The aspect of the streets and of the *cafés* showed that. One saw it and heard it in the gestures and tones of the people; one had a proof of it in oneself. The whole city was in a state of delightful anxiety; and it was happy because the result of the night, whatever fate chose to decide, could not fail to be amusing and even thrilling. All the thoroughfares converging upon the small and crowded island which is the historical kernel of Paris, were busier and livelier than usual. In particular, automobiles thronged—the largest, glossiest, and most silent automobiles, whose horns were orchestras—automobiles which vied with motor-omnibuses for imposingness and moved forward with the smooth majesty of trains.

There came a point, near the twinkling bridges, where progress was impossible, where an impalpable obstacle intervened, and vehicles stood arrested in long treble files, and mysterious words were passed backwards from driver to driver. But nobody seemed to mind; nobody seemed impatient; for it was something to be thus definitely and materially a part of the organised excitement. Hundreds of clever resourceful persons had had the idea of avoiding the main avenues, and creeping up unobserved to the centre of attraction by the little streets. So that all these ancient, narrow, dark lanes that thread between high and picturesque architectures were busy with automobiles and carriages. And in the gloom one might see shooting round a

59

corner the brilliant interior of an automobile, with electric light and flowers and a pet dog, and a couple of extremely fashionable young women in it, their eyes sparkling with present joy and the confident expectation of joy to come. And such young women, utterly correct, were doing the utterly correct thing. But all these little streets led at last to the same impalpable obstacle. So that from a high tower, for instance, the Tour St. Jacques close by, one might have beheld the black masonry of the centre of attraction as it were beleaguered on every side by the attacking converging files that were held back by some powerful word; while the minutes elapsed, and the incandescent signs of shops and theatres increased in the sky, and the Seine, dividing to clasp the island, darkened into a lamp-reflecting mirror along which tiny half-discerned steamers restlessly plied.

Despite the powerful word, the Palace of Justice, the centre of attraction, was tremendously alive and gay with humanity. Traffic could not be stopped, and was not stopped, and those who had sufficient energy and perseverance could insinuate themselves into its precincts. The great gold lamps that flank the staircase of honour gleamed upon a crowd continually ascending and descending. The outer hall was full of laughing chatter and of smoke. And barristers, both old and young, walked to and fro in hieratic converse, waving their cigarettes in sober curves, and on every one of their faces as they gazed negligently at the public was the announcement that they could tell "an they would." All the interminable intersecting corridors were equally vivacious, with their diminishing perspectives of stoves against which groups warmed themselves. Groups of talkers made the circuit of the corridors as it might have been the circuit of a town, passing a given spot regularly, and repeating and repeating the same arguments. And the solemn arched immensity of the Hall of Lost Footsteps was like a Bourse. Here, more than anywhere else, one had the sense of audience-chambers concealed behind doors, where fatal doings were afoot; one had the sense of the terrific vastness and complexity of the Palace wherein scores

60

of separate ceremonious activities simultaneously proceeded in scores of different halls. The general public knew only that somewhere within the Palace, somewhere close at hand, at the end of some particular passage, guarded doors hid the spectacle whose slightest episode was being telegraphed to all the cities of the entire civilised world, and the general public was content, even very content, to be near by.

Cause Célèbre

The affair was in essence a trifle; merely the trial of a woman for the murder of her husband. But this woman was a heroic woman; this woman belonged by right of brain and individual force to the great race of Thérèse Humbert. Years before, she had moved safely in the background of a sensational tragedy involving the highest personages of the Republic. And now in the background of her own tragedy there moved somebody so high and so potent that no newspaper dared or cared to name his name. All that was known was that this enigmatic and awful individual existed, that he was involved, that had he been less sublime he would have had to appear before the court, that he would not appear, and that justice would suffer accordingly. In the ordeal of extremest publicity, the woman had emerged a Titaness. Throughout all her altercations with judge, advocates, witnesses, and journalists, she had held her own grandly, displaying not only an astounding force of character, but a superb appreciation of the theatrical quality of her *rôle*. She was of a piece with yellow journalism, and the multitude that gapes for yellow journalism. She was shameless. She was caught again and again in a net of lies, and she always escaped. She admitted nearly everything: lyings, adulteries, and manifold deceits; but she would not admit that she knew anything about the murder of her husband. And even though it was obvious that the knots by which she was bound when the murder was discovered were not serious knots, even though she left a hundred incriminating details unexplained, a doubt concerning her guilt would persist in the minds of the impartial. She was indubitably a terrible creature, but she was an enchantress, and she was also beyond question an exceedingly able housekeeper and hostess. She might be terrible without being a murderess.

And now the trial was closing. The verdict, it was stated, would be rendered that night even if the court sat till midnight. It would be a pity to keep an amiable public, already on the rack of impatience for many days, waiting longer. The time was ripe. Further, the woman had had enough. Her resources were exhausted, and to continue the fight would mean an anti-climax. The woman had completely lost the respect of the public—that was inevitable—but she had not lost its admiration. The attitude of the public was cruel, with the ignoble cruelty which is practised towards women in Latin countries alone; she had even been sarcastically sketched in the most respectable illustrated paper in the attitude of a famous madonna; but beneath the inconceivably base jeers, there remained admiration; and there remained, too, gratitude—the gratitude offered to a gladiator who has fought well and provided a really first-class diversion.

The supper-restaurants were visited earlier and were much more crowded than usual on that night. It was as though the influence of the trial had been aphrodisiacal. Or it may have been that the men and women of pleasure wished to receive the verdict in circumstances worthy of its importance in the annals of pleasure. Or it may have been that dinner had been deranged by the excitations connected with the trial and that people felt honestly hungry. I went into one of these restaurants, in a square whose buildings are embroidered with inviting letters of fire until dawn every morning throughout the year. A stern attendant took me up in a lift, and instantly I had quitted the sternness of the lift I was in another atmosphere. There was the bar, and there the illustrious English barman, drunk. For in these regions the barman must always be English and a little drunk. The barman knows everybody, and not to know his Christian name and the feel of his hand is to be nobody. This barman is a Parisian celebrity. But let an accident or a misadventure disqualify him from his work, and he will be forgotten utterly in less than a week. And in his martyred old age he will certainly recount to charitable acquaintances, who find him ineffably tedious, how he was barman at the unique Restaurant Lepic in the old days when fun was really fun, and the most appalling iniquity was openly tolerated by the police.

The bar and the barman and the cloak-room attendant (another man of genius) are only the prelude to the great supper-hall, which is simply and completely dazzling, with its profuse festoons of electric bulbs, its innumerable naked shoulders, arms, and bosoms, its fancy costumes, its bald heads, its music, clatter, and tinkle, and its desperate gaiety. To go into it is like going into a furnace of sensuality. It can be likened to nothing but an orange-lit scene of Roman debauch in a play written and staged by Mr. Hall Caine. One feels that one has been unjust in one's attitude to Mr. Hall Caine's claims as a realist.

Although the restaurant will positively not hold any more revellers, more revellers insist on coming in, and fresh tables are produced by conjuring and placed for them between other tables, until the whole mass of wood and flesh is wedged tight together and waiters have to perform prodigies of insinuation. The effect of these multitudinous wasters is desolating, and even pathetic. It is the enormous stupidity of the mass that is pathetic, and its secret tedium that is desolating. At their wits' end how to divert themselves, these bald heads pass the time in capers more antique and fatuous than were ever employed at a village wedding. Some of them find distraction in monstrous gorging—and beefsteaks and fried potatoes and spicy sauces go down their throats in a way to terrorise the arthritic beholder. Others merely drink. Some quarrel, with the boneless persistency of intoxication. One falls humorously under a table, and is humorously fished up by the red-coated leader of the orchestra: it is a marked success of esteem. Many are content to caress the bright odalisques with fond, monotonous vacuity. A few of these odalisques, and the waiters, alone save the spectacle from utter humiliation. The waiters are experts engaged in doing their job. The industry of each night leaves them no energy for dissoluteness. They are alert and determined. Their business is to make stupidity as lavish as possible, and they succeed. To see them surveying with cold statistical glances the field of their operations, to listen to their indestructible politeness, to divine the depth of their concealed scorn—this is a pleasure. And some of the odalisques are beautiful. Fine women in the sight of heaven! They too are experts, with the hard preoccupation of experts. They are at work; and this is the battle of life. They inspire respect. It is—it is the dignity of labour.

They inspire respect

Suddenly it is announced that the jury at the Palace are about to deliver their verdict. Nobody knows how the news has come, nor even who first spoke it in the restaurant. But there it is. Humorous guffaws of relief are vented. The fever of the place becomes acute, with a decided influence on the consumption of champagne. The accused lady is toasted again and again. Of course, she had been, throughout, the solid backbone of the chatter; but now she was all the chatter. And everybody recounted again to everybody else every suggestive rumour of her iniquity that had appeared in any newspaper for months past. She was tried over again in a moment, and condemned and insulted and defended, and consistently honoured with libations. She had never been more truly heroic, more legendary, than she was then.

The childlike company loudly demanded the verdict, with their tongues and with their feet.

A beautiful young girl of about eighteen, the significant features of whose attire were long black stockings and a necklace, said to a gentleman who was helping her to eat a vast *entrecote* and to drink champagne:

"If it comes not soon, it will be too late."

"The verdict?" said the fatuous swain. "How?—too late?"

"I shall be too drunk," said the girl, apparently meaning that she would be too drunk to savour the verdict and to get joy from it. She spoke with mournful and slightly disgusted certainty, as though anticipating a phenomenon which was absolutely regular and absolutely inevitable.

And then, on a table near the centre of the room, instead of plates and glasses appeared a child-dancer who might have been Spanish or Creole, but who probably had never been out of Montmartre. This child seemed to be surrounded by her family seated at the table—by her mother and her aunts and a cousin or so, all with simple and respectable faces, naïvely proud of and pleased with the child. From their expressions, the child might have been cutting bread and butter on the table instead of dancing. The child danced exquisitely, but her performance could not moderate the din. It was a lovely thing gloriously wasted. The one feature of it that was not wasted on the intelligence of the company was the titillating contrast between the little girl's fresh infancy and the advanced decomposition of her environment.

She ceased, and disappeared into her family. The applause began, but it was mysteriously and swiftly cut short. Why did every one by a simultaneous impulse glance eagerly in the direction of the door? Why was the hush so dramatic? A voice—whose?—cried near the doorway:

"*Acquittée!*"

And all cried triumphantly: "*Acquittée! Acquittée! Acquittée! Acquittée!*" Happy, boisterous Bedlam was created and let loose. Even the waiters forgot themselves. The whole world stood up, stood on chairs, or stood on tables; and shouted, shrieked, and whistled. But the boneless drunkards were still quarrelling, and one bald head had retained sufficient presence of mind to wear a large oyster-shell facetiously for a hat. And then the orchestra, inspired, struck into a popular refrain of the moment, perfectly apposite. And all sang with right good-will:

"*Le lendemain elle était sonnante.*"

VI

RUSSIAN IMPERIAL BALLET AT THE OPERA

Sylvain's is the only good restaurant in the centre of Paris where you can dine in the open air, that is to say, in the street. Close by, the dark, still mass of the Opéra rises hugely out of the dusk and out of the flitting traffic at its base. Sylvain's is full of diners who have no eyes to see beyond the surfaces of things.

By virtue of a contract made between Sylvain's and the city, the diners are screened off from the street and from the twentieth century by a row of high potted evergreens. Pass within the screen, and you leave behind you the modern epoch. The Third Republic recedes; the Second Empire recedes; Louis-Philippe has never been, nor even Napoleon; the Revolution has not begun to announce itself. You are become suddenly a *grand seigneur*. Every gesture and tone of every member of the *personnel* of Sylvain's implores your excellency with one word:

"Deign!"

It is curious that while a modern shopkeeper who sells you a cigar or an automobile or a quarter of lamb does not think it necessary to make you a noble of the *ancien régime* before commencing business, a shopkeeper who sells you cooked food could not omit this preliminary without losing his self-respect. And it is the more curious since all pre-democratic books of travel are full of the cheek of these particular shopkeepers. Such tales of old travellers could scarcely be credited, in spite of their unison, were it not that the ancient tradition of rapacious insolence still survives in wild and barbaric spots like the cathedral cities of England.

68

Your excellency, attended by his gentlemen-in-waiting (who apparently never eat, never want to eat), in the intervals of the ceremonious collation will gaze with interest at the Opéra, final legacy of the Empire to the Republic. A great nation owes it to itself to possess a splendid opera-palace. Art must be fostered. The gracious amenities of life must be maintained. And this is the State's affair. The State has seen to it. The most gorgeous building in Paris is not the legislative chamber, nor the hall of the University, nor the clearing-house of charity. It is the Opéra. The State has paid for it, and the State pays every year for its maintenance. That is, the peasant chiefly pays. There is not a peasant in the farthest corner of France who may not go to bed at dark comforted by the thought that the Opéra in Paris is just opening its cavalry-sentinelled doors, and lighting its fifteen thousand electric candles, and that he is helping to support all that. Paris does not pay; the *habitués* of the Opéra do not pay; the yawning tourists do not pay; the grandiose classes do not pay. It is the nation, as a nation, that accepts the burden, because the encouragement of art is a national duty. (Moreover, visiting monarchs have to be diverted.) Of one sort or another, from the tenor to the vendor of programmes, there are twelve hundred priests and priestesses of art in the superb building. A few may be artists. But it is absolutely certain that all are bureaucrats.

The Opéra is the Circumlocution Office. The Opéra is a State department. More, it is probably the most characteristic of all the State departments, and the most stubbornly reactionary. The nominal director, instead of being omnipotent and godlike, is only a poor human being whose actions are the resultant of ten thousand forces that do not fear him. The Opéra is above all the theatre of secret influences. Every mystery of its enormous and wasteful inefficiency can be explained either by the operation of the secret influence or by the operation of the bureaucratic mind. If the most tedious operas are played the most often, if the stage is held by singers who cannot sing, if original artists have no chance there, if the blight of a flaccid perfunctoriness is upon nearly all the performances, if astute mothers can sell the virginity of their dancing daughters to powerful purchasers in the wings, the reason is a reason of State. The Opéra is the splendid prey of the high officers of State. If such a one wants an evening's entertainment, or a mistress, or to get rid of a mistress, the Opéra is there, at his disposition. The *foyer de la danse* is the most wonderful seraglio in the western world, and it is reserved to the Government and to subscribers. Thus is art fostered, and for this does the peasant pay.

Nevertheless the Opéra is a beautiful and impressive sight in the late, warm dusk of June. Against the deep purple sky the monument stands up like a mountain; and through its innumerable windows—holes in the floor of heaven—can be glimpsed yellow clusters of candelabra and perspectives of marble pillars and frescoed walls. And at the foot of the gigantic *façade* little brightly coloured figures are running up the steps and disappearing eagerly within: they are the world of fashion, and they know that they are correct and that the Opéra is the Opéra.

I looked over the crimson plush edge of the box down into Egypt, where Cleopatra was indulging her desires; into a civilisation so gorgeous, primitive, and far-off that when compared to it the eighteenth and the twentieth centuries seemed as like as two peas in their sophistication and sobriety. Cleopatra had set eyes on a youth, and a whim for him had taken her. By no matter what atrocious exercise of power and infliction of suffering, that whim had to be satisfied on the instant. It was satisfied. And a swift homicide left the Queen untrammelled by any sentimental consequences. The whole affair was finished in a moment, and the curtain falling on all that violent and gorgeous scene. In a moment this Oriental episode, interpreted by semi-Oriental artists, had made all the daring prurient suggestiveness of French comedy seem timid and foolish. It was a revelation. A new standard was set, and there was not a vaudevillist in the auditorium but knew that neither he nor his interpreters could ever reach that standard. The simple and childlike gestures of

70

the slave-girls as with their bodies and their veils they formed a circular tent to hide Cleopatra and her lover—these gestures took away the breath of protest.

Les Sylphides

The St. Petersburg and the Moscow troupes, united, of the Russian Imperial Ballet, had been brought to Paris, at vast expense and considerable loss, to present this astounding spectacle of mere magnificent sanguinary lubricity to the cosmopolitan fashion of Paris. There the audience actually was, rank after rank of crowded toilettes rising to the dim ceiling, young women from the Avenue du Bois and young women from

Arizona, and their protective and possessive men. And nobody blenched, nobody swooned. The audience was taken by assault. The West End of Europe was just staggered into acceptance. As yet London has seen only fragments of Russian ballet. But London may and probably will see the whole. Let there be no qualms. London will accept also. London might be horribly scared by one-quarter of the audacity shown in *Cleopatra*, but it will not be scared by the whole of that audacity. An overdose of a fatal drug is itself an antidote. The fact is, that the spectacle was saved by a sort of moral nudity, and by a naïve assurance of its own beauty. Oh! It was extremely beautiful. It was ineffably more beautiful than any other ballet I had ever seen. An artist could feel at once that an intelligence of really remarkable genius had presided over its invention and execution. It was masterfully original from the beginning. It continually furnished new ideals of beauty. It had drawn its inspiration from some rich fountain unknown to us occidentals. Neither in its scenery, nor in its grouping, nor in its pantomime was there any clear trace of that Italian influence which still dominates the European ballet. With a vengeance it was a return to nature and a recommencement. It was brutally direct. It was beastlike; but the incomparable tiger is a beast. It was not perverse. It was too fresh, zealous, and alive to be perverse. Personally I was conscious of the most intense pleasure that I had experienced in a theatre for years. And this was Russia! This was the country that had made such a deadly and disgusting mess of the Russo-Japanese War.

The box was a stage-box. It consisted of a suite of two drawing-rooms, softly upholstered, lit with electric light, and furnished with easy-chairs and mirrors. A hostess might well have offered tea to a score of guests therein. And as a fact there were a dozen people in it. Its size indicated the dimensions of the auditorium, in which it was a mere cell. The curious thing about it was the purely incidental character of its relation to the stage. The front of it was a narrow terrace, like the mouth of a bottle, which offered a magnificent panorama of the auditorium, with a longitudinal slice of the stage at one extremity. From the terrace one glanced vertically down at the stage, as at a street-pavement from a first-storey window. Three persons could be comfortable, and four could be uncomfortable, on the terrace. One or two more, by leaning against chair-backs and coiffures, could see half of the longitudinal slice of the stage. The remaining half-dozen were at liberty to meditate in the luxurious twilight of the drawing-room. The Republic, as operatic manager, sells every night some scores, and on its brilliant nights some hundreds, of expensive seats which it is perfectly well aware give no view whatever of the stage: another illustration of the truth that the sensibility of the conscience of corporations varies inversely with the size of the corporation.

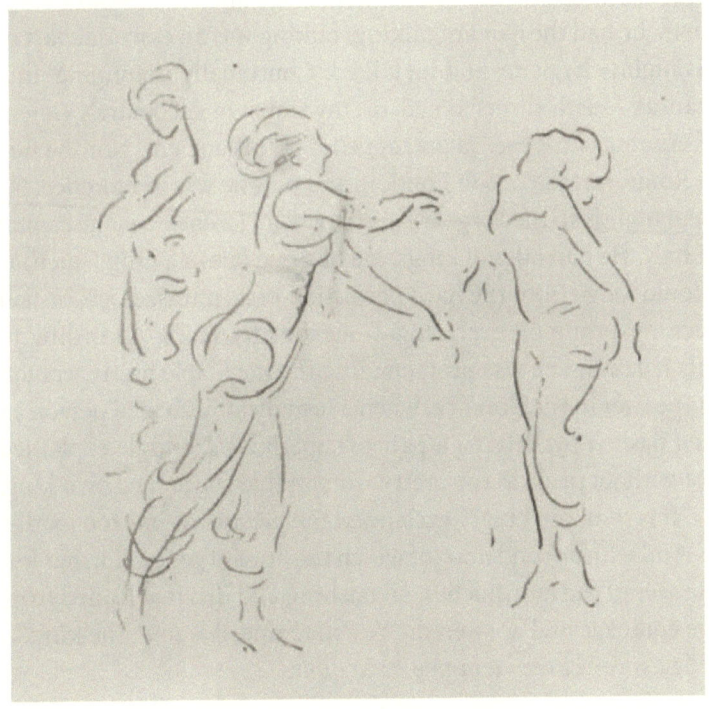

Fragile and beautiful odalisques

But this is nothing. The wonderful aspect of the transaction is that purchasers never lack. They buy and suffer; they buy again and suffer yet again; they live on and reproduce their kind. There was in the hinterland of the box a dapper, vivacious man who might (if he had wasted no time) have been grandfather to a man as old as I. He was eighty-five years old, and he had sat in boxes of an evening for over sixty years. He talked easily of the heroic age before the Revolution of '48, when, of course, every woman was an enchantress, and the farces at the Palais Royal were *really* amusing. He could pipe out whole pages of farce. Except during the *entr'actes* this man's curiosity did not extend beyond the shoulders of the young women on the terrace. For him the spectacle might have been something going on round the corner of the next street. He was in a spacious and discreet drawing-room; he had the habit of talking; talking was an essential part of his nightly hygiene; and he talked. Continually impinging, in a manner fourth-dimensional, on my vision of Cleopatra's violent afternoon, came the "*Je me rappelle*" of this ancient. Now he was in Rome, now he was in London, and now he was in Florence. He went nightly to the Pergola Theatre when Florence was the capital of Italy. He had tales of kings. He had one tale of a king which, as I could judge from the hard perfection of its phraseology, he had been repeating on every night-out for fifty years. According to this narration he was promenading the inevitable pretty woman in the Cascine at Florence, when a heavily moustached person *en civil* flashed by, driving a pair of superb bays, and he explained not without pride to the pretty woman that she looked on a king.

"It is *that*, the king?" exclaimed the pretty *ingénue* too loudly.

And with a grand bow (of which the present generation has lost the secret) the moustaches, all flashing and driving, leaned from the equipage and answered: "Yes, madame, it is *that*, the king."

"*Et si vous avez vu la tête de la dame...!*"

In those days society existed.

I should have heard many more such tales during the *entr'acte*, but I had to visit the stage. Strictly, I did not desire to visit the stage, but as I possessed the privilege of doing so, I felt bound in pride to go. I saw myself at the great age of eighty-five recounting to somebody else's grandchildren the marvels that I had witnessed in the *coulisses* of the Paris Opéra during the unforgettable season of the Russian Imperial Ballet in the early years of the century, when society existed.

At an angle of a passage which connects the auditorium with the tray (the stage is called the tray, and those who call the stage the stage at the Opéra are simpletons and lack guile) were a table and a chair, and, partly on the chair and partly on the table, a stout respectable man: one of the twelve hundred.

He looked like a town-councillor, and his life-work on this planet was to distinguish between persons who had the entry and persons who had not the entry. He doubted my genuineness at once, and all the bureaucrat in him glowered from his eyes. Yes! My card was all right, but it made no mention of madame. Therefore, I might pass, but madame might not. Moreover, save in cases very exceptional, ladies were not admitted to the tray. So it appeared! I was up against an entire department of the State. Human nature is such that at that moment, had some power offered me the choice between the ability to write a novel as fine as *Crime and Punishment* and the ability to triumph instantly over the pestilent town-councillor, I would have chosen the latter. I retired in good order. "You little suspect, town-councillor," I said to him within myself, "that I am the guest of the management, that I am extremely intimate with the management, and that, indeed, the management is my washpot!" At the next *entr'acte* I returned again with an omnipotent document which instructed the whole twelve hundred to let both monsieur and madame pass anywhere, everywhere. The town-councillor admitted that it was perfect, so far as it went. But there was the question of my hat to be considered. I was not wearing the right kind of hat! The town councillor planted both his feet firmly on tradition, and defied imperial passports. "Can you have any conception," I cried to him within myself, "how much this hat cost me at

Henry Heath's?" Useless! Nobody ever had passed, and nobody ever would pass, from the auditorium to the tray in a hat like mine. It was unthinkable. It would be an outrage on the Code Napoléon.... After all, the man had his life-work to perform. At length he offered to keep my hat for me till I came back. I yielded. I was beaten. I was put to shame. But he had earned a night's repose.

The unforgettable season

The famous, the notorious *foyer de la danse* was empty. Here was an evening given exclusively to the ballet, and not one member of the corps had had the idea of exhibiting herself in the showroom specially provided by the State as a place or rendezvous for ladies and gentlemen. The most precious quality of an annual subscription for a seat at the Opéra is that it carries with it the entry to the *foyer de la danse* (provided one's hat is right); if it did not, the subscriptions to the Opéra would assuredly diminish. And lo! the gigantic but tawdry mirror which gives a factitious amplitude to a room that is really small, did not reflect the limbs of a single dancer! The place had a mournful, shabby-genteel look, as of a resort gradually losing fashion. It was tarnished. It did not in the least correspond with a young man's dreams of it. Yawning tedium hung in it like a vapour, that tedium which is the implacable secret enemy of dissoluteness. This, the *foyer de la danse*, where the insipidly vicious heroines of Halévy's ironic masterpiece achieved, with a mother's aid, their ducal conquests! It was as cruel a disillusion as the first sight of Rome or Jerusalem. Its meretriciousness would not have deceived even a visionary parlour-maid. Nevertheless, the world of the Opéra was astounded at the neglect of its hallowed *foyer* by these young women from St. Petersburg and Moscow. I was told, with emotion, that on only two occasions in the whole season had a Russian girl wandered therein. The legend of the sobriety and the chastity of these strange Russians was abroad in the Opéra like a strange, uncanny tale. Frankly, Paris could not understand it. Because all these creatures were young, and all of them conformed to some standard or other of positive physical beauty! They could not be old, for the reason that a ukase obliged them to retire after twenty years' service at latest; that is, at about the age of thirty-six, a time of woman's life which on the Paris stage is regarded as infancy. Such a ukase must surely have been promulgated by Ivan the Terrible or Catherine!. . . No!

Paris never recovered from the wonder of the fact that when they were not dancing these lovely girls were just honest misses, with apparently no taste for bank-notes and spiced meats, even in the fever of an unexampled artistic and fashionable success.

An honest Miss

Amid the turmoil of the stage, where the prodigiously original peacock-green scenery of *Scheherazade* was being set, a dancer could be seen here and there in a corner, waiting, preoccupied, worried, practising a step or a gesture. I was clumsy enough to encounter one of the principals who did not want to be encountered; we could not escape from each other. There was nothing for it but to shake hands. His face assumed the weary, unwilling smile of conventional politeness. His fingers were limp.

"It pleases you?"

"Enormously."

I turned resolutely away at once, and with relief he lapsed back into his preoccupation concerning the half-hour's intense emotional and physical labour that lay immediately in front of him. In a few moments the curtain went up, and the terrific creative energy of the troupe began to vent itself. And I began to understand a part of the secret of the extreme brilliance of the Russian ballet.

The brutality of *Scheherazade* was shocking. It was the Arabian Nights treated with imaginative realism. In perusing the Arabian Nights we never try to picture to ourselves the manners of a real Bagdad; or we never dare. We lean on the picturesque splendour and romantic poetry of certain aspects of the existence portrayed, and we shirk the basic facts: the crudity of the passions, and the superlative cruelty informing the whole social system. For example, we should not dream of dwelling on the more serious functions of the caliphian eunuchs.

In the surpassing fury and magnificence of the Russian ballet one saw eunuchs actually at work, scimitar in hand. There was the frantic orgy, and then there was the barbarous punishment, terrible and revolting; certainly one of the most sanguinary sights ever seen on an occidental stage. The eunuchs pursued the fragile and beautiful odalisques with frenzy; in an instant the seraglio was strewn with murdered girls in all the abandoned postures of death. And then silence, save for the hard breathing of the executioners!... A thrill! It would seem incredible that such a spectacle should give pleasure. Yet it unquestionably did, and very exquisite pleasure. The artists, both the creative and the interpretative, had discovered an artistic convention which was at once grandiose and truthful. The passions displayed were primitive, but they were ennobled in their illustration. The performance was regulated to the least gesture; no detail was unstudied; and every moment was beautiful; not a few were sublime.

And all this a by-product of Russian politics! If the politics of France are subtly corrupt; if anything can be done in France by nepotism and influence, and nothing without; if the governing machine of France is fatally vitiated by an excessive and unimaginative centralisation—the same is far more shamefully true of Russia. The fantastic inefficiency of all the great departments of State in Russia is notorious and scandalous. But the Imperial ballet, where one might surely have presumed an intensification of every defect (as in Paris), happens to be far nearer perfection than any other enterprise of its kind, public or private. It is genuinely dominated by artists of the first rank; it is invigorated by a real discipline; and the results achieved approach the miraculous. The pity is that the moujik can never learn that one, at any rate, of the mysterious transactions which pass high up over his head, and for which he is robbed, is in itself honest and excellent. An alleviating thought for the moujik, if only it could be knocked into his great thick head! For during the performance of the Russian Imperial Ballet at the Paris Opéra, amid all the roods of toilettes and expensive correctness, one thinks of the moujik; or one ought to think of him. He is at the bottom of it. See him in Tchekoff's masterly tale, *The Moujiks*, in his dirt, squalor, drunkenness, lust, servitude, and despair! Realise him well at the back of your mind as you watch the ballet! Your delightful sensations before an unrivalled work of art are among the things he has paid for.

Walking home, I was attracted, within a few hundred yards of the Opéra, by the new building of the Magasins du Printemps. Instead of being lighted up and all its galleries busy with thousands of women in search of adornment, it stood dark and deserted. But at one of the entrances was a feeble ray. I could not forbear going into the porch and putting my nose against the glass. The head-watchman was seated in the centre of the ground-floor chatting with a colleague. With a lamp and chairs they had constructed a little domesticity for themselves in the middle of that acreage of silks and ribbons and feathers all covered now with pale dust-sheets. They were the centre of a small sphere of illumination, and in the surrounding gloom could be dimly discerned gallery after gallery rising in a slender lacework of iron. The vision of Bagdad had been inexpressibly romantic; but this vision also was inexpressibly romantic.

Chief Eunuch

There was something touching in the humanity of those simple men amid the vast nocturnal stillness of that organism—the most spectacular, the most characteristic, the most spontaneous, and perhaps the most beautiful symbol of an age which is just as full of romance as any other age. The human machine and the scenic panorama of the big shop have always attracted me, as in Paris so in London. And looking at this particular, wonderful shop in its repose I could contemplate better the significance of its activity. What singular ideals have the women who passionately throng it in the eternal quest! I say "passionately," because I have seen eyes glitter with fierce hope in front of a skunk boa or the tints of a new stuff, translating instantly these material things into terms of love and adoration. What cruelty is hourly practised upon the other women who must serve and smile and stand on their feet in the stuffiness of the heaped and turbulent galleries eleven hours a day six full days a week; and upon the still other women, unpresentable, who in their high garrets stitch together these confections! And how fine and how inspiriting it all is, this fever, and these delusive hopes, and this cruelty! The other women are asleep now, repairing damage; but in a very few hours they will be converging here in long hurried files from the four quarters of Paris, in their enforced black, and tying their black aprons, and pinning on their breasts the numbered discs which distinguish them from one another in the judgment-books of the shop. They will be beginning again. The fact is that Bagdad is nothing to this. Only people are so blind.

LIFE IN LONDON

1911

I

___

THE RESTAURANT

You have a certain complacency in entering it, because it is one of the twenty monster restaurants of London. The name glitters in the public mind. "Where shall we dine?" The name suggests itself; by the immense force of its notoriety it comes unsought into the conversation like a thing alive. "All right! Meet you in the Lounge at 7.45." You feel—whatever your superficial airs—that you are in the whirl of correctness as you hurry (of course late) out of a taxi into the Lounge. There is something about the word "Lounge". . .! Space and freedom in the Lounge, and a foretaste of luxury; and it is inhabited by the haughty of the earth! You are not yet a prisoner, in the Lounge. Then an official, with the metallic insignia of authority, takes you apart.

He is very deferential—but with the intimidating deference of a limited company that pays forty per cent. You can go upstairs—though he doubts if there is immediately a table—or you can go downstairs. (Strange, how in the West-End, when once you quit the street, you must always go up or down; the planet's surface is forbidden to you; you lose touch with it; the ground-landlord has taken it and hidden it-) You go downstairs; you are hypnotised into going downstairs; and you go down, and down, one of a procession, until a man, entrenched in a recess furnished to look like a ready-made tailor's, accepts half your clothing and adds it to his stock. He does not ask for it; he need not; you are hypnotised. Stripped, you go further down and down. You are now part of the tremendous organism; you have left behind not merely your clothing, but your volition; your number is in your hand.

He is very deferential

Suddenly, as you pass through a doorway, great irregular vistas of a subterranean chamber discover themselves to you, limitless. You perceive that this wondrous restaurant ramifies under all London, and that a table on one verge is beneath St. Paul's Cathedral, and a table on the other verge beneath the Albert Memorial. All the tables—all the thousands of tables—are occupied. An official comes to you, and, putting his mouth

84

to your ear (for the din is terrific), tells you that he will have a table for you in three minutes. You wait, forlorn. It reminds you of waiting at the barber's for a shave, except that the barber gives you an easy-chair and a newspaper. Here you must stand; and you must gather your skirts about you and stand firm to resist the shock of blind waiters. Others are in your case; others have been waiting longer than you, and at every moment more arrive. You wait. The diners see you waiting, and you wonder whether they are eating slowly on purpose.... At length you are led away—far, far from the pit's mouth into a remote working of the mine. You watch a man whisk away foul plates and glasses, and cover offence with a pure white cloth. You sit. You are saved! And human nature is such that you feel positively grateful to the limited company.. . .

You begin to wait again, having been deserted by your saviours. And then your wandering attention notices behind you, under all the other sounds, a steady sound of sizzling. And there fat, greasy men, clothed and capped in white, are throwing small fragments of animal carcases on to a huge, red fire, and pulling them off in the nick of time, and flinging them on to plates which are continually being snatched away by flying hands. The grill, as advertised! And you wait, helpless, through a period so long that if a live cow and a live sheep had been led into the restaurant to satisfy the British passion for realism in eating, there would have been time for both animals to be murdered, dismembered, and fried before the gaze of a delighted audience. But fear not. The deity of the organism, though unseen, is watching over you. You have not been omitted from the divine plan. Presently a man approaches with a gigantic menu, upon which are printed the names of hundreds of marvellous dishes, and you can have any of them—and at most reasonable prices. Only, you must choose at once. You must say instantly to the respectful but inexorable official exactly what you will have. You are lost in the menu as in a labyrinth, as in a jungle at nightfall.... Quick! For, as you have waited, so are others waiting! Out with it! You drop the menu. "Roast beef and Yorkshire pudding—Guinness." The magic phrase releases you. In the tenth of a second the official has vanished. A railway truck laden with the gifts of Cuba and Sumatra and the monks of the Chartreuse, sweeps majestically by, blotting out the horizon; and lo! no sooner has it glided past than you see men hastening towards you with plates and bottles. With an astounding celerity the beef and the stout have, arrived—out of the unknown and the unknowable, out of some secret place in the centre of the earth, where rows and rows of slices of beef and bottles of stout wait enchanted for your word.

All the thousands of tables scintillate with linen and glass and silver, and steel and ivory, and are bright with flowers; ten thousand blossoms have been wrenched from their beds and marshalled here in captive regiments to brighten the beef and stout on which your existence depends. The carpet is a hot crimson bed of flowers. The whole of the ceiling is carved and painted and gilded; not a square inch of repose in the entire busy expanse of it; and from it thousands of blinding electric bulbs hang down like stalactites. The walls are covered with enormous mirrors, perversely studded with gold nails, and framed in gold sculpture. And these mirrors fling everything remorselessly back at you. So that the immensity and glow of the restaurant are multiplied to infinity. The band is fighting for its life. An agonised violinist, swaying and contorting in front of the band, squeezes the last drop of juice out of his fiddle. The "selection" is "*Carmen*" But "Carmen" raised to the second power, with every *piano, forte, allegro, and adagio* exaggerated to the last limit; "*Carmen*" composed by Souza and executed by super-Sicilians; a "*Carmen*" deafening and excruciating! And amid all this light and sound, amid the music and the sizzling, and the clatter of plates and glass, and the reverberation of the mirrors, and the whirring of the ventilators, and the sheen of gold, and the harsh glitter of white, and the dull hum of hundreds of strenuous conversations, and the hoarse cries of the pale demons at the fire, and the haste, and the crowdedness, and the people waiting for your table—you eat. You practise the fine art of dining.

In a paroxysm the music expires. The effect is as disconcerting as though the mills of God had stopped. Applause, hearty and prolonged, resounds in the bowels of the earth.. . . You learn that the organism exists because people really like it.

The band

This is a fearful and a romantic place. Those artists who do not tingle to the romance of it are dead and have forgotten to be buried. The romance of it rises grandiosely storey beyond storey. For you must know that while you are dining in the depths, the courtesans, and their possessors are dining in the skies. And the most romantic and impressive thing about it all is the invisible secret thoughts, beneath the specious bravery, of the uncountable multitude gathered together under the spell of the brains that invented the organism. Can you not look through the transparent faces of the young men with fine waistcoats and neglected boots, and of the young women with concocted hats and insecure gay blouses, and of the waiters whose memories are full of Swiss mountains and Italian lakes and German beer gardens, and of the violinist who was proclaimed a Kubelik at the Conservatoire and who now is carelessly pronounced "jolly good" by eaters of beefsteaks? Can you not look through and see the wonderful secret pre-occupations? If so, you can also pierce walls and floors, and see clearly into the souls of the cooks and the sub-cooks, and the cellar-men, and the commissionaires in the rain, and the washers-up. They are all there, including the human beings with loves and ambitions who never do anything for ever, and ever but wash up. These are wistful, but they are not more wistful than the seraphim and cherubim of the upper floors. The place is grandiose and imposing; it has the dazzle of extreme success; but when you have stared it down it is wistful enough to make you cry.

Accidentally your eye rests on the gorgeous frieze in front of you, and after a few moments, among the complex scrollwork and interlaced Cupids, you discern a monogram, not large, not glaring, not leaping out at you, but concealed in fact rather modestly! You decipher the monogram. It contains the initials of the limited company paying forty per cent, and also of the very men whose brains invented the organism. They are men. They may be great men: they probably are; but they are men.

The Restaurant

II

BY THE RIVER

Every morning I get up early, and, going straight to the window, I see half London from an eighth-storey. I see factory chimneys poetised, and the sign of a great lion against the sky, and the dome of St. Paul's rising magically out of the mist, and pearl-coloured minarets round about the horizon, and Waterloo Bridge suspended like a dream over the majestic river-, and all that sort of thing. I am obliged, in spite of myself, to see London through the medium of the artistic sentimentalism of ages. I am obliged even to see it through the individual eyes of Claude Monet, whose visions of it I nevertheless resent. I do not want to see, for example, Waterloo Bridge suspended like a dream over the majestic river. I much prefer to see it firmly planted in the plain water. And I ultimately insist on so seeing it. The Victoria Embankment has been, and still is, full of pitfalls for the sentimentalist in art as in sociology; I would walk warily to avoid them. The river at dawn, the river at sunset, the river at midnight (with its myriad lamps, of course)!... Let me have the river at eleven a. m. for a change, or at tea-time. And let me patrol its banks without indulging in an orgy of melodramatic contrasts.

I will not be carried away by the fact that the grand hotels, with their rosy saloons and fair women (not invariably or even generally fair!), look directly down upon the homeless wretches huddled on the Embankment benches. Such a juxtaposition is accidental and falsifying. Nor will I be imposed upon by the light burning high in the tower of St. Stephen's to indicate that the legislators are watching over Israel. I think of the House of Commons at question-time, and I hear the rustling as two hundred schoolboyish human beings (not legislators nor fathers of their country) simultaneously turn over a leaf of two hundred question-papers, and I observe the self-consciousness of honourable members as they walk in and out, and the naïve pleasure of the Labour member in his enormous grey wideawake, and the flower in the buttonhole of the white-haired and simple ferocious veteran of democracy, and the hobnobbing over stewed tea and sultana on the draughty terrace.

Nor, when I look at the finely symbolic architecture of New Scotland Yard, will I be obsessed by the horrors of the police system and of the prison system and by the wrongness of the world. I regard with fraternal interest the policeman in his shirt-sleeves lolling at a fourth-floor window. Thirty, twenty, years ago people used to be staggered by the sudden discovery that, in the old Hebraic sense of the word, there was no God. It winded them, and some of them have never got over it. Nowadays people are being staggered by the sudden discovery that there is something fundamentally wrong with the structure of society. This discovery induces a nervous disease which runs through whole thoughtful multitudes. I suffer from it myself. Nevertheless, just as it is certain that there is a God, of some kind, so it is certain that there is nothing fundamentally wrong with the structure of society. There is something wrong—but it is not fundamental. There always has been and always will be something wrong. Do you suppose, O reformer, that when land-values are taxed, and war and poverty and slavery and overwork and underfeeding and disease and cruelty have disappeared, that the structure of society will seem a whit the less wrong? Never! A moderate sense of its wrongness is precisely what most makes life worth living.

In the embankment gardens

Between my lofty dwelling and the river is a large and beautiful garden, ornamented with statues of heroes. It occupies ground whose annual value is probably quite ten thousand pounds—that is to say, the interest on a quarter of a million. It is tended by several County Council gardeners, who spend comfortable lives in it, and doubtless thereby support their families in dignity. Its lawns are wondrous; its parterres are full of flowers, and its statues are cleansed perhaps more thoroughly than the children of the poor. This garden is, as a rule, almost empty. I use it a great deal, and sometimes I am the only person in it. Its principal occupants are well-dressed men of affairs, who apparently employ it, as I do, as a ground for reflection. Nursemaids bring into it the children of the rich. The children of the poor are not to be seen in it—they might impair the lawns, or even commit the horrible sin of picking the blossoms. During the only hours when the poor could frequent it, it is thoughtfully closed. The poor pay, and the rich enjoy. If I paid my proper share of the cost of that garden, each of my visits would run me into something like half-a-sovereign. My pleasure is being paid for up all manner of side-streets. This is wrong; it is scandalous. I would, and I will, support any measure that promises to rectify the wrongness. But in the meantime I intend to have my fill of that garden, and to savour the great sensations thereof. I will not be obsessed by one aspect of it.

The great sensations are not perhaps what one would have expected to be the great sensations. Neither domes, nor towers, nor pinnacles, nor spectacular contrasts, nor atmospheric effects, nor the Wordsworthian "mighty heart"! It is the County Council tram, as copied from Glasgow and Manchester, that appeals more constantly and more profoundly than anything else of human creation to my romantic sensibility "Yes," I am told, "the tram-cars look splendid at night!" I do not mean specially at night. I mean in the day. And further, I have no desire to call them ships, or to call them aught but tram-cars. For me they resemble just tram-cars, though I admit that when forty or fifty of them are crowded together, they remind me somewhat of a herd of elephants. They are enormous and beautiful; they are admirably designed, and they function perfectly; they are picturesque, inexplicable, and uncanny. They pome to rest with the gentleness of doves, and they hurtle through the air like shells. Their motion—smooth, delicate and horizontal—is always delightful. They are absolutely modern, new, and original. There was never anything like them before, and only when something different and better supersedes them will their extraordinary gliding picturesqueness be appreciated. They never cease. They roll along day and night without a pause; in the middle of the night you can see them glittering away to the ends of the county. At six o'clock in the morning they roll up over the horizon of Westminster

Bridge in hundreds incessantly, and swing downwards and round sharply away from the Parliament which for decades refused them access to their natural gathering-place. They are a thrilling sight. And see the pigmy in the forefront of each one, rather like a mahout on the neck of an elephant, doing as he likes with the obedient monster! And see the scores of pigmies inside, each of them, black dots that jump out like fleas and disappear like fleas! The loaded tram stops, and in a moment it is empty, and of the contents there is no trace. The contents are dissolved in London.. . . And then see London precipitate the contents again; and watch the leviathans, gorged, glide off in endless procession to spill immortal souls in the evening suburbs!

But the greatest sensation offered by the garden, though it happens to be a mechanical contrivance, is entirely independent of the County Council. It is—not the river—but the movement of the tide. Imagination is required in order to conceive the magnitude, the irresistibility, and the consequences of this tremendous shuttle-work, which is regulated from the skies, rules the existence of tens of thousands of people, and casually displaces incalculable masses of physical matter. And the curious human thing is that it fails to rouse the imagination of the town. It cleaves through the town, and yet is utterly foreign to it, having been estranged from it by the slow evolutionary process. All those tram-cars roll up over the horizon of Westminster Bridge, and cross the flood and run for a mile on its bank, and not one man in every tenth tram-car gives the faintest attention to the state of the river. A few may carelessly notice that the tide is "in" or "out," but how many realise the implications? For all they feel, the river might be a painted stream! Yo wonder that the touts crying "Steamboat! Steamboat!" have a mournful gesture, and the "music on board" sounds thin, like a hallucination, as the shabby paddle-wheels pound the water! The cause of the failure of municipal steamers is more recondite than the yellow motor-cars of the journals which took pride in having ruined them.

And the one satisfactory inference from the failure is that

human nature is far less dependent on nonhuman nature than vague detractors of the former and devotees of the latter would admit. It is, after all, rather fine to have succeeded in ignoring the Thames!

III

THE CLUB

It was founded for an ideal. Its scope is national, and its object to regenerate the race, to remedy injustice, and to proclaim the brotherhood of mankind. It is for the poor against the plutocrat, and for the slave against the tyrant, and for democracy against feudalism. It is, in a word, of the kingdom of heaven. It was born amid immense collisions, and in the holy war it is the official headquarters of those who are on the side of the angels. In its gigantic shadow the weak and the oppressed sell newspapers and touch their hats to the warriors as they pass in and pass out.

The place is as superb as its ideal. No half measures were taken when it was conceived and constructed. Its situation is among the most expensive and beautiful in the world of cities. Its architecture is grandiose, its square columned hall and its vast staircase (hewn from Carrara) are two of the sights of London. It is like a town, but a town of Paradise. When the warrior enters its portals he is confronted by instruments and documents which inform him with silent precision of the time, the temperature, the barometric pressure, the catalogue of nocturnal amusements, and the colour of the government that happens to be in power. The last word spoken in Parliament, the last quotation on the Stock Exchange, the last wager at Newmarket, the last run scored at cricket, the result of the last race, the last scandal, the last disaster—all these things are specially printed for him hour by hour, and pinned up unavoidably before his eyes. If he wants to bet, he has only to put his name on a card entitled "Derby Sweepstake." Valets take his hat and stick; others (working seventy hours a week) shave him;

others polish his hoots.

The staircase being not for use, but merely to immortalise the memory of the architect, he is wafted upwards by a lift into a Titanic apartment studded with a thousand easy-chairs, and furnished with newspapers, cigars, cigarettes, implements of play, and all the possibilities of light refection. He lapses into a chair, and lo! a hell is under his hand. Ting! And a uniformed and initialled being stands at attention in front of him, not speaking till he speaks, and receiving his command with the formalities of deference. He wishes to write a letter—a table is at his side, with all imaginable stationery; a machine offers him a stamp, another licks the stamp, and an Imperial letter-box is within reach of his arm,—it is not considered sufficient that there should be a post-office, with young girls who have passed examinations, in the building itself. He then chats, while sipping and smoking, or nibbling a cake, with other reclining warriors; and the hum of their clatter rises steadily from the groups of chairs, inspiring the uniformed and initialled beings who must not speak till spoken to with hopes of triumphant democracy and the millennium. For when they are not discussing more pacific and less heavenly matters, the warriors really do discuss the war, and how they fought yesterday, and how they will fight to-morrow. If at one moment the warrior is talking about "a perfectly pure Chianti that I have brought from Italy in a cask," at the next he is planning to close public-houses on election days.

When he has had enough of such amiable gossip he quits the easy chair, in order to occupy another one in another room where he is surrounded by all the periodical literature of the entire world, and by the hushed murmur of intellectual conversation and the discreet stirring of spoons in tea-cups. Here he acquaints himself with the progress of the war and the fluctuations of his investments and the price of slaves. And when even the solemnity of this chamber begins to offend his earnestness, he glides into the speechless glamour of an enormous library, where the tidings of the day are repeated a third time, and, amid the companionship of a hundred thousand volumes and all the complex apparatus of research, he slumbers, utterly alone.

He slumbers alone

Late at night, when he has eaten and drunk, and played cards and billiards and dominoes and draughts and chess, he finds himself once more in the smoking-room—somehow more intimate now—with a few cronies, including one or two who out in the world are disguised as the enemy. The atmosphere of the place has put him and them into a sort of exquisite coma. Their physical desires are assuaged, and they know by proof that they are in control of the most perfectly organised mechanism of comfort that was ever devised. Naught is forgotten, from the famous wines cooling a long age in the sub-basement, to the inanimate chauffeur in the dark, windy street, waiting and waiting till a curt whistle shall start him into assiduous life. They know that never an Oriental despot was better served than they. Here alone, and in the mansions of the enemy, has the true tradition of service been conserved. In comparison, the most select hotels and restaurants are a hurly-burly of crude socialism. The bell is under the hand, and the labelled menial stands with everlasting patience near; and home and women are far away. And the world is not.

Forgetting the platitudes of the war, they talk of things as they are. All the goodness of them comes to the surface, and all the weakness. They state their real ambitions and their real preferences. They narrate without reserve their secret grievances and disappointments. They are naked and unashamed. They demand sympathy, and they render it, in generous quantities. And while thus dissipating their energy, they honestly imagine that they are renewing it. The sense of reality gradually goes, and illusion reigns—the illusion that, after all, God is geometrically just, and that strength will be vouchsafed to them according to their need, and that they will receive the reward of perfect virtue.

And their illusive satisfaction is chastened and beautified by the consciousness that the sublime institution of the club is scarcely what it was,—is in fact decadent; and that if it were not vitalised by a splendid ideal, even *their* club might wilt under the sirocco of modernity. And then the echoing voice of an attendant warns them, with deep respect, that the clock moves. But they will not listen, cannot listen. And the voice of the attendant echoes again, and half the lights shockingly expire. But still they do not listen; they cannot credit. And then, suddenly, they are in utter darkness, and by the glimmer of a match are stumbling against easy-chairs and tables, real easy-chairs and real tables. The spell of illusion is broken. And in a moment they are thrust out, by the wisdom of their own orders, into Pall Mall, into actuality, into the world of two sexes once more.

And yet the sublime institution of the club is not a bit anæmic. Within a quarter of a mile is the monumental proof that the institution has been rejuvenated and ensanguined and empowered. Colossal, victorious, expensive, counting its adherents in thousands upon thousands, this monument scorns even the pretence of any ancient ideal, and adopts no new one. The aim of the club used ostensibly to be peace, idealism, a retreat, a refuge. The new aim is pandemonium, and it is achieved. The new aim is to let in the world, and it is achieved. The new aim is muscular, and it is achieved. Arms, natation, racquets—anything to subdue the soul and stifle thought! And in the reading-room, dummy hooks and dummy book-cases! And a dining-room full of bright women; and such a mad competition for meals that glasses and carafes will scarce go round, and strangers must sit together at the same small table without protest! And, to crown the hullaballoo, an orchestra of red-coated Tziganes swaying and yearning and ogling in order to soothe your digestion and to prevent you from meditating.

This club marks the point to which the evolution of the sublime institution has attained. It has come from the shore of Lake Michigan; it is the club of the future, and the forerunner of its kind. Stand on its pavement, and watch 'its entering heterogeneous crowds, and then throw the glance no more than the length of a cricket-pitch, and watch the brilliantly surviving representatives of feudalism itself ascending and descending the steps of the most exclusive club in England; and you will comprehend that even when the House of Lords goes, something will go—something unconsciously cocksure, and perfectly creased, and urbane, and dazzlingly stupid—that was valuable and beautiful. And you will comprehend politics better, and the profound truth that it takes all sorts to make a world.

The club of the future

IV

THE CIRCUS

The flowers heaped about the bronze fountain are for them. And so that they may have flowers all day long, older and fatter and shabbier women make their home round the fountain (modelled by a genius to the memory of one whose dream was to abolish the hardships of poverty), with a sugar-box for a drawing-room suite and a sack for a curtain; these needy ones live there, to the noise of water, with a secret society of newspaper-sellers, knowing intimately all the capacities of the sugar-box and sack; and on hot days they revolve round the fountain with the sun, for their only sunshade is the shadow of the dolphins. On every side of their habituated tranquillity the odours of petrol swirl. The great gaudy-coloured autobuses, brilliant as the flowers, swing and swerve and grind and sink and recover, and in the forehead of each is a blackened demon, tremendously preoccupied, and so small and withdrawn as to be often unnoticed; and this demon rushes forward all day with his life in his hand and scores of other lives in his hand, for two pounds a week. When he stops by the fountain, he glances at the flowers unseeing, out of the depths of his absorption. He is piloting cargoes of the bright beings for whom the flowers are heaped.

Stand on the steps of the fountain, and look between the autobuses and over the roofs of taxis and the shoulders of policemen, and you will see at every hand a proof that the whole glowing place, with its flags gaily waving and its hubbub of rich hues, exists first and last for those same bright beings. If there is a cigar shop, if there is a necktie shop like Joseph's coat, it is to enable the male to cut a dash with those beings. And the life insurance office—would it continue if there were no bright beings to be provided for? And the restaurants I And the I chemists! And the music-hall! The sandwich-men are walking round and round with the names of the most beauteous lifted high on their shoulders. The leather shop is crammed with dressing-cases and hat-boxes for them. The jeweller is offering solid gold slave-bangles (because they like the feel of the shackle) at six pound ten.

And above all there is the great establishment on the corner! An establishment raised by tradition and advertisement and sheer skill to the rank of a national institution, famous from Calgary to the Himalayas, far more famous and beloved than even the greatest poets and philanthropists. An institution established on one of the seven supreme sites of the world! And it is all theirs, all for them! Coloured shoes, coloured frocks, coloured necklaces, coloured parasols, coloured stockings, jabots, scents, hats, and all manner of flimsy stuffs whose names—such as Shantung—summon up in an instant the deep orientalism of the Occident: the innumerable windows are a perfect riot of these delicious affairs! Who could pass them by? This is a wondrous institution. Of a morning, before the heat of the day, you can see coming out of its private half-hidden portals (not the ceremonious glazed doors) black-robed young girls, with their hair down their backs, and the free gestures learnt at school and not yet forgotten, skipping off on I know, not what important errands, earning part of a livelihood already in the service of those others. And at its upper windows appear at times more black-robed girls, and disappear, like charming prisoners in a castle.

The beings for whom the place exists come down all the curved vistas towards it, on foot or on wheel, all day in radiant droves. They are obliged at any rate to pass through it, for the Circus is their Clap-ham Junction, and the very gate of finery. Impossible to miss it! It leads to all coquetry, and all delights and dangers. And not only down the vistas are they coming, but they are shot along subterranean tubes, and hurried through endless passages, and flung up at last by lifts from the depths into the open air. And when you look at them you are completely baffled. Because they are English, and the most mysterious women on earth, save the Scandinavians. You cannot get at their secret; it consists in an impenetrable ideal. With the Latin you do come in the end to the solid marble of Latin practicalness; the Latin is perfectly unromantic. But the romanticism of these English is something so recondite that no research and no analysis can approach it. Ibsen could never have made a play out of a Latin woman; but I tell you that, for me, every woman stepping off an autobus and exposing her ankles and her character as she dodges across the Circus, has the look in her face of an Ibsen heroine; she emanates romance and enigma; she is the potential mainspring of a late-Ibsen drama, the kind whose import no critic is ever quite sure of. This it is to be Anglo-Saxon, and herein is one of the grand major qualities of the streets of London.

They are in this matter, I do believe, all alike, these creatures. You may encounter one so ugly and mannish and grotesque that none but an Englishman could take her to his arms, and even she has the ineffable romantic gaze. All the countless middle-aged women who support circulating libraries have it; the hair of a woman of fifty blows about her face romantically. All the nice, youngish married women have it, those who think they know a thing or two. And as for the girls, the young girls, they show a romantic naïveté which transcends belief; they are so fresh and so virginal and so loose-limbed and so obsessed by a mysterious ideal, that really (you think) the street is too perilous a place for them. And yet they go confidently about, either alone or in couples, or with young men at bottom as simple as themselves, and naught happens to them; they must be protected by their idealism. And now and then you will see a woman who is strictly and truly *chic*, in the extreme French sense—an amazing spectacle in our city of sloppy women who, while dreaming of dress for ten hours a day, cannot even make their blouses fasten decently—and this *chic* Parisianised creature herself will have kept her idealistic gaze! They all keep it. They die with it at seventy-five. Whatever adventure occurs to an Englishwoman, she remains spiritually innocent and naïve. The Circus is bathed in the mood of these qualities.

Flower women

Towards dark it alters and is still the same. See it after the performances on a matinée day, surging with heroines. See it at eight o'clock at night, a packed mass of taxis and automobiles, each the casket of a romantic creature, hurrying in pursuit of that ideal without a name. Later, the place is becalmed, and scarcely an Englishwoman is to be seen in it until after the theatres, when once again it is nationalised and feminised to an intense degree. The shops are black, and the flower-sellers are gone; but the electric sky-signs are in violent activity, and there is light enough to see those baffling faces as they flash or wander by. And the trains are now bearing the creatures away in the deep-laid tubes.

And then there comes an hour when the hidden trains have ceased, and the autobuses have nearly ceased, and the bright beings have withdrawn themselves until the morrow; and now, on all the footpaths of the Circus, move crowded processions of men young and old, slowly, as though in the performance of a rite. It leads to nothing, this tramping; it serves no end; it is merely idiotic, in a peculiarly Anglo-Saxon way. But only heavy rain can interfere with it. It persists obstinately. And the reason of it is that the Circus is the Circus. And after all, though idiotic, it has the merit and significance of being instinctive. The Circus symbolises the secret force which drives forward the social organism through succeeding stages of evolution. The origin of every effort can be seen at some time of day emerging from a crimson autobus in the Circus, or speeding across the Circus in a green taxi. The answer to the singular conundrum of the City is to be found early or late in the Circus. The imponderable spirit of the basic fact of society broods in the Circus forever. Despite all changes, there is no change. I say no change. You may gaze into the jeweller's shop at the gold slave-bangles, which cannot be dear at six pound ten, since they express the secret attitude of an entire sex. And then you may turn and gaze at the face of a Suffragette, with her poster and her armful of papers, and her quiet voice and her mien of pride. And you may think you see a change fundamental and terrific. Look again.

Piccadilly Circus

V

THE BANQUET

In every large London restaurant, and in many small ones, there is a spacious hall (or several) curtained away from the public, in which every night strange secret things go on. Few suspect, and still fewer realise, the strangeness of these secret things.

In the richly decorated interior (sometimes marked with mystic signs), at a table which in space reaches from everlasting to everlasting, and has the form of a grill or a currycomb or the end of a rake—at such a table sit fifty or five hundred males. They are all dressed exactly alike, in black and white; but occasionally they display a coloured flower, and each man bears exactly the same species and tint and size of flower, so that you think of regiments of flowers trained throughout their lives in barracks to the end of shining for a night in unison on the black and white bosoms of these males. Although there is not even a buffet in the great room, and no sign of the apparatus of a restaurant, all these males are eating a dinner, and it is the same dinner. They do not wish to choose; they accept, reading the menu like a decree of fate. They do not inquire upon the machinery; a slave, unglanced at, places a certain quantity of a dish in front of them—and lo! the same quantity of the same dish is in front of all of them; they do not ask whence nor how it came; they eat, with industry, knowing that at a given moment, whether they have finished or not, a hand will steal round from behind them, and the plate will vanish into limbo. Thus the repast continues, ruthlessly, under the aquiline gaze of a slave who is also a commander-in-chief, manoeuvring his men silently, manoeuvring them with naught but a glance. With one glance he causes to disappear five hundred salad-plates, and with another he conjures from behind a screen five hundred ices, each duly below zero, and each calculated to impede the digesting of a salad. The service of the dinner is a miracle, but the diners, absorbed in the expectancy of rites to come, reck not; they assume the service as they assume the rising of the sun. Only a few remember the old, old days, in the 'eighties (before a cabal of international Jews had put their heads together and inaugurated a new age of miracles), when these solemn repasts were a scramble and a guerilla, after which one half of the combatants went home starving, and the other half went home glutted and drenched. Nowadays these repasts are the most perfectly democratic in England; and anybody who has ever assisted at one knows by a morsel of experience what life would be if the imaginative Tory's nightmare of Socialism were to become a reality. But each person has enough, and has it promptly.

From Bayswater to the Circus

The ceremonial begins with a meal, because it would be impossible on an empty stomach. Its object is ostensibly either to celebrate the memory of some deed or some dead man, or to signalise the triumph of some living contemporary. Clubs and societies exist throughout London in hundreds expressly for the execution of these purposes, and each! of them is a remunerative client of a large restaurant. Societies even exist solely in order to watch for the triumphs of contemporaries, and to gather in the triumphant to a repast and inform them positively that they are great. So much so that it is difficult to accomplish anything unusual, such as the discovery of one pole or another, or the successful defence of a libel action, without submitting to the ordeal of these societies one after the other in a chain, and emerging therefrom with modesty ruined and the brazen conceit of a star actor. But the ostensible object is merely a cover for the real object, the unadmitted and often unsuspected object: which is, to indulge in a debauch of universal mutual admiration. When the physical appetite is assuaged, then the appetite for praise and sentimentality is whetted, and the design of the mighty institution of the banquet is to minister, in a manner majestic and unexceptionable, to this base appetite, whose one excuse is its *naïveté*.

A pleasurable and even voluptuous thrill of anticipation runs through the assemblage when the chairman rises to open the orgy. Everybody screws himself up, as a fiddler screwing the pegs of a fiddle, to what he deems the correct pitch of appreciativeness; and almost the breath is held. And the chairman says: "Whatever differences may divide us upon other subjects, I am absolutely convinced, and I do not hesitate to state my conviction in the clearest possible way, that we are enthusiastically and completely agreed upon one point," the point being that such and such a person or such and such a work is the greatest person or the greatest work of the kind in the whole history of the human race. And although the point is one utterly inadmissible upon an empty stomach, although it is indeed a glaring falsity, everybody at once feverishly endorses it, either with shrill articulate cries, or with deep inarticulate booming, or with noises produced by the shock of flesh on flesh, or ivory on wood, or steel on crystal. The uproar is enormous. The chairman grows into a sacramental priest, or a philosopher of amazing insight and courage. And everybody says to himself: "I had not screwed myself up quite high enough," and proceeds to a further screwing. And in every heart is the thought: "This is grand! This is worth living for! This alone is the true reward of endeavour!" And the corporate soul muses ecstatically: "This work, or this man, is ours, by reason of our appreciation and our enthusiasm. And he, or it, is ours exclusively." And, since the soul and the body are locked together in the closest sympathetic intimacy, all those cautious dyspeptic ones who have hitherto shirked danger, immediately put on courage like a splendid garment, and order the strongest drinks and the longest cigars that the establishment can offer. The real world fades into unreality; the morrow is lost in eternity; the moment and the illusion alone are real.

The key of the mood is to be sought less in the speeches as they succeed each other than in the applause. For the applauders are not influenced by a sense of responsibility, or made self-conscious by publicity. They can be natural, and they are. What fear can prevent them from translating instantly their emotions into sound? By the applause, if you are a slave and non-participator, you may correct your too kindly estimate of men in the mass. Note how the most outrageous exaggeration, the grossest flattery, the most banal platitude, the most fatuous optimism, gain the loudest approval. Note how any reservation produces a fall of temperature. Note how the smallest jokes are seized on ravenously, as a worm by a young bird. And note always the girlish sentimentality, ever gushing forth, of these strong, hard-headed males whose habit is to proverbialise the sentimentality of women.

From South London to the Circus

The emotional crisis arrives. Feeling transcends the vehicle of speech, and escapes in song. And one guest, honoured either; for some special deed of his own or because his name has been "coupled" with some historic deed or movement, remains sitting, in the most exquisite self-consciousness that human ingenuity ever brought about, while all the rest fling hoarsely at him the fifteen sacred words of a refrain which in its incredible vulgarity surpasses even the National Anthem.

The reaction is now not far off. But owing to several reasons it is postponed yet awhile. The honoured guest's response is one of the chief attractions of the night. Very many diners have been drawn to the banquet by the desire to inspect the honoured guest at their leisure, to see his antics, to divine his human weaknesses and his ridiculous side. And, moreover, the honoured guest must give praise for praise, and lie for lie. He is bound by the strictest conventions of social intercourse to say in so many words: "Gentlemen, you are the most enlightened body of men that I ever had the good fortune to meet; and your hospitality is the greatest compliment that I have ever had, or ever shall have, or could conceive. Each of you is a prince of the earth. And I am a worm." And then there are the minor speeches, finishing off in detail the vast embroidery of laudation which was begun by the Chairman. Everybody is more or less enfolded in that immense mantle. And everybody is satisfied and sated, save those who have sat through the night awaiting the sweet mention of their own names, and who have been disappointed. At every banquet there are such. And it is they who, by their impatience, definitely cause the reaction at last. The speakers who terminate the affair fight against the reaction in vain. The applause at the close is perfunctory—how different from the fever of the commencement and the hysteria of the middle! The illusion is over. The emotional debauch is finished. The adult and bearded boys have played the delicious make-believe of being truly great, and the game is at an end; and each boy, looking within, perceives without too much surprise that he is after all only himself. A cohort "of the best," foregathered in the cloakroom, say to each other, "Delightful evening! Splendid! Ripping!" And then one says, ironically leering, in a low voice, and a tone heavy with realistic disesteem: "Well, what do you think of—?" Naming the lion of the night.

VI

ONE OF THE CROWD

He comes out of the office, which is a pretty large one, with a series of nods—condescending, curt, indifferent, friendly, and deferential. He has detestations and preferences, even cronies; and if he has superiors, he has also inferiors. But whereas his fate depends on the esteem of a superior, the fate of no inferior depends on his esteem. When he nods deferentially he is bowing to an august power before which all others are in essence equal; the least of his inferiors knows that. And the least of his inferiors will light, on the stairs, a cigarette with the same gesture, and of perhaps the same brand, as his own—to signalise the moment of freedom, of emergence from the machine into human citizenship. Presently he is walking down the crammed street with one or two preferences or indifferences, and they are communicating with each other in slang, across the shoulders of jostling interrupters, and amid the shouts of newsboys and the immense roaring of the roadway. And at the back of his mind, while he talks and smiles, or frowns, is a clear vision of a terminus and a clock and a train. Just as the water-side man, wherever he may be, is aware, night and day, of the exact state of the tide, so this man carries in his brain a time-table of a particular series of trains, and subconsciously he is always aware whether he can catch a particular train, and if so, whether he must hurry or may loiter. His case, is not peculiar. He is just an indistinguishable man on the crowded footpaths, and all the men on the footpaths, like him, are secretly obsessed by the vision of a train just moving out of a station.

From West Kensington to the Circus

He arrives at the terminus with only one companion; the rest, with nods, have vanished away at one street corner or another. Gradually he is sorting himself out. Both he and his companion know that there are a hundred and twenty seconds to spare. The companion relates a new humorous story of something unprintable, alleged to have happened between a man and a woman. The receiver of the story laughs with honest glee, and is grateful, and the companion has the air of a benefactor; which indeed he is, for these stories are the ready-money of social intercourse. The companion strides off, with a nod. The

115

other remains solitary. He has sorted himself out, but only for a minute. In a minute he is an indistinguishable unit again, with nine others, in the compartment of a moving train. He reads an evening newspaper, which seems to have come into his hand of its own agency, for he catches it every night with a purely mechanical grasp as it flies in the street. He reads of deeds and misdeeds, and glances aside uneasily from the disturbing tides of restless men who will not let the social order alone. Suddenly, after the train has stopped several times, he folds up the newspaper as it is stopping again, and gets blindly out. As he surges up into the street on a torrent of his brothers, he seems less sorted than ever. The street into which he comes is broad and busy, and the same newspapers are flying in it. Nevertheless, the street is different from the streets of the centre. It has a reddish or a yellowish quality of colour, and there is not the same haste in it. He walks more quickly now. He walks a long way up another broad street, in which rare autobuses and tradesmen's carts rattle and thunder. The street gets imperceptibly quieter, and more verdurous. He passes a dozen side-streets, and at last he turns into a side-street. And this side-street is full of trees and tranquillity. It is so silent that to reach it he might have travelled seventy miles instead of seven. There are glimpses of yellow and red houses behind thick summer verdure. His pace still quickens. He smiles to himself at the story, and wonders to whom he can present it on the morrow. And then he halts and pushes open a gate upon which is painted a name. And he is in a small garden, with a vista of a larger garden behind. And down the vista is a young girl, with the innocence and grace and awkwardness and knowingness of her years—sixteen; a little shabby, or perhaps careless, in her attire, but enchanting. She starts forward, smiling, and exclaims: "Father!"

Now he is definitely sorted out.

Though this man is one of the crowd, though nobody would look twice at him in Cannon Street, yet it is to the successful and felicitous crowd that he belongs. There are tens of thousands of his grade; but he has the right to fancy himself a bit. He can do certain difficult things very well—else how, in the fierce and gigantic struggle for money, should he contrive to get hold of five hundred pounds a year?

He is a lord in his demesne; nay, even a sort of eternal father. Two servants go in fear of him, because his wife uses him as a bogey to intimidate them. His son, the schoolboy, a mighty one at school, knows there is no appeal from him, and quite sincerely has an idea that his pockets are inexhaustible. Whenever his son has seen him called upon to pay he has always paid, and money has always been left in his pocket. His daughter adores and exasperates him. His wife, with her private system of visits, and her suffragetting, and her independences, recognises ultimately in every conflict that the resultant of forces is against her and for him. When he is very benevolent he joins her in the game of pretending that they are equals. He is the distributor of joy. When he laughs, all laugh, and word shoots through the demesne that father is in a good humour.

Waiting for the bus at the Circus

He laughs to-night. The weather is superb; it is the best time of the year in the suburbs. Twilight is endless; the silver will not die out of the sky. He wanders in the garden, the others with him. He works potteringly. He shows himself more powerful than his son, both physically and mentally. He spoils his daughter, who is daily growing more mysterious. He administers flattery to his wife. He throws scraps of kindness to the servants. It is his wife who at last insists on the children going to bed. Lights show at the upper windows. The kitchen is dark and silent. His wife calls to him from upstairs. He strolls round to the front patch of garden, stares down the side-road, sees an autobus slide past the end of it, shuts and secures the gate, comes into the house, bolts the front door, bolts the back door, inspects the windows, glances at the kitchen; finally, he extinguishes the gas in the hall. Then he leaves the ground floor to its solitude, and on the first-floor peeps in at his snoring son, and admonishes his daughter through a door ajar not to read in bed. He goes to the chief bedroom, and locks himself therein with his wife; and yawns. The night has come. He has made his dispositions for the night. And now he must trust himself, and all that is his, to the night. A vague, faint anxiety penetrates him. He can feel the weight of five human beings depending on him; their faith in him lies heavy.

In the middle of the night he wakes up, and is reminded of such-and-such a dish of which he partook. He remembers what his wife said: "There's no doing anything with that girl"—the daughter—"I don't know what's come over her." And he thinks of all his son's faults and stupidities, and of what it will be to have two children adult. It is true—there *is* no doing anything with either one or the other. Their characters are unchangeable—to be taken or left. This is one lesson he has learnt in the last ten years. And his wife. . . ! The whole organism of the demesne presents itself to him, lying awake, as most extraordinarily complicated. The garden alone, the rose-trees alone,—what a constant cause of solicitude! The friction of the servants,—was one of them a thief or was she not? The landlord must be bullied about the roof. Then, new wall-papers! A hinge! His clothes! His boots! His wife's clothes, and her occasional strange disconcerting apathy! The children's clothes! Rent! Taxes! Rates! Season-ticket! Subscriptions! Negligence of the newsvendor! Bills! Seaside holiday! Erratic striking of the drawing-room clock! The pain in his daughter's back! The singular pain in his own groin— nothing, and yet. . . ! Insurance premium! And above all, the office! Who knew, who could tell, what might happen? There was no margin of safety, not fifty pounds margin of safety. He walked in success and happiness on a thin brittle crust! Crack! And where would they all be? Where would be the illusion of his son and daughter that he was an impregnable and unshakable rock? What would his son think if he knew that his father often calculated to half-a-crown, and economised in cigarettes and a great deal in lunches?. . .

He asks, "Why did I bring all this on myself? Where do I come in, after all?". . . The dawn, very early; and he goes to sleep once more!

The next morning, factitiously bright after his bath, he is eating his breakfast, reading his newspaper, and looking at his watch. The night is over; the complicated organism is in full work again, with its air of absolute security. His newspaper, inspired by a millionaire to gain a millionaire's ends by appealing to the ingenuousness of this clever struggler, is uneasy with accounts of attacks meditated on the established order. His mind is made up. The established order may not be perfect, but he is in favour of it. He has arrived at an equilibrium, unstable possibly, but an equilibrium. One push, and he would be over! Therefore, no push! He hardens his heart against the complaint of the unjustly treated. He has his own folk to think about.

The station is now drawing him like a magnet. He sees in his mind's eye every yard of the way between the side-street and the office, and in imagination he can hear the clock striking at the other end. He must go; he must go! Several persons help him to go, and at the garden-gate he stoops and kisses that mysterious daughter. He strides down the side-street. Only a moment ago, it seems, he was striding up it! He turns into the long road. It is a grinding walk in the already hot sun. He reaches the station and descends into it, and is diminished from an eternal father to a mere unit of a throng. But on the platform he meets a jolly acquaintance. His face relaxes as they salute. "I say," he says after an instant, bursting with a good thing, "Have you heard the tale about the—?"

ITALY

1910

I

NIGHT AND MORNING IN FLORENCE

Amid the infantile fluttering confusion caused by the arrival of the Milan express at Florence railway station, the thoughts of the artist as he falls sheer out of the compartment upon the soft bodies of hold-alls and struggling women, are not solely on the platform. This moment has grandeur. This city was the home of the supreme ones—Dante, Leonardo, Michael Angelo, and Brunelleschi. You have entered it.... Awe? I have never been aware of sentiments of awe towards any artists, save Charles Baudelaire. My secret attitude to them has always been that I would like to shake their hands and tell them briefly in their private slang, whatever their private slang was, that they had given immense pleasure to another artist. I have excepted Charles Baudelaire ever since I read his correspondence, in which he is eternally trying to borrow ten francs from some one, and if they cannot make it ten—then five. There is something so excessively poignant, and to me so humiliating, in the spectacle of the grand author of La Charogne going about among his acquaintance in search of a dollar, that I would only think about it when I wished to inflict on myself a penance. It is a spectacle unique. Like the King of Thule song in Berlioz's Damnation of Faust, it resembles nothing else of its kind. If the artist does not stand in awe before that monumental enigma of human pride which called itself Charles Baudelaire, how shall the artist's posture be described?

No, I will tell you what occupied the withdrawn and undefiled spaces of my mind as I entered Florence, drifting on the stream of labelled menials and determined ladies with their teeth hard-set: Was it more interesting for an artist to be born into a great age of art, where he was beloved and appreciated, if not wholly comprehended, by relatively large masses of people; where his senses were on every hand indulged and pampered by the caress of the obviously beautiful; where he lived among equals, and saw himself continually surrounded by innumerable acts creative of beauty; and where he could feel in the very air a divine palpitation—or, on the other hand, was it more spiritually voluptuous for the artist to be born into a stone age, an age deaf and dumb, an age insensible to the sublime, ignorantly rejecting beauty, and occupying itself with the most damnable and offensive futilities that the soul of an artist can conceive? For I was going, in my fancy, out of the one age into the other. And I decided, upon reflection, that I would just as soon be in the age in which I in fact was; I said that I would not change places even with the most fortunate and miraculous of men—Leonardo da Vinci. There is an agreeable bitterness, an exquisite *tang*, in the thought of the loneliness of artists in an age whose greatness and whose epic quality are quite divorced from art. And when I think of the artist in this age, I think of the Invisible Man of H. G. Wells, in the first pride of his invisibility (when he was not yet hunted), walking unseen and unseeing amid multitudes, and it is long before? anybody in the multitudes even notices the phenomenon of mysterious footmarks that cannot be accounted for! I like to be that man. I like to think that my fellows are few, and that even I, not having eyes to see most of them, must now and then be disconcerted by the appearance of unaccountable footmarks. There is something beyond happiness, and that is, to know intensely and painfully that you are what you are. The great Florentines of course had that knowledge, but their circumstances were; not so favourable as mine to its cultivation in an artist. Therein lay their disadvantage and lies my advantage.

The Orchestra proves that its instruments are real

Besides, you do not suppose that I would wish to alter this age by a single iota of its ugliness and its preposterousness! You do not suppose I do not love it! You do not suppose I do not wallow in the trough of it with delight! There is not one stockbroker, not one musical comedy star, not one philanthropic giver of free libraries, not one noble brewer, not one pander, not one titled musician, not one fashionable bishop, not one pro-consul, that I would wish away. Where should my pride bitterly exercise itself if not in proving that my age, exactly as it exists now, contains nothing that is not the raw material of beauty? If I wished to do so, I would force some among you to see that even the hotel-tout within the portals of the city of Giotto is beautiful.

At dinner I am waited upon by a young and beautiful girl who, having almost certainly never heard of Gabriele d'Annunzio, yet speaks his language and none other. But she wears the apron and the cap of the English parlour-maid, in plenary correctness, and, knowing exactly how I should be served in England, she humours me; and above us is a vaulted ceiling. Such is the terrible might of England. I am surrounded by ladies; the room is crammed with ladies. By the perfection of their virtuosity in the nice conduct of forks alone is demonstrated their ladyship. (And I who, like a savage, cannot eat pudding without a spoon!) There is a middle-aged gentleman, whose eyeglasses are wandering down his fine nose, lost in a bosky dell of women at the other end of the room; and there is myself; and there is a boy, obviously in Hades. And there are some fifty dames. Their voices, high, and with the sublime unconscious arrogance of the English, fight quietly and steadily among each other up in the vaulting. "Of course, I used to play cricket with my brothers. But, will you believe me, I've never seen a football match in my life!"

"No, we haven't seen the new rector yet, but they say he's frightfully nice."

"Benozzo Gozzoli—ye-es." It is impossible not to believe, listening to these astounding conversations, that nature, tired of imitating Balzac any longer, has now taken to imitating the novels of Mrs. Humphry Ward.

The drawing-room is an English drawing-room—yes, with the *Queen* and "the authoress of *Elizabeth and her German Garden*" and a Bechstein grand. There are forty-five chairs and easy chairs in it, and fifty ladies; the odd five ladies sit low upon hassocks or recline on each other in attitudes of intense affection. And at the other end is a male, neither the man with the pincenez nor the boy in Hades, but a third who has mysteriously come out of nothing into existence. I have entered, and I am held, as by a spell, in the doorway, the electric light raining upon me, a San Sebastian for the fatal arrows of the fifty, who fix on me their ingenuous eyes—

And dart delicious danger thence

(to cull an incomparable phrase from one of the secular poems of Dr. Isaac Watts). And now there are more ladies behind me, filling the doorway with hushed expectation. For in the appalling silence, a young sad-orbed creature is lifting a violin delicately from its case on the Bechstein, at which waits a sister-spirit. "Do tell me," says an American voice, intrepidly breasting the silence, "what was that perfectly heavenly thing you played last night—was it Debussy? We thought it must be Debussy." And the violinist answers: "No; I expect you mean the Goltermann. It *is* pretty, isn't it?" And as she holds up the violin, interrogating its strings with an anxious and a critical ear, I observe that beneath the strings lies a layer of rosin-dust. Thirty years ago, in the fastnesses of the Five Towns, amateurs used to deem it necessary to keep their violins dirty in order to play with the soulfulness of a Norman Neruda. I would have been ready to affirm that observation of the cleanliness of the instruments of professionals had killed the superstition long since; but lo, I have tunnelled the Simplon to meet it again!

I go. Somehow, I depart, beaten off as it were with great loss. I plunge out into dark Florence, walking under the wide projecting eaves of Florence to avoid the rain. And in my mind I can still see the drawing-room, a great cube of light, with its crowded frocks whose folds merge one into the next, and the Bechstein, and the strains of Goltermann, and the attentive polite faces, and that sole man in the corner like a fly on a pin. I have run away from it. But I know that I shall go back to it, and that my curiosity will drink it to the dregs. For that drawing-room is to the working artist in me the most impressive and the most interesting thing in Florence. And when I reflect that there are dozens and dozens of it in Florence, I say that this age is the most romantic age that ever was.

I know where I am going, for my first business in entering a town, whether Florence, Hull, or Constantine, is always to examine the communicative posters on its walls and to glance through its newspapers. There is a performance of Spontini's *La Vestale* at the Teatro Verdi. Nothing, hardly, could have kept me away from that performance, which in every word of its announcement seems to me overpoweringly romantic. The name of Verdi alone.... I heard Verdi late in my life, and in Italy, long after I knew by rote all the themes in *Tristan* and *Die Meistersinger*, after *Pelleas et Mélisande* had ceased to be a novelty at the Paris Opéra Comique, after even the British discovery of Richard Strauss, and I shall never forget the ravishing effect on me of the first act of *La Traviata*; no, nor the tedium of the other acts. I would go to any theatre named Verdi. Then Spontini! What is Spontini but a name? Was it possible that I was about to hear an actual opera by this antique mediocrity whose music Berlioz loved beyond its deserts? Had anybody ever heard an opera by Spontini?

The shabbiness of the *façade* and of the box-office, and of the suits of the disillusioned but genial men within the box-office—men who knew the full meaning of existence. A seat in the *parterre* for two lire—say one and sevenpence halfpenny—it is making a gift of the spectacle! The men take my two lire with an indulgent gesture, exclaiming softly with their eyes and hands: "What are two lire more or less in the vast abyss of our deficit? Throw them down!" Then I observe that my ticket is marked *posto distinto*—prominent seat, distinguished seat. Useless to tell me that it means nothing! It means much to me: another example of Italian politeness, at once exquisite and futile.

Would the earl in the gate at Covent Garden, even for thirty-two lire on a Melba night, offer me a distinguished seat?.. . Long stone corridors, steps up, steps down, turnings, directive cries echoing amid arches; and then I am in the auditorium, vast.

It is as big as Covent Garden, and nearly as big as La Scala. It has six galleries, about a hundred boxes, and four varieties of seats on the ground floor. My distinguished seat is without the first quality of a seat—yieldingness. It does not acquiesce. It is as hard as seasoned wood can be, though roomy and well situated. And in a corner, lying against the high rampart of a box for ten people, I see negligently piled a great pyramid of ancient red cushions, scores and scores of them. And a little old ragged attendant comes and whispers alluringly, delicately in my ear: "*Cuscina.*" Two sous would hire it and a smile thrown in. But no, I won't have it. I am too English to have that cushion.. .. The immense theatre, faced all in white marble, with traces here and there in a box of crimson upholstery, is as dim as a church. There are hundreds of electric bulbs, but unlighted: the sole illumination comes from a row of perfectly mediæval gas-burners along the first gallery. After all, economy must obtain somewhere. I count an orchestra of over seventy living players; the most numerous body in the place: somehow they must support life. Over the acreage of the *parterre* are sprinkled a few dozens of audience. There is a serried ring of faces lining the fifth gallery, to which admittance is tenpence, and another lining the sixth gallery, to which admittance is sixpence. The rest is not even paper.

Yet a spruce and elegant conductor rises and the overture begins, and the orchestra proves that its instruments are real; and I hear Spontini, and for a little while enjoy his faded embroideries. And the curtain goes up on "a public place in Rome," upon a scale as spacious as Rome itself. Everything is genuine. There are two leading sopranos, one of whom is young and attractive, and they both have powerful and trained voices, and sing like the very dickens. No amateurishness about them! They know their business; they are accomplished and experienced artists. No hesitations, no timidities, no askings for indulgence because really I have only paid two lire! Their fine voices fill the theatre with ease, and would easily fill Covent Garden to the back row of the half-crown gallery. The same with the tenor, the same with the bass. Spontini surges onward in an excellent concourse of multitudinous sound, and I wonder what it is all about. I have a book of the words, but owing to the unfortunate absence of Welsbach mantles I cannot read it. I know it must be all about a vestal who objected to being a vestal, on account of a military uniform, and I content myself with this grand central fact. Then the stage brightens, and choruses begin to march on; one after another; at least a dozen: soldiers, wrestlers, populace, dancers, children. Yes, the show is complete even to ragamuffins larking about in the public place in Rome. I count a hundred people on the stage. And all the properties are complete. It is a complete production and an expensive production—except probably in the detail of wages. For in Italy *prime donne* with a *répertoire* of a dozen or fifteen first-class rôles seem to go about the streets dressed like shop-girls. I have seen it. All this is just as exciting to me as the Church of S. Croce, even as explained by John Ruskin with a schoolmaster's cane in his lily-hand.

Interval I I go to the refreshment *foyer* to see life. And now I can perceive that quite a crowd of people has been hidden somewhere in the nooks of the tremendous theatre. The large *caffé* is crammed. Of course, it is vaulted, like everything in Florence. The furniture of the caffé is strangely pathetic in its forlornness: marble-topped mahogany tables, and mahogany chairs in faded and frayed crimson rep. Furniture that ought to have been dead and buried long ago! The marble is yellow with extreme age and use. These tables and chairs are a most extraordinary survival; in a kind of Italian Loins Philippe style, debased First Empire; or it might be likened to earliest Victorian. Once they were new; once they were the latest thing. For fifty years perhaps the management has been meaning to refurnish the *caffé* as soon as it could afford. The name of the theatre has been changed, but not those chairs nor that marble.

And conceivably the sole waiter, gliding swiftly to and fro with indestructible politeness, is their contemporary. The customers are the equivalent of a music-hall audience in these isles. They smoke, drink, and expectorate with the casualness of men who are taking a rest after Little Tich. They do not go to the opera with prayer and fasting and the score. They just stroll into the opera. Nor does the conductor, nor do the players, have the air of high priests of art who have brought miracles to pass. And I know what those two sopranos are talking about upstairs. Here opera is in the bones of the rabble. It is a tradition: a tradition in a very bad way of decayed splendour, but alive yet.

For the second act the auditorium is brighter, and fuller, though the total receipts would not pay for five minutes of Caruso alone. The place looks half full and is perhaps a third full. Behind me a whole series of first-tier boxes are occupied by a nice, cheerful, chattering shop-keeping class of persons, simple folk that I like. A few soldiers are near. Also there is a man next but one to me who cannot any longer deprive himself of a cigarette. He bows his head and furtively strikes a match, right in the middle of the theatre, and for every puff he bows his head, and then looks up with an innocent air, as though repudiating any connection with the wisp of smoke that is floating aloft. Nobody minds. The curtain rises on the interior of the Temple, a beautiful and solid architectural scene, much superior to anything in the first act, whose effect was rich and complex without being harmonious. The vestal is attending to the fire. When the military uniform unostentatiously enters, I feel that during an impassioned dialogue she will go and let that fire out. And she does. Such is the second act., I did not see the third. I shall never see it. I convinced myself that two acts of Spontini were enough for me. It was astonishing that even in Florence Spontini had not been interred. But clearly, from the efficiency, assurance, and completeness of its production, *La Vestale* must have been in the Florentine *répertoire* perhaps ever, since its composition, and a management selling seats at two lire finds it so much easier to keep an old opera in the *répertoire* than to kick it out and bring in a new one. I had savoured the theatre, and I went, satisfied; also much preoccupied with the financial enigma of the enterprise, where indeed the real poetry of this age resides. Whence came the money to pay the wages of at least a couple of hundred skilled persons, and the lighting and the heating and the rent, and the advertisement, and the thousand minor expenses of such an affair?

When I reached the abode of the ladies it was all dark and silent. I rang, intimidated. And one of those young and beautiful girls (no, not so young and not so beautiful, but still—) in her exotic English attire opened the door. And with her sleepy eyes she looked at me as if saying: "Once in a way this sort of thing is all very well, but please don't let it occur too often. I suffer." A shame! And I crept contrite up the stairs, and along passages between hidden rows of sleeping ladies. And there was my Baedeker lying on the night-table, and not a word in it about Florentine opera and the romance thereof.

Rain still! Florentine rain, the next morning, steady and implacable! They come down to breakfast, those fifty ladies; not in a cohort, but in ones and twos and threes, appearing and disappearing, so that there are never more than half a dozen hovering together over the white and almost naked tables. They glance momentarily at the high windows and glance away, crushing by a heroic effort of self-control, impossible to any but women of the north, the impulse to criticise the order of the universe. Calm, angular, ungainly, long-suffering, and morose, Cimabue might have painted them; not Giotto. Their garb is austere, flannel above the zone and stuff below; no ornament, no fluffiness, no enticement; but passably neat, save for the untidy, irregular buttoning of the bodice down the spine. And note that they are fully and finally dressed to be seen of men; all the chill rites have been performed; they have not leapt straight from the couch into a peignoir, after the manner of Latin women—those odalisques at heart! They are astoundingly gentle with each

130

other, cooing sympathetic inquiries, emitting kind altruistic hopes, leaning intimately towards each other, fondling each other, and even sweetly kissing. They know by experience that strict observance of a strict code is the price of peace. In that voluntary mutual captivity, so full of enforced, familiar contacts, the error of a moment might produce a thousand hours of purgatory.... A fresh young girl comes swinging in, and with a gesture of which in a few years she will be incapable, caresses the chin of her desiccated mamma. And the contrast between the two figures, the thought of what lies behind the one and what lies before the other, inured so soon to this existence— is poignant. The girl perceptibly droops in that atmosphere; flourish in it she cannot. And the smiles and the sweetness continue in profusion. Nevertheless I feel that I am amid loose nitro-glycerine: one jar, and the whole affair might be blown to atoms, and the papers would be full of "mysterious fatal explosion in a *pension* at Florence." The danger-points are the jampots and the honey-pots and the marmalade-pots, of which each lady apparently has her own. And when one of them says to the maid (all in white at this hour, as is meet): "This is not my jam—I had more," I quake at the conception of the superhuman force which restrains the awful bitterness in her voice. A matter of an instant; but in that instant, in that fraction of an instant, the tigress has snarled at the bars of the cage and been dragged back. It is marvellous. It is terrifying.

We talk. We talk to prove our virtuosity in the nice conduct of the early meal. I learn that they have been here for months, and that they will be here for months. And that next year it may be Rome, or more possibly Florence again. Florence is inexhaustible, inexhaustible.

I mention the opera. I assert that there is such a thing as an opera.

"Really!" Politeness masking indifference.

I say that I went to the opera last night.

"Really!" Politeness masking a puzzled, an even slightly alarmed surprise.

I say that the opera was most diverting.

"Really!" Politeness masking boredom.

The opera is not appraised in the guide-books. The opera is no part of the official museum. Florence is a museum, and nothing but a museum. Beyond the museum they do not admit that anything exists; hence nothing exists beyond it. They do not scorn the rest of Florence. The rest of Florence simply has not occurred to them. Pride of the Medicis, bow before this pride, sublime in its absolute unconsciousness!

That morning I made my way in the rain to the Strozzi Palace, which palace is for me the great characteristic building of Florence. When I think of Florence, I do not expire in ecstasy on the syllables of Duomo, Baptistery, or Palazzo Vecchio, or even Bargello. The Strozzi Palace is in my mind. Possibly I merely prefer it to the Riccardi Palace because I cannot by paying fivepence invade it and add it up. The Strozzi Palace still holds out against the northern hordes. Filippo Strozzi, as to whom my ignorance is immaculate, must have united in a remarkable degree the qualities of savagery, austere arrogance, and fine taste; otherwise he would never have approved Maiano's plans for this residence and castle. The dimensions of it remind you of the Comédie Humaine, and it carries rectangularity and uncompromising sharpness of corners to the last limit. In form it is simply a colossal cube, of which you can only appreciate the height by standing immediately beneath the unfinished roof-cornice, the latter so vast in its beautiful enlargement of a Roman model that nobody during five hundred years has had the pluck to set about and finish it. Then you can see that in size the Strozzi ranks with cathedrals, and that the residential part of it, up in the air, only begins where three-story houses end.

To appreciate its beauty and its moral you must get away from it, opposite one of its corners, so as to have two *façades* in perspective. The small arched windows of the first and second storeys are all that it shows of a curve. Rather finicking these windows, the elegant trifling of a spirit essentially grim; some are bricked up, some show a gleam of white-painted interior woodwork, and others have the old iron-studded shutters. The lower windows are monstrously netted in iron to resist the human storm. The upper windows may each be ten feet high, but they are mere details of the *façades*, and the lower windows might be square port-holes. See the two perspectives sloping away from you under the tremendous eaves, a state-entrance in the middle of each! See the three rows of torch or banner holders and the marvellous iron lanterns at the corners! Imagine the place lit up with flame on some night of the early sixteenth century, human beings swarming about its base as at the foot of precipices. Imagine the lights out, and the dawn, and the day-gloom of those ill-lighted and splendid apartments. Imagine the traditional enemies of the Medicis trying to keep themselves warm therein during a windy Florentine winter! Imagine, from the Strozzi Palace, the ferocious altercations, and the artistic connoisseurship, and the continuous ruthless sweating of the common people, which made up the lives of the masters of Florence—and you will formulate a better idea of what life was than from any church! This palace is a supreme monument of grim force tempered by an exquisite sense of beauty. With the exception of an intervening cornice which has had a piece knocked out of it, and the damaged plinth, it stands now as it did at the commencement. Time has not accepted the challenge of its sharp corners. It might have been constructed ten years ago by Foster and Dicksee.

I go up to one of the state entrances and peep in, shamefacedly. For it is a private house. At the far end of the archway is a magnificent iron grille, and I can see a delicately arched courtyard, utterly different in style from the exterior, fruit of another brain; and beyond the courtyard, a glimpse of a fresco and the vista of the state entrance in the opposite *façade*. At each corner of the courtyard the rain is splashing down, evidently from high open spouts, splashing with a loud, careless, insolent noise, and the middle of the courtyard is a pool continuously pricked by thousands of raindrops. The glass of the large lamp swinging in the draught of the archway is broken. A huge lackey in uniform strolls in front of the grille and lolls there. I move instinctively away, for if anybody recoils before a lackey it is your socialist.

Then I see a lady hurrying across the square enveloped in a great cloak and sheltered beneath an umbrella. She makes straight for the state entrance, and passes me, dripping up the archway. I say to myself:

"She belongs to the house. Now I am going to see the gates yield. The lackey was expecting her." And I had quite a thrill at sight of this living inhabitant of the Strozzi Palace.

But not She went right up to the grille, as though the lackey was in prison and she visiting him, and stopped there and stared silently into the courtyard. The lackey, dumbfounded and craven, moved off. She had only come to look. This was her manner of coming to look. I ought to have divined by the solidity of her heels that she was one of ours; not one of my particular band at breakfast, but in Florence there are dozens upon dozens of such breakfasts every morning, and from some Anglican breakfast she had risen.

Our breakfast took place in a palace. Not the Strozzi, not nearly so large nor so fine as the Strozzi, but a real Florentine palazzo. It has been transformed within to suit the needs and the caprices of those stern ladies. They have come, and they have come again, and they have calmly insisted, and they have had their will. Hygienic appliances authentically signed by the great English artists in this *genre!* Radiators in each room! Electric bulbs over the bed and in the ceiling! Iron beds! The inconvenient height of the windows from the floor lessened by a little wooden platform on which are a little chair and a little table and a little piece of needlework and a little vase of flowers!... Steadily they are occupying the palaces, each lady in her nook, and the slow force of their will moulds even the granite to the desired uses.

Why do they come?

Why do they come? It cannot be out of passion for the great art of the world. Nobody who had a glimmering of the real sense of beauty could dress as they dress, move as they move, buy what they buy, or talk as they talk. They mingle in their heads

135

Goltermann with Debussy, and Botticelli with Maude Goodman. Their drawing-room is full of Maude Goodman in her rich first period.. .. It cannot be out of a love of history, for they never unseal their lips in a spot where history has been made without demonstrating in the most painful manner an entire lack of historical imagination. They nibble daintily at crumbs of art and of archæology in special booklets which some of themselves have written and others of themselves have illustrated, and which make the coarse male turn with an almost animal satisfaction to Carl Baedeker or even the Reverend Herbert H.

Jeaffreson, M. A. It is impossible that these excellent creatures, whose only real defect has to do with the hooks and eyes down their spines, can ever comprehend the beauty and the significance of that by which they are surrounded. They have not the temperament. Temperamentally, they would be much more at home in Riga. Also it is impossible to believe that they are happy in Florence. They do not wear the look of joy. Their gestures are not those of happiness. Nevertheless they can only be in Florence because they have discovered that they are less unhappy here than at home. What deep malady of society is it that drives them out of their natural frame—the frame in which they are comely and even delectable, the frame which best sets off their finer qualities—into unnatural exile and the poor despised companionship of their own sex?

And what must be the force of that malady which drives them I The long levers that ultimately exert their power on the palaces of Florence are worked from England. Behind each of these solitary ladies, in the English background, there must be a mysterious male—relative, friend, lawyer, stockbroker—advising, controlling, forwarding cheques and cheques and cheques, always. These ladies, economically, are dolls of a financial system. Or you may call them the waste products of an arthritic civilisation. What a force is behind them, that they should possess themselves of another age and genius, and live in it as conquerors, modifying manners, architecture, and even perhaps language! The cloaked lady in front of the grille shall, if you choose, fairly be likened to a barbarian on the threshold of a philosopher's dead court; hut as regards mere force, one may say that in her the Strozzis are up against an equal.

II

_____

THE SEVENTH OF MAY, 1910

It was an exquisitely beautiful Italian morning, promising heat that a mild and constant breeze would temper. The East was one glitter. Harmless clouds were loitering across the pale sky, and across the Piazza children were taking the longest way to early school, as I passed from the clear sunshine into the soft transparent gloom of one of the great pantheons of Italy—a vast thirteenth-century Franciscan church, the largest church ever built by any mendicant Order—carved and decorated and painted by Donatello, Giotto, Andrea della Robbia, Rossellino, Maiano, Taddeo Gaddi, Verrocchio, the incomparable Mino da Fiesole, Vasari, Canova.

Already the whole place had been cleansed and swept, but at one of the remotest altars a charwoman was dusting. Little by little I descried other visitors in the distance, moving quietly under the intimidation of that calm, afraid to be the first to break the morning stillness. There was the red gleam of a Baedeker. At a nearer altar a widow in black was kneeling in one of those attitudes of impassioned surrender and appeal that strike you so curiously, when for instance, you go out of Harrods' Stores suddenly into the Brompton Oratory. From an unseen chapel came the sound of chanting, perfunctory, a part of the silence; and last of all, at still another altar, I made out a richly coloured priest genuflecting, all alone, save for a black acolyte. In a corner two guides were talking business, and by the doors the beggars were talking business in ordinary tones before the official whining of the day should commence. The immense interior had spaciousness for innumerable separate and diverse activities, each undisturbed by the others. And all around me were the tombs and cenotaphs of great or notorious men, who had made the glory and the destiny of Italy; Dante, Galileo, Michael Angelo, Donatello, Machiavelli; and Alfieri, Rossini, Aretino, Cherubini, Alberti; and even St. Louis, and a famous fourteenth century English Bishop, and a couple of Bonapartes; many ages, races, climes.

I sat down and opened the damp newspaper which I had just bought outside at the foot of the steps leading up to the dazzling marble façade. And when I had been staring at the newspaper some time I became aware that the widow at the altar in the middle distance had risen and was leaving the church, and then I saw to my surprise that she was an Irish lady staying in my hotel. She passed near me. Should I stop her, or should I not? I wanted to stop her, from the naïve pride which one feels in being able to communicate a startling piece of news of the first magnitude. But on the other hand, I really was nervous about telling her. To tell her seemed brutal, seemed like knocking her down. This was my feeling. She decided the question for me by deviating from her path to greet me.

"What a lovely morning!" she said.

"Have you heard about the King?" I asked her gruffly, well knowing that she had not.

"No," she answered smiling. And then, as she looked at me, her smile faded.

"Well," I said, "he's dead!"

"What! *Our* King?"

"Yes. He died at midnight. Here it is." And I showed her the "*Recentissime*" or Latest News page of the newspaper, two lines in leaded type: "*Londra, 7, ore 2:30 (Urgenza). Re Edoardo è morto a mezzanotte.*" She knew enough Italian to comprehend that.

"This last midnight?" She was breathless.

"Yes."

Less unhappy here than at home

"But—but—no one even knew anything about him being ill?" she protested.

"Yesterday evening's Italian papers had columns about the illness—it was bronchitis," I said grimly.

"Oh!" she said, "I never see the Italian papers."

Yet the name of Edward the Seventh had been on every newspaper placard in the land on Friday night.

But in Italy these British have literally no sight for anything later than the sixteenth century.

Tears stood in her eyes. On my part it would have been just as kindly to knock her down.

"Just think of that little fellow at Osborne—he's got to be Prince of Wales now, and I suppose they'll take him away from there," she murmured brokenly, as she went off, aghast.

I sat down again. It seemed to me, as I reflected among these tombs and cenotaphs, that a woman's eyes, on such an occasion, were a good test of the genuineness of popular affection.

I then noticed that, while the Irish lady and I had been whispering, another acquaintance of mine had mysteriously entered the church without my cognizance and had set up his tent in the south transept. This was a young man who, having gained a prominent place in a certain competition at the Royal College of Art, had been sent off with money in his pocket, at the expense of the British nation, to study art and to paint in Italy. He possessed what is called a travelling scholarship, and the treasures of Italy were at his feet as at the feet of a conqueror. Already he had visited me at my hotel, and filled my room with the odour of his fresh oil-sketches. There were only two things in his head—the art of painting, and the prospect of an immediate visit to Venice. He had lodged his easel on a memorial-stone among the flags of the pavement, and was painting a vista of tombs ending in a bright light of stained glass. His habit was to paint before the museums opened and after they closed. I went and accosted him. Again I was conscious of the naïve pride of a bringer of tragic tidings. He was young and strong, with fire in his eye. I need not be afraid of knocking him down, at any rate.

"The King's dead," I said.

He lifted his brush.

"Not—?"

I nodded.

He burst out with a tremendous, "By Jove!" that broke that fresh morning stillness once for all, and faintly echoed into silence among those tombs. "By Jove!"

His imagination had at once risen to the solemn grandeur of the event, as an event; but the sharp significance of death did not penetrate the armour of that enthusiastic youthfulness. "What a pity!" he exclaimed nicely; but he could not get the iridescent vision of Venice out of his head, nor the problems of his canvas. He continued painting—what else could he do?—and then, after a few moments, he said eagerly, "I wish I was in London!"

"Me too!" I said.

Probably most of the thousands of Englishmen in Italy had the same wish.

I departed from the church. The chanting had ceased; the guides were still talking business, but the beggars had begun to whine.

In the dining-room of the hotel there was absolute silence. A lady near the door, with an Italian newspaper over her coffee-cup, who had never spoken to me before, and would probably never speak to me again, said:

"I suppose you've heard about—"

"Yes," I said.

Everybody in the room knew. Everybody was

English. And nobody spoke. As the guests came down by ones and twos to breakfast, the lady near the door stopped each of them: "I suppose you've heard—" But none of them had. I was her sole failure. At length a retired military officer came down, already informed. "Where does this news come from?" he demanded of the room, impatiently, cautiously, half-incredulously, as one who would hesitate to trust any information that he had not seen in a London daily. With a single inflection of his commanding voice he wiped out the whole Press of Italy—that country of excellent newspapers. He got little answer. We all sat silent.

III

MORE ITALIAN OPERA

Geographical considerations made it impossible for me to be present at the performance of *La Traviata*, which opened the Covent Garden season. I solaced myself by going to hear, on that very night, another and better opera of Verdi's, *Aida*, in a theatre certainly more capacious than Covent Garden, namely, the Politeamo Fiorentino, at Florence. Florence is a city of huge theatres, which seem to be generally empty, even during performances, and often on sale. In the majority of them the weather is little by little getting the better of the ceiling; and the multifarious attendants, young and old, go about their casual vague business of letting cushions or selling cigars in raiment that has the rich, storied interest of antiquity. But on this particular occasion prosperity attended a Florentine theatrical enterprise. I was one of three thousand or so excited and crowded beings, most of whom had paid a fair price for admission to hear the brassiest opera ever composed.

Once I used to condescend to Verdi. That was in the early nineties, when, at an impressionable and violent age, I got caught in the first genuine Wagner craze that attacked this country. We used to go to the special German seasons at Drury Lane, as it were to High Mass. And although Max Alvary and Frau Klafsky would be singing in *Tristan*, you might comfortably have put all the occupants of the upper circle into a Pullman car. Once a cat walked across the stage during a solemn moment in the career of Isolde, and nearly everybody laughed; a few tittered, which was even more odious. Only a handful, of such as myself, scowled angrily—not at the cat, which was really rather fine in the garden, completing it—but at the infantile unseriousness of these sniggering so-called Wagnerians. I felt that laughter would have been very well at a Verdi performance, might even have enhanced it. Meanwhile, over the way at Convent Garden, Verdi performances were being given to the usual full houses. It never occurred to me to attend them. Verdi was vulgar. I cannot explain my conviction that Verdi was vulgar, because I had not heard a single opera of Verdi's, save his Wagnerian imitations. No doubt it arose out of the deep human instinct to intensify the pleasure of admiring one thing by simultaneously disparaging another thing.

Then, a long time afterwards, in the comparatively calm interval between the first and the second Wagner crazes, I heard the real Verdi. It was *La Traviata*, in a little town in Italy, and it was the first operatic performance I had attended in Italy. I adored it, when I was not privately laughing at it; and there are one or two airs in it, which I would sit through the whole opera to hear, if I could not hear them otherwise. (Happily they occur in the first act.) Yes, Verdi's name does not begin with W; but it very nearly does. I stuck him up at once a little lower than the angels, and I have never pulled him down. It is certain, however, that *La Traviata* at any rate cannot live, unless as a comic opera. I personally did not laugh aloud, because the English are seldom cruel in a theatre; but the tragical parts are undoubtedly very funny indeed, funnier even than the tragical parts of the exquisitely absurd play, *La Dame aux Camélias*, upon which the opera is founded. When *La Traviata* was first produced, about fifty-five years ago, in Venice, its unconscious humour brought about an absolute, a disastrous failure. The performance ended amid roars of laughter. Unhappily the enormous proportions of Signora Donatelli, who sang Violetta, aided the fiasco. When the doctor announced that this lady was in an advanced stage of consumption and had but a few hours to live, Harry Lauder himself could not have had a greater success of hilarity with the mob. Italians are like that. They may be devoted to music—though there are reasons for doubting it—but as opera-goers and concert-goers they are a godless crew. An Englishman would have laughed at Violetta's unconsumptive waist, but he would have laughed in the street, or the next morning. The English have reverence, and when they go to the opera, they go to hear the opera.

When Italians go to the opera, they are apparently out for a lark, and they have some of the qualities of the Roman multitude enjoying wild beasts in the amphitheatre. I think I have never been to an operatic performance in Italy without acutely noticing this. When I went to hear *Aida*, the colossal interior of the Politeamo Fiorentino had the very look of an amphitheatre, with its row of heads and hats stretching away smaller and smaller into a haze. There were notices about appealing to the gentleness of the public not to smoke. But do you suppose the public did not smoke? Especially considering that the management thoughtfully offered cigars, cigarettes, and matches for sale! In a very large assemblage of tightly-packed people, unauthorised noises are bound to occur from time to time. Now, an Italian audience will never leave an unauthorised noise alone. If a chair creaks, or a glass on the bar tinkles, an Italian audience will hiss savagely and loudly for several seconds—which seem like several minutes. Not in the hope of stopping the noise, for the noise has stopped! Not because it wishes not to miss a note of the music, for it misses about twenty-five per cent, of the notes through its own fugal hissing! But from simple, truculent savagery! It cares naught for the susceptibilities of the artists. Whether a singer is in the midst of a tender pianissimo, or the band is blaring its best, if an Italian audience hears a noise, however innocent, it will multiply that noise by a hundred. Yet the individual politeness of the Italian people is perfectly delightful.

Further: In the middle of the performance a shabby gentleman came on to the stage and begged indulgence for an artist who was "gravely indisposed." The audience received him with cynical laughter; he made a gesture of cynical resignation and departed. The artist received no indulgence. The artist was silly enough to hold on powerfully to a high note at the end of a long solo; and that solo had to be given again—and let there be no mistake about it!—despite the protests of a minority against such insistence. The Latin temperament! If you sing in opera in Italy, your career may be unremunerative, but it will be exciting. You may be deified, or you may be half-killed. But be assured that the audience is sincere, as sincere as a tiger.

Composers also must beware. When Pasini's new opera, *Don Quixote*, was produced lately, it had a glorious run of two performances. It was, indeed, received with execration. After the second night the leading newspaper appeared with a few brief, barbed remarks: "The season of the Teatro Verdi is ended. It would have been better if it had never started.. . . The maestro Pasini has written an opera which may be very pleasing—to deaf mutes." Yet *Don Quixote* was not worse than many other operas which people pay to see. Imagine these manners in unmusical England.

France is less crude, but not always very much less crude. The most musical city in France is Toulouse. An extraordinary number of singers, composers, and poets seem to be born in Toulouse.

But the *debuts* of an operatic artist at the Toulouse municipal opera are among the most dangerous and terrible experiences that can fall to a singer. The audience is merciless, and recks not of youth nor sex. If it is not satisfied, it expresses its opinion frankly, and for the more frank and effective expression of its opinion it goes to the performance suitably provided with decayed vegetables. And I am told that Marseilles candour is carried even further. As for Naples—.

Perhaps, after all, our admirable politeness and the solemnity of our attitude towards the whole subject of opera merely prove that Continental nations are right in regarding us as fundamentally unmusical. With us opera is a cultivated exotic.

In Italy, what does it matter if you ruin a composer's career, or even kill a young soprano who has not reached your standard! There are quantities of composers and sopranos all over Italy. You can see them active in the very streets. You can't keep them down. We say Miss —————-, the English soprano, in startled accents of pride. Italians don't say Signorina ————— ', the Italian soprano. In Italy you get a new opera about once a month. The last English grand opera that held the English stage was *Artaxerœes*, and it is so long ago that not one person in a hundred who reads these lines will be able to give the name of the composer. Can any nation be musical which does not listen chiefly to its own music?

THE RIVIERA

1907

I

THE HÔTEL TRISTE

Because I am a light and uneasy sleeper I can hear, at a quarter to six every morning, the distant subterranean sound of a peculiarly energetic bell. It rings for about one minute, and it is a signal at which They quit their drowsy beds. And all along the Riviera coast, from Toulon to San Remo, in the misty and chill dawn, They are doing the same thing, beginning the great daily conspiracy to persuade me, and those like me, that we are really the Sultan, and that our previous life has been a dream. I sink back into slumber and hear the monotonous roar of the tideless Mediterranean in my sleep. The Mediterranean, too, is in the conspiracy. It is extremely inconvenient and annoying to have to go running about after a sea which wanders across half a mile of beach twice a day; appreciating this, and knowing the violent objection of sultans to any sort of trouble, the Mediterranean dispenses with a tide; at any hour it may be found tirelessly washing the same stone. After an interval of time, during which a quarter to six in the morning has receded to the middle of the night, I wake up wide, and instantly, in Whitman's phrase,

I know I am august.

I put my hand through the mosquito curtains and touch an electrical contrivance placed there for my benefit, and immediately there appears before me a woman neatly clothed to delight my eye, and I gaze out at her through my mosquito curtains. She wishes me "Good morning" in my own language, in order to save the trouble of unnecessary comprehension, and if I had happened to be Italian, French, or German she could still greet me in my own language, because she has been taught to do so in order to save me trouble. She takes my commands for the morning, and then I notice that the sun has thoughtfully got round to my window and is casting a respectful beam or two on my hyacinthine locks. In the vast palace the sultans are arising, and I catch the rumour thereof. Presently, with various and intricate aid, I have laved the imperial limbs and assumed the robes of state. The window is opened for me, and I pass out on to the balcony and languidly applaud the Mediterranean, like a king diverting himself for half an hour at the opera. It is a great sight, me applauding the Mediterranean as I drink a cup of tea; stockbrokers clapping the dinner-band at the Trocadero would be nothing to it. After this I do an unmonarchical act, an act of which I ought to be ashamed, and which I keep a profound secret from the other sultans in the vast palace—I earn my living by sheer hard labour.

Then I descend to the banqueting-hall, and no sooner do I appear than I am surrounded by minions in black, an extraordinary race of persons. At different hours I see these mysterious minions in black, and sometimes I observe them surreptitiously. They have no names. They never eat, never drink, never smile, never love, never do anything except offer me prepared meats with respectful complacency. Their god is my stomach, and they have made up their minds that it must be appeased with frequent burnt sacrifices and libations. They watch my glance as mariners the sky, and the slightest hint sends them flying. At the conclusion of the ceremony they usher me out of the hall with obeisances into other halls and other deferential silences.

And when the entire rite has been repeated twice we recline on sofas, I and the other sultans, and spend the final hours of the imperial day in being sad and silent together. We are sad because we are sultans. It is in the nature of things that sultans should be sad; it is not the cares of state which make us sad, but merely a high imperial instinct for the correct. Silence is, of course, a necessity to sultans, and for this reason the activity of the immense palace is conducted solely in hushed tones. The minions in black never raise their dulcet voices more than half an inch or so. Late at night, as I pass on my solitary, sad way to the chamber of sleep, I see them, those mysterious minions with no names and no passions and no heed for food, still hovering expectant, still bowing, still silent. And lastly I retire. I find my couch beautifully laid out, I cautiously place myself upon it, I savour the soundless calm of the palace, and I sleep again; and my closing thought is the thought that I am august, and that all the other sultans, in this and all the other palaces from Toulon to San Remo, are august.

Strange things happen. Once a week a very-strange thing happens. I find an envelope lying about. It is never given to me openly. I may discover it propped up against the teapot on my tea-tray, or on my writing-desk, or sandwiched in my "post," between a love-letter and a picture post card. But I invariably do find it; measures are taken that I shall succeed promptly in finding it. All the minions pretend that this envelope is a matter of no importance whatever; I also pretend the same. Now, the fact is that I simply hate this envelope; I hate the sight of it; I hate to open it; I dread its contents. Every week it shocks me. I carry it about with me in my imperial pocket for several hours, fighting against the inevitable. Then at length I dismally yield to a compulsion. And I wander, by accident on purpose, in the direction of a little glass-partitioned room, where a malevolent man sits like a spider sits in its web. We both pretend I am there by chance, but since I am in fact there, I may as well—a pure formality! And a keen listener might hear a golden chink or the rustle of paper. And then I feel feeble but relieved, as if I had come out of the dentist's. And I am aware that I am not so excessively august after all, and that I am in the middle of the Riviera season, when one must expect, etc., etc., and that even the scenery was scientifically reduced to figures in that envelope, and that anyhow the Hôtel Triste is the Hôtel Triste. (Triste is not its real name; one of my fellow sultans, who also does the shameful act in secret, so baptised it in a ribald moment.)

The strangest thing of all occurred one night. I was walking moodily along the convenient marge of the Mediterranean when I saw a man, a human being, dressed in a check suit and a howler hat, talking to another human being dressed in a blouse and a skirt. I passed them. The man was smiling, and chattering loudly and rapidly and even passionately to the soul within the blouse. Soon they parted, with proofs of affection, and the man strode away and overtook and left me behind. You could have knocked me down with a feather when I perceived he was one of the mysterious nameless minions who I thought always wore mourning and never ate, drank, smiled, or loved. "Fellow wanderer in the Infinite," I addressed his back as soon as I had recovered, "What are your opinions upon life and death and love, and the advisability of being august?"

A human being talking to another human being

II

WAR!

We were in the billiard-room—English men and women collected from various parts of the earth, and enjoying that state of intimacy which is somehow produced by the comfortable click of billiard balls. It is extraordinary what pretty things the balls say of a night in the billiard-room of a good hotel. They say: "You are very good-natured and jolly people. Click. Women spoil the play, but it's nice to have them here. Click. And so well-dressed and smiling and feminine I Click. Click. Cigars are good and digestion is good. Click. How correct and refined and broad-minded you all are! All's right with the world. Click." A stockbroker sat near me by the fire. My previous experience of stockbrokers had led me to suppose that all stockbrokers were pursy, middle-aged, hard-breathers, thick-fingered, with a sure taste in wines, steaks, and musical comedies. But this one was very different—except perhaps on the point of musical comedies. He was quite young, quite thin, quite simple. In fact, he was what is known as an English gentleman. He frankly enjoyed showing young ladies aged twenty-three how to make a loser off the red, and talking about waltzes, travel, and sport. He never said anything original, and so never surprised one nor made one feel uncomfortable. He was extremely amiable, and we all liked him. The sole fact about the Stock Exchange which I gleamed from him was that the Stock Exchange comprised many bounders, and "you had to be civil to 'em, too."

"You've heard the news?" I said to him. "About Japan?" he asked. No, he had not heard. It took the English papers two days to reach us, and, of course, for the English there are no newspapers but English newspapers. There was a first-class local daily; with a complete service of foreign news, and a hundred thousand readers; but I do not believe that one English person in ten even knew of its existence. So I took the local daily out of my pocket, and translated to him the Russian note informing the Powers that ambassadors were packing up. "Looks rather bad!" he murmured. I could have jumped up and slain him on the spot with the jigger, for every English person in that hotel every night for three weeks past had exclaimed on glancing at the "Times": "Looks bad!" And here this amiable young stockbroker, with war practically broken out, was saying it again! I am perfectly convinced that everyone said this, and this only, because no one had any ideas beyond it. There had appeared some masterly articles in the "Times" on the Manchurian question. But nobody read them: I am sure of that. No one had even a passable notion of Far Eastern geography, and no one could have explained, lucidly or otherwise, the origin of the gigantic altercation. How strange it is that the causes of war never excite interest! (What was the cause of the Franco-German war, you who are omniscient?)

In response to another question, the young stockbroker said that his particular market would be seriously affected. "I should like to be there," [on the Exchange], he remarked, and added dreamily: "It would be rather fun." Then we began a four-handed game, a game whose stupidities were atoned for by the charming gestures of women. And the stockbroker found himself in enormous form. The stone of the Russian Note had sunk into the placid lake and not a ripple was left. Nothing but billiards had existed since the beginning of the world, or ever would exist. Nothing, I reflected, will rouse the average sensible man to an imaginative conception of what a war is, not even the descriptions of a Stephen Crane. Nay, not even income tax at fifteen pence in the pound!

The next morning I went out for a solitary walk by the coast road. And I had not gone a mile before I came to an unkempt building, with a few officials lounging in front of it. "French Custom House" was painted across its pale face. Then the road began to climb up among the outlying spurs of the Maritime Alps. It went higher and higher till it was cut out of the solid rock. Half a mile further, and there was another French Custom House. Still further, where the rock became crags, and the crags beetled above and beetled below, there occurred a profound gorge, and from the stone bridge which spanned it one could see, and faintly hear, a thin torrent rushing to the sea perhaps a couple of hundred feet below. Immediately to the west of this bridge the surface of the crags had been chiselled smooth, and on the expanse had been pictured a large black triangle with a white border—about twelve feet across. And under the triangle was a common little milestone arrangement, smaller than many English milestones, and on one side of the milestone was painted "France" and on the other "Italia." This was the division between the two greatest Latin countries; across this imaginary line had been waged the bloodless but disastrous tariff war of ten years ago. I was in France; a step, and I was in Italy! And it is on account of similar imaginary, artificial, and unconvincing lines, one here, one there—they straggle over the whole earth's crust— that most wars, military, naval, and financial, take place.

Across the gorge was a high, brown tenement, and towards the tenement strutted an Italian soldier in the full, impossible panoply of war. He carried two rifles, a mile or so of braid, gilt enough to gild the dome of St. Paul's and Heaven knows what contrivances besides. And he was smoking a cigarette out of a long holder. Two young girls, aged perhaps six or eight, bounded out of the slatternly tenement, and began to chatter to him in a high infantile treble. The formidable warrior smiled affectionately, and bending down, offered them a few paternal words; they were evidently spoiled little things. Close by a vendor of picture post cards had set up shop on a stone wall. Far below, the Mediterranean was stretched out like a blue cloth without a crease in it, and a brig in full sail was crawling across the offing.

The sun shone brilliantly. Roses in perfect bloom had escaped from gardens and hung free over hedges. Everything was steeped in a tremendous and impressive calm—a calm at once pastoral and marine, and the calm of obdurate mountains that no plough would ever conquer. And breaking against this mighty calm was the high, thin chatter of the little girls, with their quick and beautiful movements of childhood.

And as I watched the ragged little girls, and followed the brig on the flat and peaceful sea, and sniffed the wonderful air, and was impregnated by the spirit of the incomparable coast and the morning hour, something overcame me, some new perception of the universality of humanity. (It was the little girls that did it.) And I thought intensely how absurd, how artificial, how grotesque, how accidental, how inessential, was all that rigmarole of boundaries and limits and frontiers. It seemed to me incredible, then, that people could go to war about such matters. The peace, the natural universal peace, seemed so profound and so inherent in the secret essence of things, that it could not be broken. And at the very moment, though I knew it not, while the brig was slipping by, and the little girls were imposing upon the good-nature of their terrible father, and the hawker was arranging his trumpery, pathetic post cards, they were killing each other—Russia and Japan were—in a row about "spheres of influence."

III

"MONTE"

Monte Carlo—the initiated call it merely "Monte"—has often been described, in fiction and out of it, but the frank confession of a ruined gambler is a rare thing; partly because the ruined gambler can't often write well enough to express himself accurately, partly because he isn't in the mood for literary composition, and partly because he is sometimes dead. So, since I am not dead, and since it is only by means of literary composition that I can hope to restore my shattered fortunes, I will give you the frank confession of a ruined gambler. Before I went to Monte Carlo I had all the usual ideas of the average sensible man about gambling in general, and about Monte Carlo in particular. "Where does all the exterior brilliance of Monte Carlo come from?" I asked sagely. And I said further: "The Casino administration does not disguise the fact that it makes a profit of about 50,000 francs a day. Where does that profit come from?" And I answered my own question with wonderful wisdom: "Out of the pockets of the foolish gamblers." I specially despised the gambler who gambles "on a system"; I despised him as a creature of superstition. For the "system" gambler will argue that if I toss a penny up six times and it falls "tail" every time, there is a strong probability that it will fall "head" the seventh time. "Now," I said, "can any rational creature be so foolish as to suppose that the six previous and done-with spins can possibly affect the seventh spin? What connection is there between them?" And I replied: "No rational creature can be so foolish. And there is no connection."

In this spirit, superior, omniscient, I went to Monte Carlo.

Of course, I went to study human nature and find material. The sole advantage of being a novelist is that when you are discovered in a place where, as a serious person, you would prefer not to be discovered, you can always aver that you are studying human nature and seeking material. I was much impressed by the fact of my being in Monte Carlo. I said to myself: "I am actually in Monte Carlo!" I was proud. And when I got into the gorgeous gaming saloons, amid that throng at once glittering and shabby, I said: "I am actually in the gaming saloons!" And the thought at the back of my mind was: "Henceforth I shall be able to say that I have been in the gaming saloons at Monte Carlo." After studying human nature at large, I began to study it at a roulette table. I had gambled before—notably with impassive Arab chiefs in that singular oasis of the Sahara desert, Biskra—but only a little, and always at *petits chevaux*, But I understood roulette, and I knew several "systems." I found the human nature very interesting; also the roulette. The sight of real gold, silver, and notes flung about in heaps warmed my imagination. At this point I felt a solitary five-franc piece in my pocket. And then the red turned up three times running, and I remembered a simple "system" that began after a sequence of three.

I don't know how it was, but long before I had formally decided to gamble I knew by instinct that I should stake that five-franc piece. I fought against the idea, but I couldn't take my hand empty out of my pocket. Then at last (the whole experience occupying perhaps ten seconds) I drew forth the five-franc piece and bashfully put it on black. I thought that all the fifty or sixty persons crowded round the table were staring at me and thinking to themselves: "There's a beginner!" However, black won, and the croupier pushed another five-franc piece alongside of mine, and I picked them both up very smartly, remembering all the tales I had ever heard of thieves leaning over you at Monte Carlo and snatching your ill-gotten gains. I then thought: "This is a bit of all right. Just for fun I'll continue the system." I did so.

In an hour I had made fifty francs, without breaking into gold. Once a croupier made a slip and was raking in red stakes when red had won, and people hesitated (because croupiers never make mistakes, you know, and you have to be careful how you quarrel with the table at Monte Carlo), and I was the first to give vent to a protest, and the croupier looked at me and smiled and apologised, and the winners looked at me gratefully, and I began to think myself the deuce and all of a Monte Carlo habitué.

Gambling at Monte Carlo

Having made fifty francs, I decided that I would prove my self-control by ceasing to play. So I did prove it, and went to have tea in the Casino *café*. In those moments fifty francs seemed to me to be a really enormous sum. I was as happy as though I had shot a reviewer without being found out. I gradually began to perceive, too, that though no rational creature could suppose that a spin could be affected by previous spins, nevertheless, it undoubtedly was so affected. I began to scorn a little the average sensible man who scorned the gambler. "There is more in roulette than is dreamt of in your philosophy, my conceited friend," I murmured. I was like a woman—I couldn't argue, but I knew infallibly. Then it suddenly occurred to me that if I had gambled with louis instead of five-franc pieces I should have made 200 francs—200 francs in rather over an hour! Oh, luxury! Oh, being-in-the-swim! Oh, smartness! Oh, gilded and delicious sin!

Five days afterwards I went to Monte Carlo again, to lunch with some brother authors. In the meantime, though I had been chained to my desk by unalterable engagements, I had thought constantly upon the art and craft of gambling. One of these authors knew Monte Carlo, and all that therein is, as I know Fleet Street. And to my equal astonishment and pleasure he said, when I explained my system to him: "Couldn't have a better!" And he proceeded to remark positively that the man who had a decent system and the nerve to stick to it through all crises, would infallibly win from the tables—not a lot, but an average of several louis per sitting of two hours. "Gambling," he said, "is a matter of character. You have the right character," he added. You may guess whether I did not glow with joyous pride. "The tables make their money from the plunging fools," I said, privately, "and I am not a fool." A man was pointed out to me who extracted a regular income from the tables. "But why don't the authorities forbid him the rooms?" I demanded, "Because he's such a good advertisement. Can't you see?" I saw.

We went to the Casino late after lunch. I cut myself adrift from the rest of the party and began instantly to play. In forty-five minutes, with my "system," I had made forty-five francs. And then the rest of the party reappeared and talked about tea, and trains, and dinner. "Tea!" I murmured disgusted (yet I have a profound passion for tea), "when I am netting a franc a minute!" However, I yielded, and we went and had tea at the Restaurant de Paris across the way. And over the white-and-silver of the tea-table, in the falling twilight, with the incomparable mountain landscape in front of us, and the most *chic* and decadent Parisianism around us, we talked roulette. Then the Russian Grand Duke who had won several thousand pounds in a few minutes a week or two before, came veritably and ducally in, and sat at the next table. There was no mistaking his likeness to the Tsar. It is most extraordinary how the propinquity of a Grand Duke, experienced for the first time, affects even the proverbial phlegm of a British novelist. I seemed to be moving in a perfect atmosphere of Grand Dukes! And I, too, had won! The art of literature seemed a very little thing.

After I had made fifty and forty-five francs at two sittings, I developed suddenly, without visiting the tables again, into a complete and thorough gambler. I picked up all the technical terms like picking up marbles—the greater martingale, the lesser martingale, "en plein," "à cheval," "the horses of seventeen," "last square," and so on, and so on—and I had my own original theories about the alleged superiority of red-or-black to odd-or-even in betting on the even chances. In short, for many hours I lived roulette. I ate roulette for dinner, drank it in my Vichy, and smoked it in my cigar. At first I pretended that I was only pretending to be interested in gambling as a means of earning a livelihood (call it honest or dishonest, as you please). Then the average sensible man in me began to have rather a bad time, really. I frankly acknowledged to myself that I was veritably keen on the thing. I said: "Of course, ordinary people believe that the tables must win, but we who are initiated know better. All you want in order to win is a prudent system and great force of character." And I decided that it would be idle, that it would be falsely modest, that it would be inane, to deny that I had exceptional force of character. And beautiful schemes formed themselves in my mind: how I would gain a certain sum, and then increase my "units" from five-franc pieces to louis, and so quadruple the winnings, and how I would get a friend to practise the same system, and so double them again, and how generally we would have a quietly merry time at the expense of the tables during the next month.

And I was so calm, cool, collected, impassive. There was no hurry. I would not go to Monte Carlo the next day, but perhaps the day after. However, the next day proved to be very wet, and I was alone and idle, my friends being otherwise engaged, and hence I was simply obliged to go to Monte Carlo. I didn't wish to go, but what could one do? Before starting, I reflected: "Well, there's just a *chance*—such things have been known," and I took a substantial part of my financial resources out of my pocketbook, and locked that reserve up in a drawer. After this, who will dare to say that I was not cool and sagacious? The journey to Monte Carlo seemed very long. Just as I was entering the ornate portals I met some friends who had seen me there the previous day. The thought flashed through my mind: "These people will think I have got caught in the meshes of the vice just like ordinary idiots, whereas, of course my case is not ordinary at all." So I quickly explained to them that it was very wet (as if they couldn't see), and that my other friends had left me, and that I had come to Monte Carlo merely to kill time. They appeared to regard this explanation as unnecessary.

I had a fancy for the table where I had previously played and won. I went to it, and by extraordinary good fortune secured a chair—a difficult thing to get in the afternoons. Behold me seated next door to a croupier, side by side with regular frequenters, regular practisers of systems, and doubtless envied by the outer ring of players and spectators! I was annoyed to find that every other occupant of a chair had a little printed card in black and red on which he marked the winning numbers. I had neglected to provide myself with this contrivance, and I felt conspicuous; I felt that I was not correct. However, I changed some gold for silver with the croupier, and laid the noble pieces in little piles in front of me, and looked as knowing and as initiated as I could. And at the first opening offered by the play I began the operation of my system, backing red, after black had won three times. Black won the fourth time, and I had lost five francs.... Black won the sixth time and I had lost thirty-five francs. Black won the seventh time, and I had lost seventy-five francs. "Steady, cool customer!" I addressed myself. I put down four louis (and kindly remember that in these hard times four louis is four louis—three English pounds and four English shillings), and, incredible to relate, black won the eighth time, and I had lost a hundred and fifty-five francs. The time occupied was a mere nine minutes. It was at this point that the "nerve" and the "force of character" were required, for it was an essential part of my system to "cut the loss" at the eighth turn. I said: "Hadn't I better put down eight louis and win all back again, *just this once?* Red's absolutely certain to win next time." But my confounded force of character came in, and forced me to cut the loss, and stick strictly to the system. And at the ninth spin red did win. If I had only put down that eight louis I should have been all right. I was extremely annoyed, especially when I realised that, even with decent luck, it would take me the best part of three hours to regain that hundred and fifty-five francs.

I was shaken. I was like a pugilist who had been knocked down in a prize fight, and hasn't quite made up his mind whether, on the whole, he won't be more comfortable, in the long run, where he is. I was like a soldier under a heavy fire, arguing with himself rapidly whether he prefers to be a Balaclava hero with death or the workhouse, or just a plain, ordinary, prudent Tommy. I was struck amidships. Then an American person behind my chair, just a casual foolish plunger, of the class out of which the Casino makes its profits, put a thousand franc note on the odd numbers, and thirty-three turned up. "A thousand for a thousand," said the croupier mechanically and nonchalantly, and handed to the foolish plunger the equivalent of eighty pounds sterling. And about two minutes afterwards the same foolish plunger made a hundred and sixty pounds at another single stroke. It was odious; I tell you positively it was odious. I collected the shattered bits of my character out of my boots, and recommenced my system; made a bit; felt better; and then zero turned up twice—most unsettling, even when zero means only that your stake is "held over." Then two old and fussy ladies came and gambled very seriously over my head, and deranged my hair with the end of the rake in raking up their miserable winnings.... At five o'clock I had lost a hundred and ninety-five francs. I don't mind working hard, at great nervous tension, in a vitiated atmosphere, if I can reckon on netting a franc a minute; but I have a sort of objection to three laborious sittings such as I endured that week when the grand result is a dead loss of four pounds. I somehow failed to see the point. I departed in disgust, and ordered tea at the Café de Paris, not the Restaurant de Paris (I was in no mood for Grand Dukes). And while I imbibed the tea, a heated altercation went on inside me between the average sensible man and the man who knew that money could be made out of the tables and that gambling was a question of nerves, etc. It was a pretty show, that altercation. In about ten rounds the average sensible man had knocked his opponent right out of the ring. I breathed a long breath, and seemed to wake up out of a nightmare. Did I regret the episode? I regretted the ruin, not the episode. For had I not all the time been studying human nature and getting material? Besides that, as I grow older I grow too wise. Says Montaigne: "*Wisdome hath hir excesses, and no leise need of moderation, then follie.*" (The italics are Montaigne's)... And there's a good deal in my system after all.

IV

_____

A DIVERSION AT SAN REMO

The Royal Hotel, San Remo, has the reputation of being the best hotel, and the most expensive, on the Italian Riviera. It is the abode of correctness and wealth, and if a stray novelist or so is discovered there, that is only an accident. It provides distractions of all kinds for its guests: bands of music, conjuring shows, dances; and that week it provided quite a new thing in the way of distraction, namely, an address from Prebendary Carlile, head of the Church Army, which was quite truthfully described as a "national antidote to indiscriminate charity." We looked forward to that address; it was a novelty. And if we of the Royal Hotel had a fault, our fault was a tendency, after we had paid our hotel bills, to indiscriminate charity. Indiscriminate charity salves the conscience just as well as the other kind, and though it costs as much in money, it costs less in trouble. However, we liked to be castigated for our sins, and, in the absence of Father Vaughan, we anticipated with pleasure Mr. Carlile. We did not all go. None of the representatives of ten different Continental aristocracies and plutocracies went. Nor did any young and beautiful persons of any nation go. As a fact, it was a lovely afternoon.

To atone for these defections, the solid respectability of all San Remo swarmed into the hotel. (A notice had been posted that it might order its carriages for 3.30.) We made an unprepossessing assemblage. I am far removed from the first blush of youth; but I believe I was almost the youngest person present, save a boy who had been meanly "pressed" by his white-haired father. We were chiefly old, stout, plain, and of dissatisfied visage. Many of us had never been married, and never would be. We were prepared to be very grave. But the mischief was that Mr. Carlile would not be grave.

Mr. Carlile looked like a retired colonel who had dressed by mistake in clerical raiment. His hue was ruddy, his eye clear, and his moustache martial. He is of a naturally cheerful disposition. It is impossible not to like him, not to admire him, not to respect him. It really requires considerable selfrestraint, after he has been speaking for a few minutes, not to pelt him with sovereigns for the prosecution of his work. Still, appreciation of humour was scarcely our strong point. We could not laugh without severe effort. We were unaccustomed to laugh. It is no use pretending that we were not a serious conclave (we were not basking in the sun, nor dashing across the country in our Fiat cars; we had the interests of the Empire at heart). Therefore, though we took the Prebendary's humorous denunciation of our indiscriminate charity with fairly good grace, we should have preferred it with a little less facetiousness. People burdened as we were with the responsibilities of Empire ought not to be expected to laugh. As protectionists, we were not, if the truth is to be told, in a mood for gaiety. Hence we did not laugh; we hardly smiled. We just listened soberly to the Prebendary, who, after he had told us what we ought not to do, told us what we ought to do.

"What we try to do," he said, "is to bridge the gulf—to bridge the gulf between the East End and the West End. We don't want your money, we want your help, we want each of you to take up one person and look after him. *That* is the only way to bridge the gulf." He kept on emphasising the phrase "bridge the gulf"; and to illustrate it, he mentioned a Christmas pudding that was sent from a Royal palace to his "Pudding Sunday" orgy labelled for "the poorest and loneliest widow."

"We soon found her," he said. "She worked from 8.30 A.M. to 6:30 p.m. and again two hours at night, sewing buttons, and in a good week she earned six shillings. Her right hand was all distorted by rheumatism, so that to sew gave her great pain. We found her, and we pushed her upstairs, with great difficulty—because she was so bad with bronchitis—and she had her pudding. Someone insisted on giving her 1s. a week for life, and someone else insisted on giving her 2s. a week for life, so now she's a blooming millionaire. Give us money, if you like, but please don't give us any more money for her...."

"There's another class of women," continued the Prebendary, "the drunkards. Drunkenness is growing among women owing to the evil of grocers' licences. We should like some of you to take up a drunken woman apiece and look after her. We can easily find you a nice, gentle creature, to whom getting drunk is no more than getting cross is to us. Very nice women are drunkards, and they can be reclaimed by bridging the gulf. Then there's the hooligans—you have them on the Riviera, too. I've had a good deal of experience of them myself. I was once picked up for dead near the Army and Navy Stores after meeting a hooligan. Only the other day a man put his fist in my face and said: 'You've ruined our trade.' 'What trade? The begging trade?' I said, 'I wish I had.' And then the discharged prisoners. We offer five months' work to any discharged prisoner who cares to take it; there are 200,000 every year. I was talking to a prison official the other day, who told me that 90 per cent, of his 'cases' he sent to us. We reclaim about half of these. The other half break our hearts. One broke all our windows not long since. .."

And the Prebendary said also: "My greatest pleasure is a day, a whole day, in a thoroughly bad slum. I went down to Wigan for such a day, and at a meeting, when I asked whether anyone would come forward and speak up for beer, not for Christ, a man came along and threw three pence at my feet—remains of pawning his waistcoat—and then fell down dead drunk. We picked him up, and I charged a helper with 6d., so that he could be filled up with tea or coffee beyond his capacity to drink any more beer at all. I don't know whether it was the beer or the tea, but he joined us. All due to emotion, or excitement, perhaps! Yes, but the next morning I was going out to the 7.30 prayer-meeting and I came across a Wigan collier dead drunk in the road. I tried to pick *him*, up. I had my surplice on: I always wear my surplice, for the advertisement, and because people like to see it. And I couldn't pick him up. I was carrying my trombone in one hand. Then another man came along, and we couldn't get that drunkard up between us. And then who should come along but my reclaimed drunkard of the night before! He managed it."

And the Prebendary further said: "Come some day and have lunch with me. It will take you two hours. You ought to chop ten bundles of firewood, but I'll let you off that. Or come and have tea. That will take four hours. There's a Starvation Supper to end it at 8.30, and something going on all the time. We have a brass band, thirty players, all very bad. I'm the worst, with my trombone. We also have a women's concertina band. It's terrible. But it goes down. As one man said, 'It mykes me 'ead ache, but it do do me 'eart good.'"

Then Lord Dundonald proposed a vote of thanks to everybody who deserved to be thanked. He indicated that we ought to help Mr. Carlile, just to show our repentance for having allowed the people free access to public-houses for several centuries. (Faint applause.) Unless we prevented the people from getting at beer and unless we prevented aliens from entering England—(Loud applause)—Mr. Carlile's efforts would not succeed. If we stopped the supply of beer and of aliens then the principal steps [towards Utopia?] would have been accomplished. This simple and comprehensible method of straightening out the social system appealed to us very strongly. I think we preferred it to "bridging the gulf." At the back of our minds was the idea that if we lent our motor-cars or our husbands' or brothers' motor-cars to the right candidates at election time we should be doing all that was necessary to ensure the millennium. Upon this we departed. In the glow of the meeting the scheme of attaching ourselves each to a nice, gentle drunken woman seemed attractive; but really, on reflection....! There was a plate at the door. However, Mr. Carlile had himself said, "I don't depend much on the plate at the door."

FONTAINEBLEAU

1904-1909

I

FIRST JOURNEY INTO THE FOREST

Just to show how strange, mysterious, and romantic life is, I will relate to you in a faithful narrative a few of my experiences the other day—it was a common Saturday. Some people may say that my experiences were after all quite ordinary experiences. After *all*, they were not. I was staying in a little house, unfamiliar to me, and beyond a radius of a few hundred yards I knew nothing of my surroundings, for I had arrived by train, and slept in the train. I felt that if I wandered far from that little house I should step into the unknown and the surprising. Even *in* the house I had to speak a foreign tongue; the bells rang in French. During the morning I walked about alone, not daring to go beyond the influence of the little house; I might have been a fly wandering within the small circle of lamplight on a tablecloth; all about me lay vast undiscovered spaces. Then after lunch a curious machine came by itself up to the door of the little house. I daresay you have seen these machines. You sit over something mysterious, with something still more mysterious in front of you. A singular liquid is poured into a tank; one drop explodes at a spark, and the explosion pushes the machine infinitesimally forward, another drop explodes and pushes the machine infinitesimally forward, and so on, and so on, and quicker and quicker, till you can outstrip trains. Such is the explanation given to me. I have a difficulty in believing it, but it seems to find general acceptance. However, the machine came up to the door of the little house, and took us off, four of us, all by itself; and after twisting about several lanes for a couple of minutes it ran us into a forest. I had somehow known all the time that that little house was on the edge of a great forest.

Without being informed, I knew that it was a great forest, because against the first trees there was a large board which said "General Instructions for reading the signposts in the forest," and then a lot of details. No forest that was not a great forest, a mazy forest, and a dangerous forest to get lost in, would have had a notice board like that. As a matter of fact the forest was fifty miles in circumference. We plunged into it, further and further, exploding our way at the rate of twenty or thirty miles an hour, along a superb road which had a beginning and no end. Sometimes we saw a solitary horseman caracoling by the roadside; sometimes we passed a team of horses slowly dragging a dead tree; sometimes we heard the sound of the woodman's saw in the distance. Once or twice we detected a cloud of dust on the horizon of the road, and it came nearer and nearer, and proved to be a machine like ours, speeding on some mysterious errand in the forest. And as we progressed we looked at each other, and noticed that we were getting whiter and whiter—not merely our faces, but even our clothes. And for an extraordinary time we saw nothing but the road running away from under our wheels, and on either side trees, trees, trees—the beech, the oak, the hornbeam, the birch, the pine—interminable and impenetrable millions of them, prodigious in size, and holding strange glooms in the net of their leafless branches. And at intervals we passed cross-roads, disclosing glimpses, come and gone in a second, of other immense avenues of the same trees. And then, quite startlingly, quite without notice, we were out of the forest; it was just as if we were in a train and had come out of a tunnel.

And we had fallen into the midst of a very little village, sleeping on the edge of the forest, and watched over by a very large cathedral. Most of the cathedral had ceased to exist, including one side of the dizzy tower, but enough was left to instil awe. A butcher came with great keys (why a butcher, if the world is so commonplace as people make out?), and we entered the cathedral; and though outside the sun was hot, the interior of the vast fane was ice-cold, chilling the bones. And the cathedral was full of realistic statues of the Virgin, such as could only have been allowed to survive in an ice-cold cathedral on the edge of a magic forest. And then we climbed a dark corkscrew staircase for about an hour, and came out (as startlingly as we had come out of the forest) on the brink of a precipice two hundred feet deep. There was no rail. One little step, and that night our ghosts would have begun to haunt the remoter glades of the forest. The butcher laughed, and leaned over; perhaps he could do this with impunity because he was dressed in blue; I don't know.

Soon afterwards the curious untiring machine had swept us into the forest again. And now the forest became more and more sinister, and beautiful with a dreadful beauty. Great processions of mighty and tremendous rocks straggled over hillocks, and made chasms and promontories, and lairs for tigers—tigers that burn bright in the night. But the road was always smooth, and it seemed nonchalant towards all these wonders. And presently it took us safely out of the forest once again. And this time we were in a town, a town that by some mistake of chronology had got into the wrong century; the mistake was a very gross one indeed. For this town had a fort with dungeons and things, and a moat all round it, and the quaintest streets and bridges and roofs and river and craft. And processions in charge of nuns were walking to and fro in the grass grown streets. And not only were the houses and shops quaint in the highest degree, but the shopkeepers also were all quaint. A greyheaded tailor dressed in black stood at the door of his shop, and his figure offered such a quaint spectacle that one of my friends and myself exclaimed at the same instant: "How Balzacian!" And we began to talk about Balzac's great novel "Ursule Mirouët." It was as if that novel had come into actuality, and we were in the middle of it. Everything was Balzacian; those who have read Balzac's provincial stories will realise what that means. Yet we were able to buy modern cakes at a confectioner's. And we ordered tea, and sat at a table on the pavement in front of an antique inn. And close by us the landlady sat on a chair, and sewed, and watched us. I ventured into the great Balzacian kitchen of the inn, all rafters and copper pans, and found a pretty girl boiling water for our tea in one pan and milk for our tea in another pan. I told her it was wrong to boil the milk, but I could see she did not believe me. We were on the edge of the forest.

And then the machine had carried us back into the forest. And this time we could see that it meant business. For it had chosen a road mightier than the others, and a road more determined to penetrate the very heart of the forest. We travelled many miles with scarcely a curve, until there were more trees behind us than a thousand men, could count in a thousand years. And then— you know what happened next. At least you ought to be able to guess. We came to a castle. In the centre of all forests there is an enchanted castle, and there was an enchanted castle in the centre of this forest. And as the forest was vast, so was the castle vast. And as the forest was beautiful, so was the castle beautiful. It was a sleeping castle; the night of history had overtaken it. We entered its portals by a magnificent double staircase, and there was one watchman there, like a lizard, under the great doorway. He showed us the wonders of the castle, conducting us through an endless series of noble and splendid interiors, furnished to the last detail of luxury, but silent, unpeopled, and forlorn. Only the clocks were alive. "There are sixty-eight clocks in the castle." (And ever since I have thought of those sixty-eight clocks ticking away there, with ten miles of trees on every side of them.) And the interiors grew still more imposing. And at length we arrived at an immense apartment whose gorgeous and yet restrained magnificence drew from us audible murmurs of admiration. Prominent among the furniture was a great bed, hung with green and gold, and a glittering cradle; at the head of the cradle was poised a gold angel bearing a crown. Said the sleepy watchman: "Bed-chamber of Napoleon, with cradle of the King of Rome." This was the secret of the forest.

How Balzacian!

II

SECOND JOURNEY INTO THE FOREST

We glided swiftly into the forest as into a tunnel. But after a while could be seen a silvered lane of stars overhead, a ceiling to the invisible double wall of trees. There were these stars, the rush of tonic wind in our faces, and the glare of the low-hung lanterns on the road that raced to meet us. The car swerved twice in its flight, the second time violently. We understood that there had been danger. As the engine stopped, a great cross loomed up above us, intercepting certain rays; it stood in the middle of the road, which, dividing, enveloped its base, as the current of a river strokes an island. The doctor leaned over from the driving-seat and peered behind. In avoiding the cross he had mistaken for part of the macadam an expanse of dust which rain and wind had caked; and on this treachery the wheels had skidded. "Ça aurait pu être une sale histoire!" he said briefly and drily. In the pause we pictured ourselves flung against the cross, dead or dying. I noticed that other roads joined ours at the cross, and that a large grassy space, circular, separated us from the trees. As soon as we had recovered a little from the disconcerting glimpse of the next world, the doctor got down and restarted the engine, and our road began to race forward to us again, under the narrow ceiling of stars. After monotonous miles, during which I pondered upon eternity, nature, the meaning of life, the precariousness of my earthly situation, and the incipient hole in my boot-sole—all the common night-thoughts—we passed by a high obelisk (the primitive phallic symbol succeeding to the other), and turning to the right, followed an obscure gas-lit street of walls relieved by

176

sculptured porticoes. Then came the vast and sombre courtyard of a vague palace, screened from us by a grille; we overtook a tram-car, a long, glazed box of electric light; and then we were suddenly in a bright and living town. We descended upon the terrace of a calm *café*, in front of which were ranged twin red-blossomed trees in green tubs, and a waiter in a large white apron and a tiny black jacket.

The lights of the town lit the earth to an elevation of about fifteen feet; above that was the primeval and mysterious darkness, hiding even the housetops. Within the planes of radiance people moved to and fro, appearing and disappearing on their secret errands; and glittering tramcars continually threaded the Square, attended by blue sparks. A monumental bull occupied a pedestal in the centre of the Square; parts of its body were lustrous, others intensely black, according to the incidence of the lights. My friends said it was the bull of Rosa Bonheur, the Amazon. Pointing to a dark void beyond the flanks of the bull, they said, too, that the palace was there, and spoke of the Council-Chamber of Napoleon, the cradle of the King of Rome, the boudoir of Marie Antoinette. I had to summon my faith in order to realise that I was in Fontainebleau, which hitherto had been to me chiefly a romantic name. In the deep and half-fearful pleasure of realisation—-"This also has happened to me!"—I was aware of the thrill which has shaken me on many similar occasions, each however unique: as when I first stepped on a foreign shore; when I first saw the Alps, the Pyrenees; when I first strolled on the grand boulevards; when I first staked a coin at Monte Carlo; when I walked over the French frontier and read on a thing like a mile-post the sacred name "Italia"; and, most marvellous, when I stood alone in the Sahara and saw the vermilions and ochres of the Aurès Mountains. This thrill, ever returning, is the reward of a perfect ingenuousness.

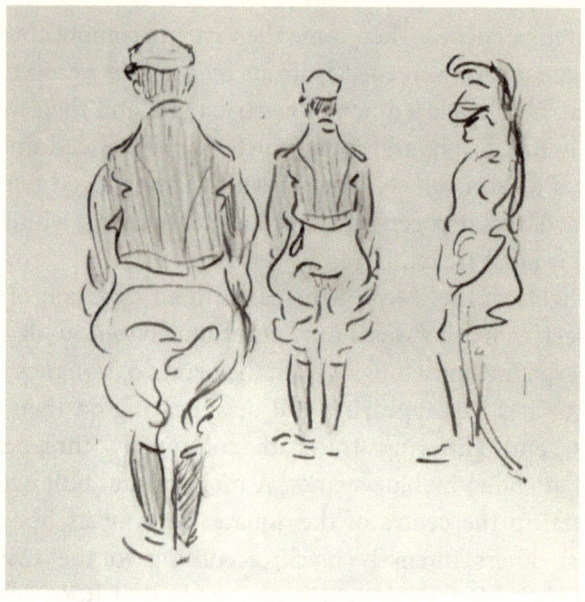

Guards of the castle

I was shown a map, and as I studied it, the strangeness of the town's situation seduced me more than the thought of its history. For the town, with its lights, cars, cafés, shops, halls, palaces, theatres, hotels, and sponging-houses, was lost in the midst of the great forest. Impossible to enter it, or to leave it, without winding through those dark woods! On the map I could trace all the roads, a dozen like ours, converging on the town. I had a vision of them, palely stretching through the interminable and sinister labyrinth of unquiet trees, and gradually reaching the humanity of the town. And I had a vision of the recesses of the forest, where the deer wandered or couched. All around, on the rim of the forest, were significant names: the Moret and the Grez and the Franchard of Stevenson; Barbizon; the Nemours of Balzac; Larchant. Nor did I forget the forest scene of George Moore's "Mildred Lawson."

After we had sat half an hour in front of glasses, we rushed back through the forest to the house on its confines whence we had come. The fascination of the town did not cease to draw me until, years later, I yielded and went definitely to live in it.

III

THE CASTLE GARDENS

On the night of the Feast of Saint Louis the gardens of the palace are not locked as on other nights. The gardens are within the park, and the park is within the forest. I walked on that hot, clear night amid the parterres of flowers; and across shining water, over the regular tops of clipped trees, I saw the long façades and the courts of the palace: pale walls of stone surmounted by steep slated roofs, and high red chimneys cut out against the glittering sky. An architecture whose character is set by the exaggerated slope of its immense roofs, which dwarf the walls they should only protect! All the interest of the style is in these eventful roofs, chequered continually by the facings of upright dormers, pierced by little ovals, and continually interrupted by the perpendicularity of huge chimneys. The palace seems to live chiefly in its roof, and to be top-heavy.

It is a forest of brick chimneys growing out of stone. Millions upon millions of red bricks had been raised and piled in elegant forms solely that the smoke of fires below might escape above the roof ridge: fires which in theory heated rooms, but which had never heated aught but their own chimneys: inefficient and beautiful chimneys of picturesque, ineffectual hearths! Tin pipes and cowls, such as sprout thickly on the roofs of Paris and London, would have been cheaper and better. (It is always thus to practical matters that my mind runs.) In these monstrous and innumerable chimneys one saw eccentricity causing an absurd expense of means for a trifling end: sure mask of a debased style!

The Castle Gardens

With malicious sadness I reflected that in most of those chimneys smoke would never ascend again. I thought of the hundreds of rooms, designed before architects understood the art of planning, crowded with gilt and mahogany furniture, smothered in hangings, tapestries, and carpets, sparkling with crystal whose cold gaiety is reflected in the polish of oak floors! And not a room but conjures up the splendour of the monarchs and the misery of the people of France! Not an object that is associated with the real welfare of the folk, the makers of the country! A museum now—the palace, the gardens, and

181

the fountained vistas of lake and canal—or shall I not say a mausoleum?—whose title to fame, in the esteem of the open-mouthed, is that here Napoleon, the supreme scourge of families and costly spreader of ruin,-wrote an illegible abdication. The document of abdication, which is, after all, only a facsimile, and the greedy carp in the lake—these two phenomena divide the eyes of the open-mouthed.

And not all the starers that come from the quarters of the world are more than sufficient to dot very sparsely the interminable polished floors and the great spaces of the gardens. The fantastic monument is preserved ostensibly as one of the glories of France! (*Gloire*, thou art French! Fontainebleau, Pasteur, the Eiffel Tower, Victor Hugo, the Paris-Lyons-Mediterranean Railway—each has been termed a *gloire* of France!) But the true reason of the monument's preservation is that it is too big to destroy. The later age has not the force nor the courage to raze it and parcel it and sell it, and give to the poor. It is a defiance to the later age of the age departed. Like a gigantic idol, it is kept gilded and tidy at terrific expense by a cult which tempers fear with disdain.

IV

AN ITINERARY

I have lived for years in the forest of Fontainebleau, the largest forest in France, and one of the classic forests—I suppose—of the world. Not in a charcoal-burner's hut, nor in a cave, but in a town; for the united towns of Avon and Fontainebleau happen to be in the forest itself, and you cannot either enter or quit them without passing through the forest; thus it happens that, while inhabiting the recesses of a forest you can enjoy all the graces and conveniences of an imperial city (Fontainebleau is nothing if not Napoleonic), even to *cafés chantants*, cinematograph theatres, and expensive fruiterers. I tramp daily, and often twice daily, in this forest, seldom reaching its edge, unless I do my tramping on a bicycle, and it is probably this familiarity with its fastnesses and this unfamiliarity with its periphery as a continuous whole that has given me what I believe to be a new idea for a tramping excursion: namely, a circuit of the forest of Fontainebleau. It is an enterprise which might take two days or two months. I may never accomplish it myself, but it ought to be accomplished by somebody, and I can guarantee its exceeding diversity and interest. The forest is surrounded by a ring of towns, townships, and villages of the most varied character. I think I know every one of them, having arrived somehow at each of them by following radii from the centre. I propose to put down some un-Baedekerish but practical notes on each place, for the use and benefit of the tramp er who has the wisdom to pursue my suggestion.

One must begin with Moret. Moret is the show-place on the

edge of the forest, and perhaps the oldest. I assisted some years ago at the celebration of its thousandth anniversary. It is only forty-three miles from Paris, on the main line of the Paris-Lyons-Mediterranean railway, an important junction; two hundred and fifty trains a day pass through the station. And yet it is one of the deadest places I ever had tea in. It lies low, on the banks of the Loing, about a mile above the confluence of the Seine and the Loing. It is dirty, not very healthy, and exceedingly picturesque. Its bridge, church, gates and donjon have been painted and sketched by millions of artists, professional and amateur. It appears several times in each year's Salon. This is its curse—the same curse as that of Bruges: it is overrun by amateur artists. I am an amateur artist myself; in summer I am not to be seen abroad without a sketching-stool, a portfolio, and a water-bottle in my hip pocket. But I hate, loathe and despise other amateur artists. Nothing would induce me to make one of the group of earnest dabbers and scratchers by the bridge at Moret. When I attack Nature, I must be alone, or, if another artist is to be there, he must be a certified professional. I have nothing else to say against Moret. There are several hotels, all mediocre.

A more amusing and bracing place than Moret is its suburb St. Mammès, the port at the afore-mentioned confluence, magnificently situated, and always brightened by the traffic of barges, tugs, and other craft. There is an hotel and a *pension*. The Seine is a great and noble stream here, and absolutely unused by pleasure-craft. I do not know why. I once made a canoe and navigated the Amazonian flood, but the contrivance was too frail. Tugs would come rushing down, causing waves twelve inches high at least, and I was afraid, especially as I had had the temerity to put a sail to the canoe.

The tramper should cross the Seine here, and go through Champagne, a horrible town erected by the Creusot Steel Company—called, quite seriously, a "garden city." He then crosses the river again to Thomery—the grape town. The finest table grapes in France are grown at Thomery. Vines flourish in public on both sides of most streets, and public opinion is so powerful (on this one point) that the fruit is never stolen. Thomery's lesser neighbour, By, is equally vinous. These large villages offer very interesting studies in the results of specialisation. Hotels and *pensions* exist.

From Thomery, going in a general direction north by west, it is necessary to penetrate a little into the forest, as the Seine is its boundary here, and there is no practical towing-path on the forest side of the river. You come down to the river at Yalvins Bridge, and, following the left bank, you arrive at the little village of Les Plâtreries, which consists of about six houses and an hotel where the food is excellent and whose garden rises steeply straight into the forest. A mile farther on is the large village of Samois, also on the Seine. Lower Samois is too pretty—-as pretty as a Christmas card. It is much frequented in summer; its hotel accommodation is inferior and expensive, and its reputation for strictly conventional propriety is scarcely excessive. 'However, a picturesque spot! Climb the very abrupt stony high street, and you come to Upper Samois, which is less sophisticated.

From Samois (unless you choose to ferry across to Féricy and reach Melun by Fontaine-le-Port) you must cut through an arm of the forest to Bois-le-Roi. You are now getting toward the northern and less interesting extremity of the forest. Bois-le-Roi looks a perfect dream of a place from the station. But it is no such thing. It is residential. It is even respectably residential. All trains except the big expresses stop at Bois-le-Roi, which fact is a proof that the residents exert secret influences upon the railway directors, and that therefore they are the kind of resident whose notion of architecture is merely distressing. You can stay at Bois-le-Roi and live therein comfortably, but there is no reason why you should.

The next place is Melun, which lies just to the north of the forest. It is the county town. It is noted for its brewery. It is well situated on a curve of the Seine, and it is more provincial (in the stodgy sense) and more ineffably tedious even than Moret.

It possesses neither monuments nor charm. Yet the distant view of it—say from the height above Fontaine-le-Port, is ravishing at morn.

Arbonne

From Melun you face about and strike due south, again cutting through a bit of the forest, to Chailly-en-Bière. (All the villages about here are "*en bière*") Chailly is just a nice plain average forest-edge village, and that is why I like it. I doubt if you could sleep there with advantage. But if you travel with your own tea, you might have excellent tea there.

The next village is Barbizon, the most renowned place in all the Fontainebleau region; a name full of romantic associations. It is utterly vulgarised, like Stratford-on-Avon. "Les Charmettes" has become a fashionable hotel with a private theatre and an orchestra during dinner. What would Rousseau, Daubigny and Millet say if they could see it now? Curiosity shops, art exhibitions, and a very large *café*! An appalling light railway, and all over everything the sticky slime of sophistication! Walking about the lanes you have glimpses of superb studio interiors, furnished doubtless by Waring or Lazard. Indeed Barbizon has now become naught but a target for the staring eyes of tourists from Arizona, and a place of abode for persons whose mentality leads them to believe that the atmosphere of this village is favourable to high-class painting.

All the country round about here is exquisite. I have seen purple mornings in the fields nearly as good as any that Millet ever painted. A lane westward should be followed so that other nice average villages, St. Martin-en-Bière and Fleury-en-Bière can be seen. At Fleury there is a glorious castle, partly falling to ruin, and partly in process of restoration. Thence, south-easterly, to Arbonne.

Arbonne is only a few miles from Barbizon, and I fancy that it resembles what Barbizon used to be before Barbizon was discovered by London and New York. It is a long, straggling place, with one impossible and one quite possible hotel. As a field of action for the tramping painter I should say that it is unsurpassed in the department. From Arbonne you must cross another arm of the forest, and pass from the department of Seine-et-Marne to that of Seine-et-Oise, to the market town of Milly. From Milly onwards the human interest is less than the landscape interest until you come to Chapelle-la-Reine; from there you are soon at Larchant, whose ruined cathedral is one of the leading attractions of the forest edge.

You are now within the sphere of Nemours. From Larchant to Nemours the only agreeable method of locomotion is by aeroplane. The high road is straight and level, and, owing to heavy traffic caused by quarries, atrociously bad. It reaches the acme of boredom. Its one merit is its brevity, about five miles. Nemours is a fine Balzacian town, on the Loing, with a picturesque canal in the heart of it, a frowning castle, a goodish church and bridge, a good hotel and delightful suburbs.

At Nemours, cross the river, and keep to the high road which follows the Loing canal through Episy back to Moret. Or, in the alternative, refrain from crossing the river, and take the Paris high road, leaving it to the left at Bourron, and so reach Moret through Marlotte and Montigny. Marlotte and Montigny are Parisian villages in July, August, and September, new, artistic, snobbish; in winter they are quite tolerable. Montigny is "picturesquely situated" on the Loing, and Marlotte has a huge hotel. The road thence on the rim of the forest back to Moret is delightful.

I do not know how many miles you will have done—anything from sixty to a hundred and twenty probably—when you arrive for the second time in Moret. But you must find strength to struggle onwards from Moret to Fontainebleau itself, about seven miles off in the forest. Fontainebleau contains one of the dearest hotels in the world. Ask for it, and go somewhere else.

SWITZERLAND

1909-1911

I

THE HOTEL ON THE LANDSCAPE

I do not mean the picturesque and gabled construction which on our own country-side has been restored to prosperity, though not to efficiency, by Americans travelling with money and motor-cars. I mean the uncompromising grand hotel— Majestic, Palace, Métropole, Royal, Splendide, Victoria, Belle Vue, Ritz, Savoy, Windsor, Continental, and supereminently Grand—which was perhaps first invented and compiled in Northumberland Avenue, and has now spread with its thousand windows and balconies over the entire world. I mean the hotel which is invariably referred to in daily newspapers as a "huge modern caravanserai." This hotel cannot be judged in a town. In a town, unless it possesses a river-front or a sea-esplanade, the eye never gets higher than its second storey, and as a spectacle the hotel resolves itself usually into a row of shops (for the sale of uselessness), with a large square hole in the middle manned by laced officials who die after a career devoted exclusively to the opening and shutting of glazed double-doors.

To be fairly judged, the grand hotel must be seen alone on a landscape as vast as itself. The best country in which to see it is therefore Switzerland. True, the Riviera is regularly fringed with grand hotels from Toulon to the other side of San Remo; but there they are so closely packed as to interfere with each other's impressiveness, and as a rule they are at too low an altitude. In Switzerland they occur in all conceivable and inconceivable situations. The official guide of the Swiss Society of Hotel Keepers gives us photographs of over eight hundred grand hotels, and it is by no means complete; in fact, some of the grandest consider themselves too grand to be in it, pictorially. Just as Germany is the land of pundits and aniline dyes, France of revolutions, England of beautiful women, and Scotland of sixpences, so is Switzerland the land of huge modern caravanserais.

You may put Snowdon on the top of Ben Nevis and climb up the height of the total by the aid of railways, funiculars, racks and pinions, diligences and sledges; and when nothing but your own feet will take you any farther, you will see, in Switzerland, a grand hotel, magically and incredibly raised aloft in the mountains; solitary—no town, no houses, nothing but this hotel hemmed in on all sides by snowy crags, and made impregnable by precipices and treacherous snow and ice. I always imagine that at the next great re-drawing of the map of Europe, when the lesser nationalities are to disappear, the Switzers will take armed refuge in their farthest grand hotels, and there defy the mandates of the Concert. For the hotel, no matter how remote it be, lacks nothing that is mentioned in the dictionary of comfort. Beyond its walls your life is not worth twelve hours' purchase. You would not die of hunger, because you would perish of cold. At best you might hit on some peasant's cottage in which the standards of existence had not changed for a century. But once pass within the portals of the grand hotel, and you become the spoiled darling of an intricate organisation that laughts at mountains, avalanches, and frost. You are surrounded by luxuries surpassing even the luxuries off ered by the huge modern caravanserais of London.

(For example, I believe that no London caravanserai was, until quite lately, steam-heated throughout.) You have the temperature of the South, or of the North, by turning a handle, and the light of suns at midnight. You have the restaurants of Piccadilly and the tea-rooms of St. James's Street. You eat to the music of wild artistes in red uniforms. You are amused by conjurers, bridge-drives, and cotillons. You can read the periodical literature of the world while reclining on upholstery from the most expensive houses in Tottenham Court Road and Oxford Street. You have a post-office, a telegraph-office, and a telephone; pianos, pianolas, and musical-boxes. You go up to bed in a lift, and come down again to lunch in one. You need only ring a bell, and a specially trained man in clothes more glittering than yours will answer you softly in any language you please, and do anything you want except carry you bodily.... And on the other side of a pane of glass is the white peak, the virgin glacier, twenty degrees of frost, starvation, death—and Nature as obdurate as she was ten thousand years ago. Within the grand hotel civilisation is so powerful that it governs the very colour of your necktie of an evening. Without it, cut off from it, in those mountains you would be fighting your fellows for existence according to the codes of primitive humanity. Put your nose against the dark window, after dinner, while the band is soothing your digestion with a waltz, and in the distance you may see a greenish light. It is a star. And a little below it you may see a yellow light glimmering. It is another grand hotel, by day generally invisible, another eyrie *de luxe*.

You go home and calmly say that you have been staying at the Grand Hotel Blank. But does it ever occur to you to wonder how it was all done? Does it ever occur to you that orchestras, lampshades, fresh eggs, fresh fish, vanilla ices, champagne, and cut flowers do not grow on snow-wreathed crags? You have not been staying in a hotel, but in a miracle of seven storeys. In the sub-basement lie the wines. In the basement women are for ever washing linen and men for ever cooking. On the ground-floor

191

all is eating and drinking and rhythm. Then come five storeys of slumber; and above that the attics where the tips are divided.

In judging the hotel on the landscape, you must thus imaginatively realise what it is and what it means.

The eye needs to be trained before it can look seeingly at a grand hotel and disengage its beauty from the mists and distortions which prejudice has created. This age (like any other age, for the matter of that) has so little confidence in itself that it cannot believe that it has created anything beautiful. It is incapable of conceiving that an insurance office may be beautiful. It is convinced, with the late Sir William Harcourt, that New Scotland Yard is a monstrosity. It talks of the cost, not of the beauty, of the Piccadilly Hotel. No doubt the Romans, who were nevertheless a sound artistic race of the second rank, talked of the cost (in slaves) of their aqueducts, and would have been puzzled could they have seen us staring at the imperfect remains of the said aqueducts as interesting works of art. The notion that a hotel, even the most comfortable, is anything but a blot on the landscape, has probably never yet occurred to a single one of the thousands of dilettanti who wander restlessly over the face of Europe admiring architecture and scenery. Hotels as visual objects are condemned offhand, without leave to appeal, unheard, or rather unseen—I mean really *unseen*.

For several weeks, once, I passed daily in the vicinity of a huge modern caravanserai, which stood by itself on a mountain side in Switzerland; and my attitude towards that hotel was as abusive and violent as Ruskin's towards railways. And then one evening, early, in the middle dusk, I came across it unexpectedly, when I was not prepared for it: it took me unawares and suddenly conquered me. I saw it in the mass, rising in an immense, irregular rectangle out of a floor of snow and a background of pines and firs. Its details had vanished. What I saw was not a series of parts, but the whole hotel, as one organism and entity. Only its eight floors were indicated by illuminated windows, and behind those windows I seemed to have a mysterious sense of its lifts continually ascending and descending. The apparition was impressive, poetic, almost overwhelming. It was of a piece with the mountains. It had simplicity, severity, grandeur. It was indubitably and movingly ground of pines and firs. Its details had vanished. What I saw was not a series of parts, but the whole hotel, as one organism and entity. Only its eight floors were indicated by illuminated windows, and behind those windows I seemed to have a mysterious sense of its lifts continually ascending and descending. The apparition was impressive, poetic, almost overwhelming. It was of a piece with the mountains. It had simplicity, severity, grandeur. It was indubitably and movingly beautiful. My eye had been opened; the training had been begun.

I expected, naturally, that the next morning I should see the hotel again in its original ugliness. But no! My view of it had been permanently altered. I had glimpsed the secret of the true manner of seeing a grand hotel. A grand hotel must be seen grandiosely—that is to say, it must be seen with a large sweep of the eye, and from a distance, and while the eye is upon its form the brain must appreciate its moral significance; for the one explains the other. You do not examine Mont Blanc or an oil painting by Turner with a microscope, and you must not look at a grand hotel as you would look at a marble fountain or a miniature.

Since the crepuscular hour above described, I have learnt to observe sympathetically the physiognomy of grand hotels, and I have discovered a new source of æsthetic pleasure. I remember on a morning in autumn, standing on a suspension bridge over the Dordogne and gazing at a feudal castle perched on a pre-feudal crag. I could not decide whether the feudal castle or the suspension bridge was the more romantic fact (for I am so constituted as to see the phenomena of the nineteenth century with the vision of the twenty-third), but the feudal castle, silhouetted against the flank of a great hill that shimmered in the sunshine, had an extraordinary beauty—moral as well as physical, possibly more moral than physical. As architecture it could not compare with the Parthenon or New Scotland Yard. But it was far from ugly, and it had an exquisite rightness in the landscape. I understood that it had been put precisely there because that was the unique place for it. And I understood that its turrets and windows and roofs and walls had been constructed precisely as they were constructed because a whole series of complicated ends had to be attained which could have been attained in no other way. Here was a simple result of an unaffected human activity which had endeavoured to achieve an honest utilitarian end, and, while succeeding, had succeeded also in producing a work of art that gave pleasure to a mind entirely unfeudal. A feudal castle on a crag as impossible to climb as to descend is, and always was, exotic, artificial, and against nature—like every effort of man!—but it does, and always did, contribute to the happiness of peoples.

Similarly I remember, on a morning in winter, standing on a wild country, road, gazing at another castle perched on a pre-feudal crag. But this castle was about fifteen times as big as the former one, and the crag had its earthy foot in a lake about a mile below. The scale of everything was terrifically larger. Still, the two castles, seen at proportionate distances, bore a strange, disconcerting, resemblance the one to the other. The architecture of the second, as of the first, would not compare with the Parthenon or New Scotland Yard. But it was not ugly. And assuredly it had an exquisite rightness in the landscape. I understood, far better than in the former instance, that it had been put precisely where it was, because no other spot would have been so suited to its purposes; its geographical relation to the sun and the lake and the mountains had been perfectly adjusted. I understood profoundly the meaning of all those rows of windows and all those balconies facing the south and southeast. I understood profoundly the intention of the great glazed box at the base of the castle. I could read the words that the wreath of smoke from behind the turreted roof was writing on the slate of the sky, and those words were "*Chauffage central*"

From the façades I could construct the plan and arrangement of the interior of the castle. I could instantly decide which of its two hundred chambers were the costliest, and which would be the last to be occupied and the first to be left. I could feel the valves of its heart rising and falling. Here was the simple result of an unaffected human activity, which had endeavoured to achieve an honest utilitarian end, and, while succeeding, had succeeded also in giving pleasure to a mind representative of the twenty-third century. A grand hotel on a crag as impossible to climb as to descend is, and always will be, exotic, artificial, and against nature—like every effort of man! Why should a man want to leave that pancake, England, and reside for weeks at a time in dizzy altitudes in order to stare at mountains and propel himself over snow and ice by means of skis, skates, sledges, and other unnatural dodges? No one knows. But the ultimate sequel, gathered up and symbolised in the grand hotel, contributes to the happiness of peoples and gives joy to the eye that is not afflicted with moral cataract.

And I am under no compulsion to confine myself to Switzerland. I do not object to go to the other extreme and flit to the Sahara. Who that from afar off in the Algerian desert has seen the white tower of the Royal Hotel at Biskra, oasis of a hundred thousand palm-trees and twenty grand hotels, will deny either its moral or its physical beauty in that tremendously beautiful landscape?

Conceivably, the judgment against hotel architecture was fatally biassed in its origin by the horrible libels pictured on hotel notepapers.

In estimating the architecture of hotels, it must be borne in mind that they constitute the sole genuine contribution made by the modern epoch to the real history of architecture. The last previous contribution took the shape of railway stations, which, until the erection of the Lyons and the Orleans stations in Paris—about seventy years after the birth of stations— were almost without exception desolate failures. It will not

195

be seriously argued, I suppose, that the first twenty years of grand hotels have added as much ugliness to the world's stock of ugliness as the first twenty years of railway stations. If there exists a grand hotel as direfully squalid as King's Cross Station (palace of an undertaking with a capital of over sixty millions sterling) I should like to see it. Hotel architecture is the outcome of a new feature in the activity of society, and this fact must be taken into account. When a new grand hotel takes a page of a daily paper to announce itself as the "last word" of hotels—what it means is, roughly, the "first word," as distinguished from inarticulate babbling.

Of course it is based on strictly utilitarian principles— and rightly. Even when the grand hotel blossoms into rich ornamentation, the aim is not beauty, but the attracting of clients. And the practical conditions, the shackles of utility, in which the architecture of hotels has to evolve, are extremely severe and galling. In the end this will probably lead to a finer form of beauty than would otherwise have been achieved. In the first place a grand hotel, especially when it is situated "on the landscape," can have only one authentic face, and to this face the other three must be sacrificed. Already many hotels advertise that every bedroom without exception looks south, or at any rate looks direct at whatever prospect the visitors have come to look at. This means that the hotel must have length without depth—that it must be a sort of vast wall pierced with windows. Further, the democratic quality of the social microcosm of a hotel necessitates an external monotony of detail. In general, all the rooms on each floor must resemble each other, possessing the same advantages. If one has a balcony, all must have balconies. There must be no sacrificing of the amenities of a room here and there to demands of variety or balance in the elevation. Again, the hotel must be relatively lofty—not because of lack of space, but to facilitate a complex service. The kitchens of Buckingham Palace may be a quarter of a mile from the dining-room, and people will say, "How wonderful!" But if a pot of tea had to be carried a quarter of a mile in a grand hotel, from the kitchen to a bedroom, people would say, "How absurd!" or, "How stewed!" The "layer" system of architecture is from all points of view indispensable to the grand hotel, and its scenic disadvantages must be met by the exercise of ingenuity. There are other problems confronting the hotel architecture, such as the fitting together of very large public rooms with very small private rooms, and the obligation to minimise externally a whole vital department of the hotel (the kitchens, etc.); and I conceive that these problems are perhaps not the least exasperating.

From the utilitarian standpoint the architect of hotels has unquestionably succeeded. The latest hotels are admirably planned; and a good plan cannot result in an elevation entirely bad. One might say, indeed, that a good plan implies an elevation good in, at any rate, elementals. Save that bedrooms are seldom sound-proof, and that they are nearly always too long for their breadth (the reason is obvious), not much fault can be found with the practical features of the newest hotel architecture. In essential matters hotel architecture is good. You may dissolve in ecstasy before the façade of the Chateau de Chambord; but it is certainly the whited sepulchre of sacrificed comfort, health, and practicability. There also, but from a different and a less defensible cause, and to a different and not a better end, the importance of the main front rides roughly over numerous other considerations. In skilful planning no architecture of any period equals ours; and ours is the architecture of grand hotels.

The beholder, before abruptly condemning that uniformity of feature which is the chief characteristic of the hotel on the landscape, must reflect that this is the natural outer expression of the spirit and needs of the hotel, and that it neither can be nor ought to be disguised. It is of the very essence of the building. It may be very slightly relieved by the employment of certain devices of grouping—as some architects in the United States have shown—but it must remain patent and paramount; and the ultimate beauty of more advanced styles will undoubtedly

197

spring from it and, in a minor degree, from the other inner conditions to which I have referred. And even when the ultimate beauty has been accomplished the same thing will come to pass as has always come to pass in the gradual progress of schools of architecture. The pendulum will swing too far, and the best critics of those future days will point to the primitive erections of the early twentieth century and affirm that there has been a decadence since then, and that if the virtue of architecture is to be maintained inspiration must be sought by returning to the first models, when men did not consciously think of beauty, but produced beauty unawares!

It was ever thus.

The salvation of hotel architecture, up to this present, is that the grand hotel on the landscape, in nineteen cases out of twenty, is remuneratively occupied only during some three or four months in the year. Which means that the annual interest on capital expenditure must be earned in that brief period. Which in turn means that architects have no money to squander on ornament in an age notorious for its bad ornament. If the architect of the grand hotel were as little disturbed by the question of dividends as Francis the First was in creating his Chambord and other marvels, the consequences might have been offensive even to the sympathetic eye.

Meanwhile, in Switzerland, the hotel architect may flatter himself that he has suddenly given architecture to a country which had none. This is a highly curious phenomenon. "Next door" to the grand hotel which so surprised me in the twilight is another human habitation, fairly representative of all the non-hotel architecture on the Swiss countryside. It is quaint, and it would not hurt a fly. But surely the grand hotel is man's more fitting answer to the challenge of the mountains?

II

THE EGOIST

A little boy, aged about eight, with nearly all his front teeth gone, came down early for breakfast this morning while I was having mine. He asked me where the waiters were, and rang. When one arrived, the little boy discovered that he could speak no French. However, the waiter said "Café?" and he said "One"; but he told me that he also wanted buns. While breakfasting, he said to me that he had got up early because he was going down into the town that morning by the Funicular, as his mother was to buy him his Christmas present, a silver lever watch. He said: "I hate to be hurried for anything. Now, at home, I have to go to school, and I get up early so that I shan't be hurried, but my breakfast is *always* late; so I have too much time before breakfast, and nothing to do, and too little time after breakfast when I've a lot to do." In answer to my question, he said gravely that he was going into the Navy. He knew the exam, was very stiff, and that if you failed at a certain age you were barred out altogether; and he asked me whether I thought it was better to try the exam, early with only a little preparation, or to leave it late with a long preparation. He thought the first course was the best, because you could go in again if you failed. I asked him if he didn't want some jam. He said no, because the butter was so good, and if he had jam he wouldn't be able to taste the butter. He then rang the bell for more milk, and explained to me that he couldn't drink coffee strong, and the consequence was that he had a whole lot of coffee left and no milk to drink it with.. . . He said he lived in London, and that some shops down in the town were better than

London shops. By this time a German had descended. He and I both laughed. But the child stuck to his point. We asked him: "What shops?" He said that jerseys and watches were nicer in the town than in London. In this he was right, and we had to admit it. As a complete résumé, he said that there were fewer things in the town than in London, but some of the things were nicer. Then he explained to the German his early rising, and added an alternative explanation, namely, that he had been sent to bed at 6.45, whereas 7.15 was his legal time.

Later in the day I asked him if he would come down early again to-morrow and have breakfast with me. He said: "I don't know. I shall see." There was no pose in this. Simply a perfect preoccupation with his own interests and welfare. I should say he is absolutely egotistic. He always employs natural, direct methods to get what he wants and to avoid what lie doesn't want.

I met him again a few afternoons later on the luge-track. He was very solemn. He said he had decided not to go in for the single-luge race, as it all depended on weight. I said: "Put stones in your pocket. Eat stones for breakfast."

He laughed slightly and uncertainly. "You can't eat stones for breakfast," he said. "I'm getting on fine at skating. I can turn round on one leg."

"Do you still fall?" (He was notorious for his tumbles.)

"Yes."

"How often?"

He reflected. Then: "About twelve times an hour.... If I skated all day and all night I should fall twelve twelves—144, isn't it?"

I said it would be twenty-four twelves.

"Oh! I see——"

"Two hundred and——"

"Eighty-eight," he overtook me quickly. "But I didn't mean that. I meant all day and all *night*, you know—'evening. People don't generally skate all *through* the night, do they?" Pause. "Six from 144—138, isn't it? I'll say 138, because you'd have to take half an hour off for dinner, wouldn't you?"

He became silent, discussing seriously within himself whether half an hour would suffice for dinner, without undue hurrying.

III

THE BLAND WANDERER

In the drawing-room to-night an old and solitary, but blandly cheerful, female wanderer recounted numerous accidents at St. Moritz: legs broken in two places, shoulders broken, spines injured; also deaths. Further, the danger of catching infectious diseases at St. Moritz. "One *very* large hotel, where *everybody* had influenza," etc. These recitals seemed to give her calm and serious pleasure.

"Do you think this place is good for nerves?" she broke out suddenly at me. I told her that in my opinion a hot bath and a day in bed would make any place good for nerves. "I mean the nerves of the *body*," she said inscrutably. Then she deviated into a long set description of the historic attack of Russian influenza which she had had several years ago, and which had kept her in bed for three months, since when she had' never been the same woman. And she seemed to savour with placid joy the fact that she had never since been the same woman.

Then she flew back to St. Moritz and the prices thereof. She said you could get pretty reasonable terms, even there, "provided you didn't mind going high up." Upon my saying that I actually preferred being high up, she exclaimed: "I don't. I'm so afraid of fire. I'm always afraid of fire." She said that she had had two nephews at Cambridge. The second one took rooms at the top of the highest house in Cambridge, and the landlord was a drunkard. "My sister didn't seem to care, but I didn't know *what* to do! What *could* I do? Well, I bought him a. non-inflammable rope." She smiled blandly.

This allusion to death and inebriety prompted a sprightly young Yorkshirewoman, with the country gift for yarn-spinning, to tell a tale of something that had happened to her cousin, who gave lessons in domestic economy at a London Board School. A little girl, absent for two days, was questioned as to the reason.

"I couldn't come."

"But why not?"

"I was kept.. . Please 'm, my mother's dead."

"Well, wouldn't you be better here at school? When did she die?"

"Yesterday. I must go back, please. I only came to tell you."

"But why?"

"Well, ma'am. She's lying on the table and I have to watch her."

"Watch her?"

"Yes. Because when father comes home drunk, he knocks her off, and I have to put her on again."

This narration startled even the bridge-players, and there were protests of horror. But the philosophic wanderer, who had never been the same woman since Russian influenza, smiled placidly.

"I knew something really much more awful than that," she said. "A young woman, well-known to me, had charge of a crèche of thirty infants, and one day she took it into her head to amuse herself by changing all their clothes, so that at night they could not be identified; and many of them never *were* identified! She was *such* a merry girl! I knew all her brothers and sisters too! She wanted to go into a sisterhood, and she did, for a month. But the only thing she did there—well, one day she went down into the laundry and taught all the laundry-maids to polka. She was such a merry girl!"

She smiled with extraordinary simplicity.

"In the end," the bland wanderer continued, after a little pause, "she went to America. America is such an odd place! Once I got into a car at Philadelphia that had come from New York. The conductor showed me my berth. The bed was warm. I partly undressed and got into it, and drew the curtain. I was half asleep, when I felt a hand feeling me over through the curtain. I called out, and a man's voice said: 'It's all right. I'm only looking for my stick. I think I must have left it in the berth'! Another time a lot of student girls were in the same car with me. They all got into their beds—or berths or whatever you call it—about eight o'clock, wearing fancy jackets, and they sat up and ate candy. I was walking up and down, and every time I passed they *implored* me to have candy, and then they implored each other to try to persuade me. They were mostly named Sadie. At one in the morning they ordered iced drinks 'round. I was obliged to drink with them. They tired me out, and then made me drink. I don't know what happened just after that, but I know that, at five in the morning, they were all sitting up and eating candy. I've travelled a good deal in America and it's *such* an odd place! It was just the place for that young woman to go to."

IV

ON A MOUNTAIN

Last week I did a thing which you may call hackneyed or unhackneyed, according to your way of life. To some people an excursion to Hampstead Heath is a unique adventure: to others, a walk around the summit of Popocatapetl is all in the year's work. I went to Switzerland and spent Easter on the top of a mountain. At any rate, the mountain was less hackneyed at that season than Rome or Seville, where the price of beds rises in proportion as religious emotion falls. It was Marcus Aurelius Antoninus who sent me to the mountain. To mention Marcus Aurelius is almost as clear a sign of priggish affectation and tenth-rate preciosity as to quote Omar Khayyam; and I may interject defensively that I prefer Epictetus, the slave, to Marcus Aurelius, the neurotic emperor. Still, it was Marcus Aurelius who sent me to the mountain. He advised me, in certain circumstances, to climb high and then look down at human nature.

I did so. My luggage alone cost me four francs excess in the Funicular.

I had before me what I have been told—by others than the hotel proprietor—is one of the finest panoramas in Europe. Across a Calvinistic lake, whose renown is familiar to the profane chiefly because Byron wrote a mediocre poem about a castle on its shores, rose the five-fanged Dent du Midi, twenty-five miles off, and ten thousand feet towards the sky; other mountains, worthy companions of the illustrious Tooth, made a tremendous snowy semicircle right and left; and I on my mountain fronted this semi-circle. The weather was perfect.

Down below me, on the edge of the lake, was a continuous chain of towns, all full and crammed with the final products of civilisation, miles of them. There was everything in those towns that a nation whose destiny it is to satisfy the caprices of the English thought the English could possibly desire. Such things as baths, lifts, fish-knives, two-steps and rag-times, casinos, theatres, rackets, skates, hot-water bottles, whisky, beef-steaks, churches, chapels, cameras, puttees, jig-saws, bridge-markers, clubs, China tea, phonographs, concert-halls, charitable societies, money-changers, hygiene, picture post cards, even books—-just cheap ones! It was dizzying to think of the refined complexity of existence down there. It was impressive to think of the slow centuries of effort, struggle, discovery and invention that had gone to the production of that wondrous civilisation. It was perfectly distracting to think of the innumerable activities that were proceeding in all parts of the earth (for you could have coral from India's coral strand in those towns, and furs from Labrador, and skates from Birmingham) to keep the vast organism in working order.

And behind the chain of towns ran the railwayline, along which flew the expresses with dining-cars and fresh flowers on the tables of the dining-cars, and living drivers on the footplates of the engines, whirling the salt of the earth to and fro, threading like torpedo-shuttles between far-distant centres of refinement. And behind the railway line spread the cultivated fields of these Swiss, who, after all, in the intervals of passing dishes to stately guests in hotel-refectories, have a national life of their own; who indeed have shown more skill and commonsense in the organisation of posts, hotels, and military conscription, than any other nation; so much so, that one gazes and wonders how on earth a race so thick-headed and tedious could ever have done it.

I knew that I had all that before me, because I had been among it all, and had ascended and descended in the lifts, lolled in the casinos and the trains, and drunk the China tea. But I could not see it from the top of my mountain. All that I could see from the top of my mountain was a scattering of dolls' houses, and that scattering constituted three towns; with here and there a white cube overtopping the rest by half an inch, and that white cube was a grand hotel; and out of the upper face of the cube a wisp of vapour, and that wisp of vapour was the smoke of a furnace that sent hot-water through miles of plumbing and heated 400 radiators in 400 elegant apartments; and little stretches of ribbon, and these ribbons were boulevards bordered with great trees; and a puff of steam crawling along a fine wire, and that crawling puff was an international express; and rectangular spaces like handkerchiefs fresh from a bad laundry, and those handkerchiefs were immense fields of vine; and a water-beetle on the still surface of the lake, and that water-beetle was a steamer licensed to carry 850 persons. And there was silence. The towns were feverishly living in ten thousand fashions, and made not a sound. Even the express breathed softly, like a child in another room.

The mountains remained impassive; they were too indifferent to be even contemptuous. Humanity had only soiled their ankles: I could see all around that with all his jumping man had not found a perch higher than their ankles. It seemed to me painfully inept that humanity, having spent seven years in worming a hole through one of those mountains, should have filled the newspapers with the marvels of its hole, and should have fallen into the habit of calling its hole "the Simplon." The Simplon—that hole! It seemed to me that the excellence of Swiss conscription was merely ridiculous in its exquisite unimportance. It seemed to me that I must have been absolutely mad to get myself excited about the January elections in a trifling isle called Britain, writing articles and pamphlets and rude letters, and estranging friends and thinking myself an earnest warrior in the van of progress. Land taxes! I could not look down, or up, and see land taxes as aught but an infantile invention of comic opera. Two Chambers or one! Veto first or Budget first! Mr. F. E. Smith or Mr. Steel-Maitland! Ah! The tea-cup and the storm!

The prescription of Marcus Aurelius Antoninus had "acted."

It is an exceedingly harmful prescription if employed long or often. Go to the top of a mountain by all means, but hurry down again quickly. The top of a mountain, instead of correcting your perspective, as is generally supported by philosophers for whom human existence is not good enough, falsifies it. Because it induces self-aggrandisement. You draw illusive bigness from the mountain. You imagine that you are august, but you are not. If the man below was informed by telephone that a being august was gazing on him from above he would probably squint his eyes upwards in the sunshine and assert with calmness that he couldn't even see a living speck on the mountain-crest. You who have gone up had better come down. You couldn't remain up twenty-four hours without the aid of the ant-like evolutions below, which you grandiosely despise. You couldn't have got up at all if a procession of those miserable conceited ants had not been up there before you.

The detached philosophic mountain view of the littleness of things is a delightful and diverting amusement, and there is perhaps no harm in it so long as you don't really act on it. If you begin really to act on it you at once become ridiculous, and especially ridiculous in the sight of mountains.

You commit the fatuity of despising the corporate toil which has made you what you are, and you prove nothing except that you have found a rather specious and glittering excuse for idleness, for cowardice, and for having permitted the stuffing to be knocked out of you.

When I hear a man say, when I hear myself say: "I'm sick of politics," I always think: "What you want is six months in prison, or in a slum, or in a mine, or in a bakehouse, or in the skin of a woman. After that, we should see if you were sick of politics." And when I hear a lot of people together say that they are sick of politics, then I am quite sure that politics are more than ever urgently in need of attention. It is at such moments that a man has an excellent opportunity of showing that he is a man.

ENGLAND AGAIN

1907

I

THE GATE OF THE EMPIRE

When one comes back to it, after long absence, one sees exactly the same staring, cold white cliffs under the same stars. Ministries may have fallen; the salaries of music-hall artistes may have risen; Christmas boxes may have become a crime; war balloons may be in the air; the strange notion may have sprouted that school children must be fed before they are taught: but all these things are as nothing compared to the changeless fact of the island itself. You in the island are apt to forget that the sea is eternally beating round about all the political fuss you make; you are apt to forget that your 40-h.p. cars are rushing to and fro on a mere whale's back insecurely anchored in the Atlantic. You may call the Atlantic by soft, reassuring names, such as Irish Sea, North Sea, and silver streak; it remains the Atlantic, very careless of social progress, very rude.

The ship under the stars swirls shaking over the starlit waves, and then bumps up against granite and wood, and amid cries ropes are thrown out, and so one is lashed to the island.

Scarcely any reasonable harbours in this island! The inhabitants are obliged to throw stones into the sea till they emerge like a geometrical reef, and vessels cling hard to the reef. One climbs on to it from the steamer; it is very long and thin, like a sword, and between shouting wind and water one precariously balances oneself on it. After some eighty years of steam, nothing more comfortable than the reef has yet been achieved. But far out on the water a black line may be discerned, with the silhouettes of cranes and terrific engines. Denied a natural harbour, the island has at length determined to have an unnatural harbour at this bleak and perilous spot. In another ten years or so the peaceful invader will no longer be compelled to fight with a real train for standing room on a storm-swept reef.

And that train! Electric light, corridors, lavatories, and general brilliance! Luxuries inconceivable in the past! But, just to prove a robust conservatism, hot-water bottles remain as the sole protection against being frozen to death.

"Can I get you a seat, sir?"

It is the guard's tone that is the very essence of England. You may say he descries a shilling on the horizon. I don't care. That tone cannot be heard outside England. It is an honest tone, cheerful, kindly, the welling-up of a fundamental good nature. It is a tone which says: "I am a decent fellow, so are you; let us do the best for ourselves under difficulties." It is far more English than a beefsteak or a ground-landlord. It touches the returned exile profoundly, especially at the dreadful hour of four a. m. And in replying, "Yes, please. Second. Not a smoker," one is saying, "Hail! Fellow-islander. You have appalling faults, but for sheer straightness you cannot be matched elsewhere."

One comes to an oblong aperture on the reef, something resembling the aperture of a Punch and Judy show, and not much larger. In this aperture are a man, many thick cups, several urns, and some chunks of bread. One struggles up to the man.

"Tea or coffee, sir?"

"Hot milk," one says.

"Hot milk!" he repeats. You have shocked his Toryism. You have dragged him out of the rut of tea and coffee, and he does not like it. However—brave, resourceful fellow!—he pulls himself together for an immense effort, and gives you hot milk, and you stand there, in front of the aperture, under the stars and over the sea and in the blast, trying to keep the cup upright in a mêlée of elbows.

This is the gate, and this the hospitality, of the greatest empire that, etc.

"Can I take this cup to the train?"

"Certainly, sir!" says the Punch and Judy man genially, as who should say: "God bless my soul! Aren't you in the country where anyone can choose the portmanteau that suits him out of a luggage van?"

Now that is England! In France, Germany, Italy, there would have been a spacious golden *café* and all the drinks on earth, but one could never have got that cup out of the *café* without at least a stamped declaration signed by two commissioners of police and countersigned by a Consul. One makes a line of milk along the reef, and sits blowing and sipping what is left of the milk in the train. And when the train is ready to depart one demands of a porter:

"What am I to do with this cup?"

"Give it to me, sir."

And he planks it down on the platform next a pillar, and leaves it. And off one goes. The adventures of that thick mug are a beautiful demonstration that the new England contains a lot of the old. It will ultimately reach the Punch and Judy show once more (not broken—perhaps cracked); not, however, by rules and regulations; but higgledy-piggledy, by mutual aid and good nature and good will. He tranquil; it will regain its counter.

The fringe of villas, each primly asleep in its starlit garden, which borders the island and divides the hopfields from the Atlantic, is much wider than it used to be. But in the fields time has stood still.... Now, one has left the sea and the storm and the

reef, and already one is forgetting that the island is an island.. . .
Warmth gradually creeps up from the hot-water bottles to one's
heart and eyes, and sleep comes as the train scurries into the
empire.... A loud reverberation, and one wakes up in a vast cavern,
dimly lit, and sparsely peopled by a few brass-buttoned beings
that have the air of dwarfs under its high, invisible roof. They
give it a name, and call it Charing Cross, and one remembers
that, since one last saw it, it fell down and demolished a theatre.
Everything is shuttered in the cavern. Nothing to eat or to drink,
or to read, but shutters. And shutters are so cold, and caverns
so draughty.

"Where can I get something to eat?" one demands.

"Eat, sir?" A staggered pause, and the porter looks at one as
if one were Oliver Twist. "There's the hotels, sir," he says, finally.

Yet one has not come by a special, unique train, unexpected
and startling. No! That train knocks at the inner door of the
empire every morning in every month in every year at the
same hour, and it is always met by shutters. And the empire,
by the fact of its accredited representatives in brass buttons and
socialistic ties, is always taken aback by the desire of the peaceful
invader to eat.

One wanders out into the frozen silence. Gas lamps patiently
burning over acres of beautiful creosoted wood! A dead cab
or so! A policeman! Shutters everywhere: Nothing else. No
change here.

This is the changeless, ineffable Strand at Charing Cross,
sacred as the Ganges. One cannot see a single new building. Yet
they say London has been rebuilt.

The door of the hotel is locked. And the night watchman
opens with the same air of astonishment as the Punch and Judy
man when one asked for milk, and the railway porter when one
asked for food. Every morning at that hour the train stops within
fifty yards of the hotel door, and pitches out into London persons
who have been up all night; and London blandly continues to be
amazed at their arrival. A good English fellow, the watchman—

almost certainly the elder brother of the train-guard.

"I want a room and some breakfast."

He cautiously relocks the door.

"Yes, sir, as soon as the waiters are down. In about an hour, sir. I can take you to the lavatory now, sir, if that will do."

Who said there was a new England?

One sits overlooking the Strand, and tragically waiting. And presently, in the beginnings of the dawn, that pathetic, wistful object the first omnibus of the day rolls along—all by itself—no horses in front of it! And, after hours, a waiter descends as bright as a pin from his attic, and asks with a strong German accent whether one will have tea or coffee. The empire is waking up, and one is in the heart of it.

II

AN ESTABLISHMENT

When I returned to England I came across a terrific establishment. As it may be more or less novel to you I will attempt to describe it, though the really right words for describing it do not exist in the English language. In the first place, it is a restaurant, where meals are served at almost any hour—and not meals such as you get in ordinary restaurants, but sane meals, spread amid flowers and diaper. Then it is also a crèche, where babies are tended upon scientific principles; nothing that a baby needs is neglected. Older, children are also looked after, and the whole question of education is deeply studied, and advice given. Also young men and women of sixteen or so are started in the world, and every information concerning careers is collected and freely given out.

Another branch of the establishment is devoted to inexpensive but effective dressmaking, and still another to hats; here you will find the periodical literature of fashion, and all hints as to shopping. There is, further, a very efficient department of mending, highly curious and ingenious, which embraces men's clothing. I discovered, too, a horticultural department for the encouragement of flowers, serving secondarily as a branch of the crèche and nursery. There is a fine art department, where reproductions of the great masters are to be seen and meditated upon, and an applied art department, full of antiques. It must mention the library, where the latest and the most ancient literatures fraternise on the same shelves; also the chamber-music department.

Lastly, a portion of the establishment is simply nothing but an uncommon lodging-house for travellers, where electric light, hot water bottles, and hot baths are not extras. I scarcely expect you to believe what I say; nevertheless I have exaggerated in nothing. You would never guess where I encountered this extraordinary, this incredible establishment. It was No. 137 (the final number) in a perfectly ordinary long street in a residential suburb of a large town. When I expressed my surprise to the manager of the place, he looked at me as if I had come from Timbuctoo. "Why!" he exclaimed, "there are a hundred and thirty-six establishments much like mine in this very street!" He was right; for what I had stumbled into was just the average cultivated Englishman's home.

You must look at it as I looked at it in order to perceive what an organisation the thing is. The Englishman may totter continually on the edge of his income, but he does get value for his money. I do not mean the poor man, for he is too unskilled, and too hampered by lack of capital, to get value even for what money he has. Nor do I mean the wealthy man, who usually spends about five-sixths of his income in acquiring worries and nuisances. I mean the nice, usual professional or business islander, who by means of a small oblong piece of paper, marked £30 or so, once a month, attempts and accomplishes more than a native of the mainland would dream of on £30 a week. The immense pyramid which that man and his wife build, wrong side up, on the blowsy head of one domestic servant is a truly astonishing phenomenon, and its frequency does not impair its extraordinariness.

The mere machinery is tremendously complex. You lie awake at 6-30 in the uncommon lodging-house department, and you hear distant noises. It is the inverted apex of the pyramid starting into life. You might imagine that she would be intensely preoccupied by the complexity of her duties, and by her responsibility. Not a bit. Open her head, and you would find nothing in it but the vision of a grocer's assistant and a new frock. You then hear weird bumps and gurgling noises. It is the hot water running up behind walls to meet you half-way from the kitchen. You catch the early vivacity of the crèche. A row overhead means that a young man who has already studied the comparative anatomy of cigars is embarking on life. A tinkling of cymbals below—it is a young woman preparing to be attractive to some undiscovered young man in another street.

The Englishman's home is assuredly the most elaborate organisation for sustaining and reproducing life in the world— or at any rate, east of Sandy Hook. It becomes more and more elaborate, luxurious, and efficient. For example, illumination is not the most important of its activities. Yet, you will generally find in it four different methods of illumination—electricity, gas, a few oil lamps in case of necessity, and candles stuck about. Only yesterday, as it seems, human fancy had not got beyond candles. Much the same with cookery. Even at a simple refection like afternoon tea you may well have jam boiled over gas, cake baked in the range, and tea kept hot by alcohol or electricity.

I am not old, but I have known housewives who would neither eat nor offer to a guest, bread which they had not baked. They drew water from their own wells. And the idea of a public laundry would have horrified them. And before that generation there existed a generation which spun and wove at home. To-day the English household is dependent on cooperative methods for light, heat, much food, and several sorts of cleanliness. True (though it has abandoned baking), the idea of cooperative cookery horrifies it! However, another generation is coming! And that generation, while expending no more energy than ourselves, will live in homes more complicatedly luxurious than ours. When it is house-hunting it will turn in scorn from an abode which has not a service of hot and cold water in every bedroom and a steam device for "washing up" without human fingers. And it will as soon think of keeping a private orchestra as of keeping a private cook—with her loves and her thirst.

Leave England and come hack, and you cannot fail to see that this generation is already knocking at the door. When it once gets inside the door it will probably be more "house-proud," more

216

inclined to regard the dwelling as its toy, with which it can never tire of playing, than even the present generation. Such is a salient characteristic which strikes the returned traveller, and which the foreigner goes back to his own country and talks about—namely, the tremendous and intense pre-occupation of the English home with "comfort"—with every branch and sub-branch of comfort.

"*Le comfort anglais*" is a phrase which has passed into the French language. On spiritual and intellectual matters the Englishman may be the most sweetly reasonable of creatures— always ready to compromise, and loathing discussion. But catch him compromising about his hot-water apparatus, the texture of a beefsteak, or the flushing of a cistern!

III

AMUSEMENTS

It is when one comes to survey with a fresh eye the amusements of the English race that one realises the incomprehensibility of existence. Here is the most serious people on earth—the only people, assuredly, with a genuine grasp of the principles of political wisdom—amusing itself untiringly with a play-ball. The ball may be large and soft, as in football, or small and hard, as in golf, or small and very hard, as in billiards, or neither one thing nor the other, as in cricket—it is always a ball.. Abolish the sphere, and the flower of English manhood would perish from ennui.

The fact is, speaking broadly, there is only one amusement worth mentioning in England. Football dwarfs all the others. It has outrun cricket. This is a hard saying, but a true one. Football arouses more interest, passion, heat; it attracts far vaster crowds; it sheds more blood. Having beheld England, after absence, in the North and in the South, I seem to see my native country as an immense football ground, with a net across the Isle of Wight and another in the neighbourhood of John o' Groat's, and the entire population stamping their feet on the cold, cold ground and hoarsely roaring at the bounces of a gigantic football. It is a great game, but watching it is a mysterious and peculiar amusement, full of contradictions. The physical conditions of getting into a football ground, of keeping life in one's veins while there, and of getting away from it, appear at first sight to preclude the possibility of amusement. They remind one of the Crimean War or the passage of the Beresina. A man will freeze to within half a degree of death on a football ground, and the same man

218

will haughtily refuse to sit on anything less soft than plush at a music-hall. Such is the inexplicable virtue of football.

Further, a man will safely carry his sense of fair play past the gate of a cricket field, but he will leave it outside the turnstiles of a football ground. I refer to the relentless refusal of the man amusing himself at a football match to see any virtue in the other side. I refer to the howl of execration which can only be heard on a football ground. English public life is a series of pretences. And the greatest pretence of all is that football matches are eleven a side. Football matches are usually a battle between eleven men and ten thousand and eleven; that is why the home team so seldom loses.

The football crowd is religious, stern, grim, terrible, magnificent. It is prepared to sacrifice everything to an ideal. And even when its ideal gets tumbled out of the First League into the Second, it will not part with a single illusion. There are greater things than justice (which, after all, is a human invention, and unknown to nature), and this ferocious idealism is greater than justice. The explanation is that football is the oldest English game—far older than cricket, and it "throws back" to the true, deep sources of the English character. It is a weekly return to the beneficent and heroic simplicity of nature's methods.

Another phenomenon of the chief English amusement goes to show the religious sentiment that underlies it. A leading Spanish toreador will earn twenty thousand pounds a year. A leading English jockey will make as much. A music-hall star can lay hands on several hundreds a week. A good tea-taster receives a thousand a year, and a cloakroom attendant at a fashionable hotel can always retire at the age of forty. Now, on the same scale, a great half-back, or a miraculous goalkeeper with the indispensable gift of being in two places at once, ought to earn about half a million a year. He is the idol of innumerable multitudes of enthusiasts; he can rouse them into heavenly ecstasy, or render them homicidal, with a turn of his foot. He is the theme of hundreds of newspapers. One town will cheerfully pay another a thousand pounds for the mere privilege of his citizenship. But his total personal income would not keep a stockbroker's wife in hats! His uniform is the shabbiest uniform ever donned by a military genius, and he is taught to look forward to the tenancy of a tied public-house as an ultimate paradise!

To the unimpassioned observer, nothing in English national life seems more anomalous than this. It can be explained solely by stern religious sentiment. Call it pagan if you will, but even pagan religions were religious. The truth is that so foul a thing as money does not enter into the question. A footballer is treated like a sort of priest. "You have this rare and incommunicable gift," says the public to him in effect. "You can, for instance, do things with your head that the profane cannot do with their hands. It is no credit to you. You were born so. Yet a few years, and the gift will leave you I Then we shall cast you aside and forget you. But, in the meantime, you are like unto a precious vase. Keep yourself, therefore, holy and uncracked. There is no money in the career, no luxury, no soft cushions, nothing but sprained ankles, broken legs, abstinence, suspensions, and a pittance, followed by ingratitude and neglect. But you have the rare and incommunicable gift I And that is your exceeding reward."

In view of such an attitude, to offer the salary of a County Court judge to a footballer would be an insult.

After indulging in the spectacle and the vocal gymnastics of a football match, the British public goes home to its wife, hurries her out, and they stand in the open street at a closed door for an hour, or it may be two hours, stolidly, grimly, fiercely, with obstinate chins, on pleasure bent. They are determined to see that door open, no matter what the weather. Let it rain, let it freeze, they will stand there till the door opens. At last it does open, and they are so superbly eager to see what they shall see that they tumble over each other in order to arrive at the seats of delight. That which they long to witness with such an ardent longing is usually a scene of destruction. Let an artiste come forward and simply guarantee to smash a thousand plates in a quarter of an hour, and he will fill with enraptured souls the largest music-hall in England. Next to splendid destruction the British public is most amused by knockabout comedians, so called because they knock each other about in a manner which would be fatally tragic to any ordinary persons.

Though this freshly-obtained impression of the amusements of the folk is perfectly sincere and fair, it is fair also to assert that the folk shine far more brightly at work and at propaganda than at play. The island folk, being utterly serious, have not yet given adequate attention to the amusement of the better part of themselves. But far up in the empyrean, where culture floats, the directors of the Stage Society and Miss Horniman are devoting their lives to the question.

IV

MANCHESTER

Over thirty years ago I first used to go to Manchester on Tuesdays, in charge of people who could remember Waterloo, and I was taken into a vast and intricate palace, where we bought quantities of things without paying for them—a method of acquisition strictly forbidden in our shop. This palace was called "Rylands." I knew not what "Rylands" was, but from the accents of awe in which the name was uttered I gathered that its importance in the universe was supreme. My sole impression of Manchester was an impression of extreme noise.

Without shouting you could not make yourself heard in the streets. Ten years later, London-road Station had somehow become for me the gate of Paradise, and I was wont to escape into Manchester as a prisoner escapes into the open country.

After twenty years' absence in London and Paris I began to revisit Manchester. My earliest impression will be my last. Still the same prodigious racket; the same gigantic altercation between irresistible iron and immovable paving stones! With the addition of the growling thunder of cars that seem to be continually bumping each other as if they were college eights! Lunch in a fashionable grill-room at Manchester constitutes an auditory experience that could not be matched outside New York. In the great saloon there is no carpet on the polished planks of the floor, and the walls consist of highly resonant tiles, for Manchester would not willingly smother the slightest murmur of its immense reverberations. The tables are set close together, so that everybody can hear everybody; the waiters

222

(exactly the same waiters that one meets at Monte Carlo or in the Champs Elysées) understand all languages save English, so that the Britisher must shout at them. Doors are for ever swinging, and people rush to and fro without surcease. It is Babel. In the background, a vague somewhere, an orchestra is beating; one catches the bass notes marking the measure, and occasionally a high squeak in the upper register. And superimposed on this, the lusty voice of a man of herculean physique passionately chanting that "a-hunting we will go."

One looks through the window and, astonished, observes one of those electric cars flying hugely past without a sound. The thunder within has challenged and annihilated the heaviest thunder without. The experience is unique. One rushes forth in search of silence. Where can silence dwell in Manchester? The end of every street is a mystery of white fog, a possible home of silence. But no! Be sure that if one plucks out the heart of the mystery one will find a lorry preceded by at least eight iron hoofs. The Art Gallery! One passes in. Clack! Clack! Clack! It is the turnstile. And all afternoon the advent of each student of the fine arts, of each cultivated dilettante, is announced by Clack! Clack! Clack! Two young men come in. Clack! Clack! Clack! Turner's "Decline of Carthage" naturally arrests them. "By Jove!" says one, "that was something to tackle!" Clack! Clack! Clack! Out again, in search of silence. But over nearly every portal curves the legend: "Music all day." And outside the music-halls hired bawlers are bawling to the people to come in. At last, near the Infirmary, one sees a stationary cab, and across the window of this cab is printed, in letters of gold, the extraordinary, the magic, the wonderful, the amazing word:

"Noiseless."

Ah! The traditional, sublime humour of cabmen!

But if my impression has remained, and even waxed, that Manchester would be an ideal metropolis for a nation of deaf mutes, my other early impression, of its artistic and intellectual primacy, is sharply renewed and intensified. Of late, not only by contact with Manchester men, but by the subtle physiognomy of Manchester streets and the revealing gestures of the common intelligent person, I have been more than ever convinced that there is no place which can match its union of intellectual vigour, artistic perceptiveness, and political sagacity.

Long and close intercourse with capitals has not in the slightest degree modified my youthful conception of Manchester, my admiration for its institutions, and my deep respect for its opinion. London may patronise Manchester as it chooses, but you can catch in London's tone a secret awe, an inward conviction of essential inferiority. I have noticed this again and again. I know well that my view is shared by the fine flower of Fleet-street, and no dread of disagreeable insinuations or accusations shall prevent me from expressing my sentiments with my customary directness. There is no department of artistic, intellectual, social, or political activity in which Manchester has not corporately surpassed London. And there have been very few occasions on which, when they have differed in opinion, Manchester has been as wrong as London.

It is, of course, notorious that London is still agitated by more than one controversy which was definitely settled by Manchester twenty years ago in the way in which London will settle it twenty years hence. Manchester is too proud to proclaim its fundamental supremacy in the island (though unalterably convinced of it), and no other city would be such a fool as to proclaim it; hence it is not proclaimed. But it exists, and the general knowledge of it exists.

The explanation of Manchester is twofold. First, its geographical situation, midway between the corrupting languor of the south and the too bleak hardness of the north. And, second, that it enjoys the advantages of a population as vast as that of London, without the disadvantages of either an exaggerated centralisation or of a capital. London suffers from elephantiasis, a rush of blue blood to the head, vertigo, imperfect circulation, and other maladies. Bureaucratic and caste influences must always vitiate the existence of a capital, and I do not suppose that any great capital in Europe is the real source of its country's life and energy. Not Rome, but Milan! Not Madrid, but Barcelona! Not St. Petersburg, but Moscow! Not Berlin, but Hamburg and Munich! Not Paris, but the rest of France! Not London, but the Manchester area!

V

LONDON

There are probably other streets as ugly, as utterly bereft of the romantic, as Lots-road, Chelsea, but certainly nothing more desolating can exist in London. It was ten years since I had seen it, and now I saw it at its worst moment of the week, about ten o'clock of a Sunday morning. Some time before I reached it I heard a humming vibration which grew louder and more impressive as I approached. I passed (really) sixty-eight seagulls sitting in two straight rows on the railings of a deserted County Council pier, and on a rusty lantern at the head of the pier was a sixty-ninth seagull, no doubt the secretary of their trade union.

A mist lay over the river and over a man reading the "Referee" on an anchored barge, and nobody at all seemed to be taking any notice of the growing menace of this humming vibration. Then I came to a gigantic building, quite new to me—I had not suspected that such a thing was—a building which must be among the largest in London, a red brick building with a grandiose architectural effect, an overpowering affair, one of those affairs that man creates in order to show how small and puny he himself is. You could pile all the houses of a dozen neighbouring streets under the colossal roof, of that erection and leave room for a church or so. Extraordinary that a returned exile, interested in London, could have walked about London for days without even getting a glimpse of such hugeness.

It was shut up, closed in, mysterious, inviolable. The gates of its yards were bolted. It bore no legend of its name and owner; there was no sign of human life in it. And the humming vibration

226

came out of it, and was visibly cracking walls and windows in the doll's-houses of Lots-road that shook at its feet. Lots-road got up to that thunder, went to bed to that thunder, ate bacon to it, and generally transacted its daily life. I gazed baffled at the building. No clue anywhere to the mystery! Nothing but a proof of the determined tendency on the part of civilisation to imitate the romances of H. G. Wells!

A milkman in a striped apron was ringing and ringing angrily at the grille of a locked public-house. I hate to question people in the street, but curiosity concerning a marvel is like love, stronger than hate.

"That?" said the milkman peevishly. "That's the generating stytion for the electric rilewys."

"Which railways?" I asked.

"All of 'em," said he. "There's bin above sixty men killed there already."

Who would have supposed, a few years ago, that romance would visit unromantic Lots-road in this strange and terrible manner, cracking it, smashing it, deafening it, making the vases rattle on its mantelpieces, and robbing it of sleep? Lots-road is now the true romantic centre of London. (It would probably prefer to be something else, but it is.) It holds the true symbol of the development of London's corporate life.

You come to an unusual hole in the street, and enter it, and find yourself on a large floor surrounded by advertisements of whisky and art furniture. The whole floor suddenly sinks with you towards the centre of the earth, far below sewers. You emerge into a system of tunnels, and, guided by painted white hands, you traverse these tunnels till you arrive at a precipice. Then a suite of drawing-rooms, four or six, glides along the front of the precipice. Each saloon is lighted by scores of electric lamps, and the steel doors of each are magically thrown wide open. An attendant urges you to come in and sit down. You do so, and instantly the suite of rooms glides glittering away with you, curving through an endless subterranean passage, and stopping now and then for two seconds at a precipice. At last you get out, and hurry through more tunnels, and another flying floor wafts you up out of the earth again, and you stagger into daylight and a strange street, and when your eyes have recovered themselves you perceive that the strange street is merely Holborn.. . . And all this because of the roaring necromancers' castle in Lots-road! All this impossible without the roaring necromancers' castle!

People ejaculate, "The new Tubes!" and think they have described these astounding phenomena. But they have not.

The fact that strikes the traveller beyond all other facts of the new London is the immensity of the penalty which the Metropolis is now paying for its size. Tubes, electrified "Districts," petrol omnibuses, electric cars and cabs, and automobiles; these are only the more theatrical aspects of an activity which permeates and exhausts the life of the community. Locomotion has become an obsession in London; it has become a perfect nightmare. The city gets larger and larger, but the centre remains the centre and everybody must get to it.

See the motor cars speeding over Barnes Common to plunge into London. One after another, treading on each other's heels, scurrying, preoccupied, and malodorous, they fly past in an interminable procession for hours, to give a melodramatic interest to the streets of London. See the attack on the omnibuses by a coldly-determined mob of workers outside Putney Station, and the stream that ceaselessly descends into Putney Station. Follow the omnibuses as they rush across the bridge into Fulham-road. See the girls on the top at 8 a. m. in the frosty fog. They are glad to be anywhere, even on the top.

See the acrobatic young men who, all along the route, jump on to the step and drop off disappointed because there are already sixteen inside and eighteen out. Notice the fight at every stopping-place. Watch the gradual growth of the traffic, until the driver, from being a charioteer, is transformed into a solver of Chinese puzzles. And remember that Fulham-road is one great highway out of fifty. Bend your head, and gaze through London clay into the tunnels full of gliding drawing-rooms and the drawing-rooms jammed with people. Think of the five hundred railway stations of all sorts in London, all at the same business of transporting people to the centre! Then put yourself in front of one station, the type-terminus, Liver-pool-street, and see the incredible thick, surging, bursting torrent that it vomits (there is no other word) from long before dawn till ten o'clock. And, finally, see the silent, sanguinary battles on bridges for common tram-cars and 'buses.

Not clubs, not hotels, not cathedrals, not halls of song, not emporia, not mansions; but this is London, now; this necessary, passionate, complex locomotion! All other phenomena are insignificant beside it.

VI

INDUSTRY

My native heath, thanks to the enterprise of London newspapers and the indestructibility of picturesque lies, has the reputation of being quite unlike the rest of England, but when I set foot in it after absence, it seems to me the most English piece of England that I ever came across. With extraordinary clearness I see it as absurdly, ridiculously, splendidly English. All the English characteristics are, quite remarkably, exaggerated in the Potteries. (That is perhaps why it is a butt for the organs of London civilisation.) This intensifying of a type is due no doubt to a certain isolation, caused partly by geography and partly by the inspired genius of the gentleman who, in planning what is now the London and North-Western Railway, carefully diverted it from a populous district and sent it through a hamlet six miles away. On the 28 miles between Stafford and Crewe of the four-track way of the greatest line in England, not a town! And a solid population of a quarter of a million within gunshot! English methods! That is to say, the preposterous side of English methods.

We practise in the Potteries the fine old English plan of not calling things by their names. We are one town, one unseparated mass of streets. We are, in fact, the twelfth largest town in the United Kingdom (though you would never guess it). And the chief of our retail commerce and of our amusements are congregated in the centre of our town, as the custom is. But do not imagine that we will consent to call ourselves one town. [1] No! We pretend

---

1 Since this was written a very modified form of federation has

that we are six towns, and to carry out the pretence we have six town halls, six Mayors or chief bailiffs, six sanitary inspectors, six everything, including six jealousies. We find it so much more economical, convenient, and dignified, in dealing with public health, education, and railway, canal, and tramway companies to act by means of six mutually jealous authorities.

We make your cups and saucers—and other earthen utensils. We have been making them for over a thousand years. And, since we are English, we want to make them now as we made them a thousand years ago. We flatter ourselves that we! are a particularly hard-headed race, and we are. Steel drills would not get a new idea into our hard heads. We have a characteristic shrewd look, a sort of looking askance and suspicious. We are looking askance and suspicious at the insidious approaches of science and scientific organisation. At the present moment the twelfth largest town is proposing to find a sum of £250 (less than it spends on amusement in a single day) towards the cost of a central school of pottery. Mind, only proposing! Up to three years ago (as has been publicly stated by a master-potter) we carped at scientific methods. "Carp" is an amiable word. We hated and loathed innovation. We do still. Only a scientific, adventurous, un-English manufacturer who has dared to innovate knows the depth and height, the terrific inertia, of that hate and that loathing.

Oh, yes, we are fully aware of Germany! Yesterday a successful manufacturer said to me—and these are his exact words, which I wrote down and read over to him: "Owing to superior technical knowledge, the general body of German manufacturers are able to produce certain effects in china and in earthenware, which the general body of English manufacturers are incapable of producing." However, we have already established two outlying minor technical schools, and we are proposing to find £250 privately towards a grand and imposing central technical college.

been introduced into the Potteries.

Do not smile, you who read this. You are not archangels, either. Besides, when we like, we can produce the finest earthenware in the world. We are only just a tiny bit more English than you— that's all. And the Potteries is English industry in little—a glass for English manufacture to see itself in.

For the rest, we are the typical industrial community, presenting the typical phenomena of new England. We have made municipal parks out of wildernesses, and hired brass bands of music to play in them. We have quite six parks in our town. The character of our annual carnivals has improved out of recognition within living memory. Electricity no longer astounds us. We have public baths everywhere (though I have never heard that they rival our gasworks in contributing to the rates). Our public libraries are better and more numerous, though their chief function is still to fleet the idle hours of our daughters. Our roads are less awful. Our slums are decreasing. Our building regulations are stricter. Our sanitation is vastly improved; and in spite of asthma, lead-poisoning, and infant mortality our death-rate is midway between those of Manchester and Liverpool.

We grow steadily less drunken. Yet drunkenness remains our worst vice, and in the social hierarchy none stands higher than the brewer, precisely as in the rest of England. We grow steadily less drunken, but even the intellectuals still think it odd and cranky to meet without drinking fluids admittedly harmful; and as for the workingman's beer... Knock the glass out of his hand and see! We grow steadily less drunken, but we possess some 750 licensed houses and not a single proper bookshop. No man could make a hundred pounds a year by selling books in the Potteries. We really do know a lot, and we have as many bathrooms per thousand as any industrial hive in this island, and as many advertisements of incomparable soaps. We are in the way of perfection, and when we have conquered drunkenness, ignorance, and dirt we shall have arrived there, with the rest of England. Dirt—a public slatternliness, a public and shameless flouting of the virtues of cleanliness and tidiness—is the most spectacular of our sins.

We are the supreme land of picturesque contrasts. On one day last week I saw a Town Clerk who had never heard of H. G. Wells; I walked five hundred yards and assisted at a performance of chamber-music by Bach and a discussion of the French slang of Huysmans; walked only another hundred yards and was, literally, stuck in an unprotected bog and extricated therefrom by the kindness of two girls who were rooting in a shawd-ruck for bits of coal.

Lastly, with other industrial communities, we share the finest of all qualities—the power and the will to work. We do work. All of us work. We have no use for idlers. Climb a hill and survey our combined endeavour, and you will admit it to be magnificent.

THE MIDLANDS

1910-1911

I

THE HANBRIDGE EMPIRE

When I came into the palace, out of the streets where black human silhouettes moved on seemingly mysterious errands in the haze of high-hung electric globes, I was met at the inner portal by the word "Welcome" in large gold letters. This greeting, I saw, was part of the elaborate mechanics of the place. It reiterated its message monotonously to perhaps fifteen thousand visitors a week; nevertheless, it had a certain effectiveness, since it showed that the Hanbridge Theatres Company Limited was striving after the right attitude towards the weekly fifteen thousand. At some pit doors the seekers after pleasure are received and herded as if they were criminals, or beggars. I entered with curiosity, for, though it is the business of my life to keep an eye on the enthralling social phenomena of Hanbridge, I had never been in its Empire. When I formed part of Hanbridge there was no Empire; nothing but sing-songs conducted by convivial chairmen with rapping hammers in public-houses whose blinds were drawn and whose posters were in manuscript. Not that I have ever assisted at one of those extinct sing-songs. They were as forbidden to me as a High Church service. The only convivial rapping chairman I ever beheld was at Gatti's, under Charing Cross Station, twenty-two years ago.

Now I saw an immense carved and gilded interior, not as large as the Paris Opéra, but assuredly capable of seating as many persons. My first thought was: "Why, it's just like a real music-hall!" I was so accustomed to regard Hanbridge as a place where the great visible people went in to work at seven a.m. and emerged out of public-houses at eleven P.M., or stood movelessly mournful in packed tramcars, or bitterly partisan on chill football grounds, that I could scarcely credit their presence here, lolling on velvet amid gold Cupids and Hercules, and smoking at ease, with plentiful ash-trays to encourage them. I glanced round to find acquaintances, and the first I saw was the human being who from nine to seven was my tailor's assistant; not now an automaton wound up with deferential replies to any conceivable question that a dandy could put, but a living soul with a calabash between his teeth, as fine as anybody. Indeed, finer than most! He, like me, reclined aristocratic in the grand circle (a bob). He, like me, was offered chocolates and what not at reasonable prices by a boy whose dress indicated that his education was proceeding at Eton. I was glad to see him. I should have gone and spoken to him, only I feared that by so doing I might balefully kill a man and create a deferential automaton. And I was glad to see the vast gallery with human twopences. In nearly all public places of pleasure, the pleasure is poisoned for me by the obsession that I owe it, at last, to the underpaid labour of people who aren't there and can't be there; by the growing, deepening obsession that the whole structure of what a respectable person means, when he says with patriotic warmth "England," is reared on a stupendous and shocking injustice. I did not feel this at the Hanbridge Empire. Even the newspaper-lad and the match-girl might go to the Hanbridge Empire and, sitting together, drink the milk of paradise. Wonderful discoverers, these new music-hall directors all up and down the United Kingdom! They have discovered the folk.

The performance was timed as carefully as a prize-fight. Ting! and the curtain went unfailingly up. Ting! and it came unfailingly down. Ting! and something started. Ting! and it stopped. Everybody concerned in the show knew what he and everybody else had to do. The illuminated number-signs on either side of the proscenium changed themselves with the implacable accuracy of astronomical phenomena. It was as though some deity of ten thousand syndicated halls was controlling the show from some throne studded with electric switches in Shaftesbury Avenue. Only the uniformed shepherd of the twopences aloft seemed free to use his own discretion. His "Now then, order, *please*," a masterly union of entreaty and intimidation, was the sole feature of the entertainment not regulated to the fifth of a second by that recurrent ting.

But what the entertainment gained in efficient exactitude by this ruthless ordering, it seemed to lose in zest, in capriciousness, in rude joy. It was watched almost dully, and certainly there was nothing in it that could rouse the wayward animal that is in all of us. It was marked by an impeccable propriety. In the classic halls of London you can still hear skittish grandmothers, stars of a past age unreformed, prattling (with an amazing imitation of youthfulness) of champagne suppers. But not in the Hanbridge Empire. At the Hanbridge Empire the curtain never rises on any disclosure of the carnal core of things. Even when a young woman in a short skirt chanted of being clasped in his arms again, the tepid primness of her manner indicated that the embrace would be that of a tailor's dummy and a pretty head-and-shoulders in a hairdresser's window. The pulse never asserted itself. Only in the unconscious but overpowering temperament of a couple of acrobatic mulatto women was there the least trace of bodily fever. Male acrobats of the highest class, whose feats were a continual creation of sheer animal beauty, roused no adequate enthusiasm.

"When do the Yorkshire Songsters come on?" I asked an

attendant at the interval. In the bar, a handful of pleasure-seekers were dispassionately drinking, without a rollicking word to mar the flow of their secret reflections.

"Second item in the second part," said the attendant, and added heartily: "And very good they are, too, sir!"

He meant it. He would not have said as much of a man whom in the lounge of a London hotel I saw playing the fiddle and the piano simultaneously. He was an attendant of mature and difficult judgment, not to be carried away by clowning or grotesquerie. With him good meant good. And they were very good. And they were what they pretended to be. There were about twenty of them; the women were dressed in white, and the men wore scarlet hunting coats. The conductor, a little shrewd man, was disguised in a sort of *levée* dress, with knee-breeches and silk stockings. But he could not disguise himself from me. I had seen him, and hundreds of him, in the streets of Halifax, Wakefield, and Batley. I had seen him all over Yorkshire, Lancashire, and Staffordshire. He was a Midland type: infernally well satisfied with himself under a crust of quiet modesty; a nice man to chat with on the way to Blackpool, a man who could take a pot of beer respectably and then stop, who could argue ingeniously without heat, and who would stick a shaft into you as he left you, just to let you know that he was not quite so ordinary as he made out to be. They were all like that, in a less degree; women too; those women could cook a Welsh rarebit with any woman, and they wouldn't say all they thought all at once, either.

And there they were ranged in a flattened semicircle on a music-hall stage. Perhaps they appeared on forty music-hall stages in a year. It had come to that: another case of specialisation. Doubtless they had begun in small choirs, or in the parlours of home, singing for the pleasure of singing, and then acquiring some local renown; and then the little shrewd conductor had had the grand idea of organised professionalism. God bless my soul! The thing was an epic, or ought to be! They really could sing. They really had voices. And they would not "demean" themselves to cheapness. All their eyes said: "This is no music-hall foolery. This is uncompromisingly high-class, and if you don't like it you ought to be ashamed of yourselves!" They sang part-song music, from "Sweet and Low" to a "Lohengrin" chorus. And with a will, with finesse, with a pianissimo over which the endless drone of the electric fan could be clearly distinguished, and a fine, free fortissimo that would have enchanted Wagner! They brought the house down every time. They might have rendered encores till midnight, but for my deity in Shaftesbury Avenue. It was the "folk" themselves giving back to the folk in the form of art the very life of the folk.

The Lady clog-dancer

But the most touching instances of this giving-back was furnished by the lady clog-dancer. Hanridge used to be the centre of a land of clogs. Hundreds of times I have wakened in winter darkness to the sound of clogs on slushy pavements. And when I think of clogs I think of the knocker-up, and hurried fire-lighting, and tea and thick bread, and the icy draught from the opened front door, and the factory gates, and the terrible timekeeper therein, and his clock: all the military harshness of industrialism grimly accepted. Few are the clogs now in Hanbridge. The girls wear paper boots, for their health's sake, and I don't know what the men wear. Clogs have nearly gone out of life. But at the Hanbridge Empire they had reappeared in an art highly conventionalised. The old clog-dancing, begun in public-houses, was realistic, and was done by people who the next morning would clatter to work in clogs. But this pretty, simpering girl had never worn a clog seriously. She had never regarded a clog as a cheap and lasting protection against wind and rain, but as a contrivance that you had to dance in. I daresay she rose at eleven a.m. She had a Cockney accent. She would not let her clogs make a noise. She minced in clogs. It was no part of her scheme to lose her breath. And yet I doubt not that she constituted a romantic ideal for the young male twopences, with her clogs that had reached her natty feet from the original hack streets of, say, Stockport. As I lumbered home in the electric car, besieged by printed requests from the tram company not on any account to spit, I could not help thinking and thinking, in a very trite way, that art is a wonderful thing.

II

THE MYSTERIOUS PEOPLE

According to Whitaker's Almanac, there are something under a million of them actually at work, which means probably that the whole race numbers something over two millions. And, speaking broadly, no one knows anything about them. The most modern parents, anxious to be parental in a scientific manner, will explain to their children on the hearth the chemistry of the fire, showing how the coal releases again the carbon which was absorbed by the plant in a past age, and so on, to the end that the children may learn to understand the order of the universe.

This I have seen. But I have never seen parents explaining to their children on the hearth the effect of coal-getting on the family life of the collier, to the end that the children might learn to understand the price of coal in sweat, blood, and tears. The householder is interested only in the other insignificant part of the price of coal. And this is odd, for the majority of householders are certainly not monsters of selfish and miserly indifference to the human factor in economics. Nor—I have convinced myself, though with difficulty—are the members of the House of Lords. Yet among all the speeches against the Miners' Eight Hours Bill in this Chamber where beats the warm, generous heart of Lord Halsbury, I do not remember one which mentioned the real price of coal. Even the members of the sublime Coal Consumers' League, though phantoms, cannot be phantoms without bowels. But has the League ever issued one leaflet dealing with the psychology of the collier's wife as affected by notions of fire-damp? I doubt it.

Even artists have remained unstirred by the provocative mystery of this subterranean race, which perspires with a pick, not only beneath our cellars, but far beneath the caves of the sea itself. A working miner, Joseph Skipsey, had to write the one verse about this race which has had vigour enough to struggle into the anthologies. The only novel handling in the grand manner this tremendous and bizarre theme is Emile Zola's "Germinal." And, though it is a fine novel, though it is honest and really impressive, there are shallows in the mighty stream of its narrative, and its climax is marred by a false sentimentality, which is none the less sentimentality for being sensual. Not a great novel, but nearly great; as the child's ring was "nearly gold." And in English fiction what is there but "Miss Grace of All Souls," a wistful and painstaking book, with pages which extort respect, but which no power can save from oblivion? And in the fine arts, is there anything but pretty coloured sentimentalities of hopeless dawns at pit-heads? Well, there is! Happily there are Constantin Meunier's sculptures of miners at work—compositions over which oblivion will have no power. But I think this is all.

Journalistic reporting of great tragic events is certainly much better than it used to be, when the phraseology of the reporter was as rigidly fixed by convention as poetic phraseology in the eighteenth century. The special correspondent is now much more of an artist, because he is much more free. But he is handicapped by the fact that when he does his special work really well, he is set to doing special work always, and lives largely among abnormal and affrighting phenomena, and so his sensibility is dulled. Moreover, there are valuable effects and impressions which the greatest genius on earth could not accomplish in a telegraph office. But did you ever see the lives or the swift deaths of the mysterious people treated, descriptively by an imaginative writer in a monthly review? I noted recently with pleasure that the American magazines, characteristically alert, have awakened to the possibilities of the mysterious people as material for serious work in the more leisurely journalism. The last tremendous accident in the United States produced at any rate one careful and fairly adequate study of the psychology of the principal figures in it, and of the drama which a bundle of burning hay originated.

Even if I did not share the general incurious apathy towards the mysterious people, I should not blame that apathy, for it is so widespread that there must be some human explanation of it; my object is merely to point it out. But I share it. I lived half my life among coalpits. I never got up in the morning without seeing the double wheels at a neighbouring pit-head spin silently in opposite directions for a time, and then stop, and then begin again. I was accustomed to see coal and ironstone, not in tons, but in thousands of tons. I have been close to colliery disasters so enormous that the ambitious local paper would make special reporters of the whole of its staff, and give up to the affair the whole of its space, save a corner for the betting news. My district lives half by earthenware and half by mining. I have often philandered with pot-workers, but I have never felt a genuine, active curiosity about the mysterious people. I have never been down a coalpit, though the galleries are now white-washed and lighted by electricity. It has never occurred to me to try to write a novel about the real price of coal.

And yet how powerfully suggestive the glimpses I have had! Down there, on my heath, covered with a shuttle-work of trams, you may get on to a car about four o'clock in the afternoon to pay a visit, and you may observe a handful of silent, formidable men in the car, a greyish-yellowish-black from head to foot. Like Eugene Stratton, they are black everywhere, except the whites of their eyes. You ask yourself what these begrimed creatures that touch nothing without soiling it are doing abroad at four o'clock in the afternoon, seeing that men are not usually unyoked till six.

They have an uncanny air, especially when you reflect that there is not one arm among them that could not stretch you out with one blow. Then you remember that they have been buried in geological strata probably since five o'clock that morning, and that the sky must look strange to them.

Or you may be walking in the appalling outskirts, miles from town halls and free libraries, but miles also from flowers, and you may see a whole procession of these silent men, encrusted with carbon and perspiration, a perfect pilgrimage of them, winding its way over a down where the sparse grass is sooty and the trees are withered. And then you feel that you yourself are the exotic stranger in those regions. But the procession absolutely ignores you. You might not exist. It goes on, absorbed, ruthless, and sinister. Your feeling is that if you got in its path it would tramp right over you. And it passes out of sight.

Around, dotting the moors, are the mining villages, withdrawn, self-centred, where the entire existence of the community is regulated by a single steam-siren, where good fortune and ill-fortune are common, and where the disaster of one is the disaster of all. Little is known of the life of these villages and townlets—known, that is, by people capable of imaginative external sympathetic comprehension. And herein is probably a reason why the mysterious people remain so mysterious. They live physically separated. A large proportion of them never mingle with the general mass. They are not sufficiently seen of surface-men to maintain curiosity concerning them. They keep themselves to themselves, and circumstances so keep them. Only at elections do they seem to impinge in powerful silence on the destinies of the nation.

I have visited some of these villages. I have walked over the moors to them with local preachers, and heard them challenge God. I have talked to doctors and magistrates about them, and acquired the certainty, vague and yet vivid, that in religion, love, work, and debauch they are equally violent and splendid. It needs no insight to perceive that they live nearer even than sailors to that central tract of emotion where life and death meet. But I have never sympathetically got near them. And I don't think I ever shall.

Once I was talking to a man whose father, not himself a miner, had been the moral chieftain of one of these large villages, the individuality to which everyone turned in doubt or need. And I was getting this man to untap the memories of his childhood. "Eh!" he said, "I remember how th' women used to come to my mother sometimes of a night, and beg, 'Mrs. B., an' ye got any old white shirts to spare? They're bringing 'em up, and we mun lay 'em out!' And I remember—" But just then he had to leave me, and I obtained no more. But what a glimpse!

III

FIRST VOYAGE TO THE ISLE OF MAN

It seemed solid enough. I leaned for an instant over the rail on the quarter away from the landing-stage, and there, at the foot of the high precipice formed by the side of the vessel, was the wavy water. A self-important, self-confident man standing near me lighted a black cigar of unseemly proportions, and threw the match into the water. The match was lost at once in the waves, which far below beat up futilely against the absolutely unmoved precipice. I had never been on such a large steamer before. I said to myself: "This is all right."

However, that was not the moment to go into ecstasies over the solidity of the steamer. I had to secure a place for myself. Hundreds of people on the illimitable deck were securing places for themselves. And many of them were being aided by porters or mariners. The number of people seemed to exceed the number of seats; it certainly exceeded the number of nice sheltered corners. I picked up my portmanteau with one hand and my bag and my sticks and my rug with the other. Then I dropped the portmanteau. A portmanteau has the peculiar property of possessing different weights. You pick it up in your bedroom, and it seems a feather. You say to yourself: "I can carry that easily—save tips to porters." But in a public place its weight changes for the worse with every yard you walk. At twenty yards it weighs half a ton. At forty yards no steam-crane could support it. You drop it. Besides, the carrying of it robs your movements of all grace and style. Well, I had carried that bag myself from the cab to the steamer, across the landing-stage, and up the gangway. Economy! I had spent a shilling on a useless magazine, and I grudged three pence to a porter with a wife and family! I was wearing a necktie whose price represented the upkeep of the porter and his wife and family for a full twenty-four hours, and yet I wouldn't employ the porter to the tune of threepence. Economy! These thoughts flashed through my head with the rapidity of lightning.

You see, I could not skip about for a deck-chair with that portmanteau in my hand. But if I left it lying on the deck, which was like a street... well, thieves, professional thieves, thieves who specialise in departing steamers! They nip off with your things while you are looking for a chair; the steamer bell sounds; and there you are! Nevertheless, I accepted the horrid risk and left all my belongings in the middle of the street.

Not a free chair, not a red deck-chair, not a corner! There were seats by the rail at one extremity of the boat, and at the other extremity of the boat, but no chair to be had. Thousands of persons reclining in chairs, and thousands of others occupied by bags, fugs, and bonnet-boxes, but no empty chair.

"Want a deck-chair, governor?" a bearded mariner accosted me.

Impossible to conceal from him that I did. But, being perhaps the ship's carpenter, was he going to manufacture a chair for me on the spot? I knew not how he did it, but in about thirty seconds he produced a chair out of the entrails of the ship, and fixed it for me in a beautiful situation, just forward of the funnel, and close to a charming young woman, and a little deck-house in front for protection! It was exactly what I wanted; the most stationary part of the entire vessel.

Sixpence! Economy! Still, I couldn't give him less. Moreover, I only had two pence in coppers.

"What will the voyage be like?" I asked him with false jollity, as he touched his cap.

"Grand, sir!" he replied enthusiastically.

Yes, and if I had given him a shilling the voyage would have been the most magnificent and utterly perfect voyage that ship ever made.

No sooner was I comfortably installed in that almost horizontal deck-chair than I was aware of a desire to roam about, watch the casting-off and the behaviour of the poor stay-at-home crowd on the landing-stage; a very keen desire. But I would not risk the portmanteau again. Nothing should part us till the gangways were withdrawn. Absurd, of course! Human nature is absurd.... I caught the charming young woman's eye about a dozen times. The ship got fuller and fuller. With mean and paltry joy I perceived other passengers seeking for chairs and not finding them, and I gazed at them with haughty superiority. Then a fiendish, an incredible, an appalling screech over my head made me jump in a silly way quite unworthy of a man who is reclining next to a charming young woman, and apt to prejudice him in her eyes. It was merely the steamer announcing that we were off. I. sprang up, trying to make the spring seem part of the original jump. I looked. And lo! The whole landing-stage with all the people and horses and cabs was moving backwards, floating clean away; while the enormous ship stood quite still! A most singular effect!

In a minute we were in the middle of the river, and my portmanteau was safe. I left it in possession of the chair.

The next strange phenomenon of my mental condition was an extraordinary curiosity in regard to the ship. I had to explore it. I had to learn all about it. I began counting the people on the deck, but soon after I had come to the man with the unseemly black cigar I lost count. Then I went downstairs. There seemed to be staircases all over the place. You could scarcely move without falling down a staircase. And I came to another deck also full of people and bags, and fitted with other staircases that led still lower. And on the sloping ceiling of one of these lower staircases I saw the Board of Trade certificate of the ship. A most interesting document. It gave the tonnage as 2,000, and the legal number of passengers as about the same; and it said there were over two thousand life-belts on board, and room on the eight boats for I don't remember how many shipwrecked voyagers. It even gave the captain's Christian name. You might think that this would slake my curiosity. But, no! It urged me on. Lower down—somewhere near the caverns at the bottom of the sea, I came across marble halls, upholstered in velvet, where at snowy tables people were unconcernedly eating steaks and drinking tea. I said to myself "At such and such an hour I will come down here and have tea. It will break the monotony of the voyage." Looking through the little round windows of the restaurant I saw strips of flying green.

The Voyage

Then I thought: "The engines!" And somehow the word "reciprocating" came into my mind. I really must go and see the engines reciprocate. I had never seen anything reciprocate, except possibly my Aunt Hilda at the New Year, when she answered my letter of good wishes. I discovered that many other persons had been drawn down towards the engine-room by the attraction of the spectacle of reciprocity. And as a spectacle it was assuredly majestic, overwhelming, and odorous. I must learn the exact number of times those engines reciprocated in a minute, and I took out my watch for the purpose. Other gazers at once did the same. It seemed to be a matter of the highest importance that we should know the precise speed of those engines. Then I espied a large brass plate which appeared to have been affixed to the engine room in order to inform the engineers that the ship was built by Messrs. Macconochie and Sons, of Dumbarton. Why Dumbarton? Why not Halifax? And why must this precious information always be staring the engineers in the face? I wondered whether "Sons" were married, and, if so, what the relations were between Sons' wives and old Mrs. Macconochie. Then, far down, impossibly far down, furlongs beneath those gesticulating steely arms, I saw a coalpit on fire and demons therein with shovels. And all of a sudden it occurred to me that I might as well climb up again to my own special deck.

I did so. The wind blew my hat off, my hat ran half-way up the street before I could catch it. I caught it and clung to the rail. We were just passing a lightship; the land was vague behind; in front there was nothing but wisps of smoke here and there. Then I saw a fishing-smack, tossing like anything; its bows went down into the sea and then jerked themselves fairly out of the sea, and this process went on and on and on. And although I was not aboard the smack, it disconcerted me. However, I said to myself, "How glad I am to be on a nice firm steamer, instead of on that smack!" I looked at my watch again. We seemed to have been away from England about seven days, but it was barely three-quarters of an hour. The offensive man with the cigar went swaggering by.

And then a steward came up out of the depths of the sea with a tray full of glasses of beer, and a group of men lolling in deck chairs started to drink this beer. I cared not for the sight. I said to myself, "I will go and sit down." And as I stepped forward the deck seemed to sink away ever so slightly. A trifle! Perhaps a delusion on my part! Surely nothing so solid as that high road of a deck could sink away! Having removed my portmanteau from my chair, I sat down. The charming girl was very pale, with eyes closed. Possibly asleep I Many people had the air of being asleep. Every chair was now occupied. Still, dozens of boastful persons were walking to and fro, pretending to have the easy sea-legs of Lord Charles Beresford. The man with the atrocious cigar (that is, another atrocious cigar) swung by. Hateful individual! "You wait a bit!" I said to him (in my mind). "You'll see!"

I, too, shut my eyes, keeping very still. A grand voyage! Certainly, a grand voyage! Then I woke up. I had been asleep. It was tea-time. But I would not have descended to that marble restaurant for ten thousand pounds. For the first time I was indifferent to tea in the afternoon. However, after another quarter of an hour, I had an access of courage. I rose. I walked to the rail. The horizon was behaving improperly. I saw that I had made a mistake. But I dared not move. To move would have been death. I clung to the rail. There was my chair five yards off, but as inaccessible as if it had been five miles off. Years passed. Pale I must have been, but I retained my dignity. More years rolled by. Then, by accident, I saw what resembled a little cloud on the horizon.

It was the island! The mere sight of the island gave me hope and strength, and cheek.

In half an hour—you will never guess it—I was lighting a cigarette, partly for the benefit of the charming young woman, and partly to show that offensive man with the cigars that he was not the Shah of Persia. He had not suffered. Confound him!

IV

THE ISLAND BOARDING-HOUSE

When you first take up your brief residence in the private hotel, as they term it—though I believe it is still called boarding-house in the plain-spoken island—your attitude towards your fellow-guests is perfectly clear; I mean your secret attitude, of course. Your secret attitude is that you have got among a queer and an unsympathetic set of people. At the first meal—especially if it be breakfast—you glance at them all one by one out of the corners of your eyes, and in that shrewd way of yours you add them up (being a more than average experienced judge of human nature), and you come to the conclusion that you have seldom, if ever, encountered such a series of stupid and harsh faces. The men seem heavy, if not greedy, and sunk in mental sloth. And, really, the women might have striven a little harder to avoid resembling guys. After all, it is the duty of educated people not to offend the gaze of their fellow-creatures. And as for eating, do these men, in fact, live for naught but eating? Here are perhaps fifty or sixty immortal souls, and their unique concern, their united concern, seems to be the gross satisfaction of the body. Perhaps they do not have enough to eat at home, you reflect ironically. And you also reflect that some people, when they have contracted for bed and full board at so much per day, become absolutely lost to all sense of scruple, all sense of what is nice, and would, if they could, eat the unfortunate landlord right into the bankruptcy court. Look at that man there, near the window— doubtless, he obtained his excellent place near the window by the simple, colonizing method of grabbing it—well, he has already apportioned to himself four Manx herrings, and now, with his mouth full, he is mumbling about eggs and flesh meat.

The Island Boarding House

And then their conversation! How dull!—how lacking in point, in originality! These unhappy people appear to have in their heads no ideas that are not either trivial, tedious, or merely absurd. They do not appear to be interested in any matters that could interest a reasonable man. They babble, saying over and over again the same things. Or if they do not babble they giggle, or they may do both, which is worse; and, indeed, the uproarious way in which some of them laugh, upon no sufficient provocation, is disagreeable, especially in a woman. Or, if they neither babble, giggle, nor deafen the room with their outrageous mirth, they sit glum, speaking not a word, glowering upon humanity. How English that is—and how rude!

Commonplace—'that is what these people are! It is not their fault, but it is nevertheless a pity; and you resent it. Indubitably you are not in a sympathetic environment; you are not among kindred spirits. You grow haughty, within. When two late comers enter breezily and take seats near to you, and one of them begins at once by remarking that he is going to Port Erin for the day, and asks you if you know Port Erin, you reply "No"; the fact being that you have visited Port Erin, but the fact also being that you shirk the prospect of a sustained conversation with any of these too commonplace, uncomprehending strangers.

You meet some one on the stairs

You rise and depart from the table, and you endeavour to make your exit as majestic as possible; but there is a suspicion in your mind that your exit is only sheepish.

You meet someone on the stairs, a woman less like a guy than those you have seen, and still youthful. As you are going upstairs and she is coming down, and the two of you are staying in the same house, you wonder whether it would not be well to greet her. A simple "Good-morning." You argue about this in your head for some ten years—it is only in reality three seconds, but it seems eternal. You feel it would be nice to say good-morning to her. But at the critical point, at the psychological moment, a hard feeling comes into your heart, and a glazed blind look into your eyes, and you glance away. You perceive that she is staring straight in front of her; you perceive that she is deliberately cutting you. And so the two of you pass like ships in the night, and yet not quite like ships in the night, because ships do not hate, detest, and despise.

You go out into the sunshine (if sunshine there happens to be), between the plash of the waves and the call of the boatman on the right hand, and the front doors of all the other boarding-houses on the left, and you see that the other boarding-houses are frequented by a much superior, smarter, more intelligent, better-mannered set of pleasure-seekers than yours. You feel by a sure premonition that you are in for a dull time.

Nothing occurs for about forty-eight terrible hours, during which time, with the most strict propriety, you behave as though the other people in the boarding-house did not exist. On several occasions you have meant to exchange a few words with this individual or that, but this individual or that has not been encouraging, has made no advance. And you are the last person to risk a rebuff. You are sensitive, like all fine minds, to a degree which this coarse clay in the boarding-house cannot conceive.

Then one afternoon something occurs. It usually does occur in the afternoon. You are in the tram-car. About ten others are in the tram-car. And among them you notice the man who put a pistol to your head at the first meal and asked you if you knew Port Erin; also the young woman who so arrogantly pretended that she did not see you on the stairs. They are together. You had an idea they were together in the boarding-house; but you were not sure, because they seldom arrived in the dining-room together, or left it together, and both of them did a great deal of talking to other people. Of course, you might have asked, but the matter did not interest you; besides, you hate to seem inquisitive. He is considerably older than she is; a hale, jolly, red-faced, grey bearded man, who probably finds it easier to catch sight of his watch-chain than of his toes. She is slim, and a little arch. If she is his wife the difference between their ages is really excessive.

The car in its passage gradually empties until there is nobody in it save you and the conductor on the platform and these two inside. And a minute before it reaches the end of its journey the man opens his cigar-case, and preparing a cigar for the sacrificial burning, strolls along the car to the platform.

"We're the last on the car," he says, between two puffs, and not very articulately.

"Yes," you say. It is indubitable that you are the last on the car. You needed nobody to tell you that. Still, the information gives you pleasure, and the fellow is rather jolly. So you add, amiably, "I suppose it's these electric motors that are giving the tram-cars beans."

He laughs. He evidently thinks you have expressed yourself in an amusing manner.

And inspecting the scarlet end of his cigar, he says in a low voice: "I hope you're right. I've just bought a packet of shares in that motor company."

"Really!" you exclaim. So he is a shareholder, a member of the investing public! You are impressed. Instantly you imagine him as a very wealthy man who knows how to look after his money, and who has a hawk's eye for "a good thing." You wish you had loose money that would enable you to pick up a casual "packet of shares" here and there.

The car stops. The lady gets out. You raise your hat; it is the least you can do. Instead of pretending that you are empty air, she smiles on you charmingly, almost anxiously polite (perhaps she wants to make up for having cut you on the stairs), and offers you some remark about the weather, a banal remark, but so prettily enveloped in tissue paper and tied with pink ribbon, that you treasure it.

Your common home is only fifty yards off. Obviously you must reach it in company.

"My daughter here—" the grey-bearded man begins a remark.

So she is his daughter. Rather interesting. You talk freely, exposing all the most agreeable and polite side of your disposition.

While preparing for dinner you reflect with satisfaction and joy that at last you are on friendly terms with somebody in the house. You anticipate the dinner with eagerness. You regard the father and daughter somewhat as palm trees in the desert. During dinner you talk to them a great deal, and insensibly you find yourself exchanging remarks with other guests.

They are not so bad as they seemed, perhaps. Anyhow, one ought to make the best of things.

A whisky that night with the father! In the course of the whisky you contrive to let him gather that you, too, keep an eye on the share-market, and that you have travelled a great deal. In another twenty-four hours you are perfectly at home in the boarding-house, greeting people all over the place, and even stopping on the stairs to converse. Rather a jolly house! Really, some very decent people here, indeed! Of course there are also some with whom the ice is never broken. To the end you and they glaringly and fiercely pretend to be blind when you meet. You reconcile yourself to this; you harden yourself. As for new-comers, you wish they would not be so stiff and so absurdly aristocratic. You take pity on them, poor things!

But father and daughter remain your chief stand-by. They overstay you (certainly unlimited wealth), and they actually have the delightful idea of seeing you off at the station. You part on terms that are effusive. You feel you have made friends for life—and first-class friends. You are to meet them again; you have sworn it.

By the time you get home you have forgotten all about them.

V

TEN HOURS AT BLACKPOOL

Manchester is a right place to start from. And the vastness of Victoria Station—more like London than any other phenomenon in Manchester—with its score of platforms, and its subways romantically lighted by red lamps and beckoning pale hands, and its crowds eternally surging up and down granitic flights of stairs—-the vastness of this roaring spot prepares you better than anything else could for the dimensions and the loudness of your destination. The Blackpool excursionists fill the twelfth platform from end to end, waiting with bags and baskets: a multitude of well-marked types, some of the men rather violently smart as to their socks and neckties, but for the most part showing that defiant disregard of appearances which is perhaps the worst trait of the Midland character. The women seem particularly unattractive in their mack-intoshed blousiness—so much so that the mere continuance of the race is a proof that they must possess secret qualities which render them irresistible; they evidently consult their oculists to the neglect of their dentists: which is singular, and would be dangerous to the social success of any other type of woman.

"I never *did* see such a coal-cellar, not in all my days!" exclaims one lady, apparently outraged by sights seen in house-hunting.

And a middle-aged tradesman (or possibly he was an insurance agent) remarks: "What I say is—the man who doesn't appreciate sterling generosity—is no man!"

Such fragments of conversation illustrate the fine out-and-out idiosyncrasy of the Midlands.

The train comes forward like a victim, and in an instant is captured, and in another instant is gone, leaving an empty platform. These people ruthlessly know what they want. And for miles and many miles the train skims over canals, and tram-cars, and yards, and back-streets, and at intervals you glimpse a young woman with her hair in pins kneeling in sack-cloth to wash a grimy doorstep. And you feel convinced that in an hour or two, when she has "done," that young woman, too, will be in Blackpool; or, if not she, at any rate her sister.

* * * * *

The station of arrival is enormous; and it is as though all the passenger rolling-stock of the entire country had had an important rendezvous there. And there are about three cabs. This is not the town of cabs. On every horizon you see floating terrific tramcars which seat ninety people and which ought to be baptised Lusitania and Baltic. You wander with your fellow men down a long street of cookshops with calligraphic and undecipherable menus, and at every shopdoor is a loud-tongued man to persuade you that his is the gate of paradise and the entrance to the finest shilling dinner in Blackpool. But you have not the courage of his convictions; though you would like to partake of the finest shilling dinner, you dare not, with your southern stomach in rebellion against you. You slip miserably into the Hotel Majestic, and glide through many Lincrusta-Walton passages to an immense, empty smoking-room, where there is one barmaid and one waiter. You dare not even face the bar.... In the end the waiter chooses your *apéritif* for you, and you might be in London. The waiter, agreeably embittered by existence, tells you all about everything.

"This hotel used to be smaller," he says. "A hundred and twenty. A nice select party, you know. Now it's all changed. Our better-class clients have taken houses at St. Anne's.. . . Jews! I should say so! Two hundred and fifty out of three hundred in August.

Some of 'em all right, of course, but they try to own the place. They come in for tea, or it may be a small ginger with plenty of lemon and ice, and when they've had that they've had their principal drink for the day.. . . The lift is altered from hydraulic to electricity. . . years ago. . ."

Meanwhile a client who obviously knows his way about has taken possession of the bar and the barmaid.

"I've changed my frock, you see," says she.

"Changed it down here?" he demands.

"Yes. Well, I've been ironing. . . Oh! You monkey!"

In a mirror you catch her delicately chucking him under the chin. And, feeling that this kind of thing is not special to Blackpool, that it in fact might happen anywhere, you decide that it is time to lunch and leave the oasis of the Majestic and confront Blackpool once more.

The Fair Ground is several miles off, and on the way are three piers, loaded with toothless young women flirting, and with middle-aged women diligently crocheting or knitting. Millions of stitches must be accomplished to every waltz that the bands play; and perhaps every second a sock is finished. But you may not linger on any pier. There is the longest sea-promenade in Europe to be stepped. As you leave the shopping quarter and undertake the vista of ten thousand boarding-house windows (in each of which is a white table full of knives and forks and sauce-bottles) you are enheartened by a banneret curving in the breeze with these words: "Flor de Higginbotham. The cigar that you come back for. 2d." You know that you will, indeed, come back for it.. . . At last, footsore, amid a maze of gliding trams, your vision dizzy with the passing and re-passing of trams, you arrive at the Fair Ground. And the first thing you see is a woman knitting on a campstool as she guards the booth of a spiritualistic medium. The next is a procession of people each carrying a doormat and climbing up the central staircase of a huge lighthouse, and another procession of people, each sitting on a doormat and sliding down a corkscrew shoot that encircles the lighthouse. Why a lighthouse? A gigantic simulation of a bottle of Bass would have been better.

The scenic railway and the switchback surpass all previous dimensions in their kind. Some other method of locomotion is described as "half a mile of jolly fun." And the bowl-slide is "a riot of joy."

"Joy" is the key-word of the Fair Ground. You travel on planks over loose, unkempt sand, and under tethered circling Maxim aeroplanes, from one joy to the next. In the House of Nonsense, "joy reigns supreme." Giggling also reigns supreme. The "human spider," with a young woman's face, is a source of joy, and guaranteed by a stentorian sailor to be alive. Another genuine source of joy is "'Dante's Inferno' up to date." Another enormous booth, made mysterious, is announced as "the home of superior enjoyments." Near by is the abode of the two-headed giant, as to whom it is shouted upon oath that "he had a brother which lived to the height of twelve foot seven." Then you come to the destructive section, offering joy still more vivid. Here by kicking a football you may destroy images of your fellow men. Or—exquisitely democratic invention—you can throw deadly missiles at life-sized dolls that fly round and round in life-sized motor-cars: genius is, in fact, abroad on the Fair Ground.

All this is nothing compared to the joy-wheel, certainly the sublimest device for getting money and giving value for it that a student of human nature ever hit upon. You pay threepence for admittance into the booth of the joy-wheel, and upon entering you are specially informed that you need not practise the joy-wheel unless you like; it is your privilege to sit and watch. Having sat down, there is no reason why you should ever get up again, so diverting is the spectacle of a crowd of young men and boys clinging to each other on a large revolving floor and endeavouring to defy the centrifugal force. Every time a youth is flung against the cushions at the side you grin, and if a thousand youths were thrown off, your thousandth grin would be as hearty as the first. The secret thought of every spectator is that a mixture of men and maidens would be even more amusing. A bell rings, and the floor is cleared, and you anticipate hopefully, but the word is for children only, and you are somewhat dashed, though still inordinately amused. Then another bell, and you hope again, and the word is for ladies only. The ladies rush on to the floor with a fearful alacrity, and are flung rudely off it by an unrespecting centrifugal force (which alone the attendant, acrobatic and stately, can dominate); they slide away in all postures, head over heels, shrieking, but the angel of decency seems to watch over their skirts.. . . And at length the word is for ladies and gentlemen together, and the onslaught is frantic. The ladies and gentlemen, to the number of a score or so, clutch at each other, making a bouquet of trousers and petticoats in the centre of the floor. The revolutions commence, and gain in rapidity, and couple after couple is shot off, yelling, to the periphery. They enjoy it. Oh! They enjoy it! The ladies, abandoning themselves to dynamic law, slither away with closed eyes and muscles relaxed in a voluptuous languor. And then the attendant, braving the peril of the wheel, leaps to the middle, and taking a lady in his arms, exhibits to the swains how it is possible to keep oneself in the centre and keep one's damsel there too. And then, with a bow, he hands the lady back to her lawful possessor. Nothing could be more English, or more agreeable, than the curious contradiction of frank abandonment and chaste simplicity which characterises this extraordinary exhibition. It is a perfect revelation of the Anglo-Saxon temperament, and would absolutely baffle any one of Latin race.. . . You leave here because you must; you tear yourself away and return to the limitless beach, where the sea is going nonchalantly about its business just as if human progress had not got as far as the joy-wheel.

After you have gone back for the cigar, and faced the question of the man on the kerb, "Who says Blackpool rock?" and eaten high tea in a restaurant more gilded than the Trocadero, and visited the menagerie, and ascended to the top of the Tower in order to be badgered by rather nice girl-touts with a living to make and a powerful determination to make it, and seen the blue turn to deep purple over the sea, you reach at length the dancing-halls, which are the justification of Blackpool's existence. Blackpool is an ugly town, mean in its vastness, but its dancing-halls present a beautiful spectacle. You push your way up crowded stairs into crowded galleries, where the attendants are persuasive as with children—"*Please* don't smoke here"—and you see the throng from Victoria Station and a thousand other stations in its evening glory of drooping millinery and fragile blouses, though toothless as ever. You see it in a palatial and enormous setting of crystal and gold under a ceiling like the firmament. And you struggle to the edge and look over, and see, beneath, the glittering floor covered with couples in a strange array of straw hats and caps, and knickers, and tennis shoes, and scarcely a glove among the five hundred of them. Only the serio-comic M.C., with a delicately waved wand, conforms to the fashion of London. He has his hands full, has that M.C., as he trips to and fro, calling, with a curious stress and pause: "One—more couple please! One—more couple please!" And then the music pulsates—does really pulsate—and releases the multitude.. . . It is a sight to stir emotion. The waltz is even better. And then beings perched in the loftiest corners of the roof shoot coloured rays upon the floor, and paper snow begins to fall, and confetti to fly about, and eyes to soften and allure.. . .

And all around are subsidiary halls, equally resplendent, where people are drinking, or lounging, or flirting, or gloating over acrobats, monkeys and ballerinas. The tiger roars, the fountain tinkles, the corks go pop, the air is alive with music and giggling, the photographer cries his invitation, and everywhere there is the patter of animated feet and the contagion of a barbaric and honest gaiety.

Brains and imagination are behind this colossal phenomenon. For sixpence you can form part of it; for sixpence you can have delight, if you are young and simple and lusty enough. This is the huge flower that springs from the horrid bed of the factory system. Human creatures are half-timers for this; they are knocked up at 5.30 a.m. in winter for this; they go on strike for this; they endure for eleven months and three weeks for this. They all earn their living by hard and repulsive work, and here they are in splendour! They will work hard at joy till they drop from exhaustion. You can see men and women fast asleep on the plush, supporting each other's heads in the attitudes of affection. The railway stations and the night-trains are waiting for these.

THE BRITISH HOME

1908

I

AN EVENING AT THE SMITHS'

Mr. Smith returns to his home of an evening at 6:30. Mr. Smith's home is in a fairly long street, containing some dozens of homes exactly like Mr. Smith's. It has a drawing-room and a dining-room, two or three bedrooms, and one or two attics, also a narrow hall (with stained glass in the front door), a kitchen, a bathroom, a front garden, and a back garden. It has a service of gas and of water, and excellent drains. The kitchen range incidentally heats the water for the bathroom, so that the bath water is hottest at about noon on Sundays, when nobody, wants it, and coldest first thing in the morning, and last thing at night, when everybody wants it. (This is a detail. The fact remains that when hot water is really required it can always be had by cooking a joint of beef.)

The house and its two gardens are absolutely private. The front garden is made private by iron rails; its sole purposes are to withdraw the house a little from the road and to enable the servant to fill up her spare time by washing tiles. The back

267

garden is made private by match-boarding. The house itself is made private by a mysterious substance unsurpassed as a conductor of sound.

Mr. Smith's home is adequately furnished. There may be two beds in a room, but each person has a bed. Carpets are everywhere; easy chairs and a sofa do not lack; linen is sufficient; crockery is plenteous. As for cutlery, Mr. Smith belongs to the only race in the world which allows itself a fresh knife and fork to each course of a meal. The drawing-room is the best apartment and the least used. It has a piano, but, as the drawingroom fire is not a constant phenomenon, pianists can only practise with regularity and comfort during four months of the year—hence, perhaps, a certain mediocrity of performance.

Mr. Smith sits down to tea in the dining-room. According to fashionable newspapers, tea as a square meal has quite expired in England. On six days a week, however, tea still constitutes the chief repast in about 99 per cent, of English homes. At the table are Mrs. Smith and three children—John, aged 25; Mary, aged 22; and Harry, aged 15. For I must inform you that Mr. Smith is 50, and his wife is very near 50. Mr. Smith gazes round at his home, his wife, and his children. He has been at work in the world for 34 years, and this spectacle is what he has to show for his labour. It is his reward. It is the supreme result. He hurries through his breakfast, and spends seven industrious hours at the works in order that he may have tea nicely with his own family in his own home of a night.

Well, the food is wholesome and sufficient, and they are all neat and honest, and healthy—except Mrs. Smith, whose health is not what it ought to be. Mr. Smith conceals his pride in his children, but the pride is there. Impossible that he should not be proud! He has the right to be proud. John is a personable young man, earning more and more every year. Mary is charming in her pleasant blouse, and Harry is getting enormous, and will soon be leaving school.

This tea, which is the daily blossoming-time of the home that

Mr. Smith and his wife have constructed with 26 years' continual effort, ought to be a very agreeable affair. Surely the materials for pleasure are present! But it does not seem to be a very agreeable meal. There is no regular conversation. Everybody has the air of being preoccupied with his own affairs. A long stretch of silence; then some chaffing or sardonic remark by one child to another; then another silence; then a monosyllable from Mr. Smith; then another silence.

No subject of wide interest is ever seriously argued at that table. No discussion is ever undertaken for the sake of discussion. It has never occurred to anyone named Smith that conversation in general is an art and may be a diverting pastime, and that conversation at table is a duty. Besides, conversation is nourished on books, and books are rarer than teaspoons in that home. Further, at back of the excellent, honest, and clean mind of every Smith is the notion that politeness is something that one owes only to strangers.

When tea is over—and it is soon over—young John Smith silently departs to another home, very like his own, in the next street but one. In that other home is a girl whom John sincerely considers to be the pearl of womanhood. In a few months John, inspired and aided by this pearl, will embark in business for himself as constructor of a home.

Mary Smith wanders silently and inconspicuously into the drawing-room (it being, as you know summer) and caresses the piano in an expectant manner. John's views as to the identity of the pearl of womanhood are not shared by another young man who lives not very far off. This other young man has no doubt whatever that the pearl of womanhood is precisely Mary Smith (an idea which had never entered John's head); and he comes to see Mary every night, with the permission of her parents. The pair are, in fact, engaged. Probably Mary opens the door for him, in which case they go straight to the drawing-room. (One is glad to think that, after all, the drawingroom is turning out useful.) Young Henry has disappeared from human ken.

Mr. Smith and wife remain in the dining-room, separated from each other by a newspaper, which Mr. Smith is ostensibly reading. I say "ostensibly," for what Mr. Smith is really reading on the page of the newspaper is this: "I shall have to give something to John, something pretty handsome. Of course, there's no question of a dowry with Mary, but I shall have to give something handsome to her, too. And weddings cost money. And I have no savings, except my insurance." He keeps on reading this in every column. It is true. He is still worried about money, as he was 26 years ago. He has lived hard and honourably, ever at strain, and never had a moment's true peace of mind: once it was the fear of losing his situation; now it is the fear of his business going wrong; always it has been the tendency of expenditure to increase. The fruit of his ancient immense desire to have Mrs. Smith is now ripe for falling. The home which he and she have built is finished now, and is to be disintegrated. And John and Mary are about to begin again what their parents once began. I can almost hear Mr. Smith plaintively asking the newspaper, as he thinks over the achieved enterprise of his home: Has it been a success? Is it a success?

II

THE GREAT MANNERS QUESTION

Let us forget that it is a home. Let us conceive it as a small collection of people living in the same house. They are together by accident rather than by design, and they remain together rather by inertia than by the fitness of things. Supposing that the adult occupants of the average house had to begin domestic life again (I do not speak of husbands and wives), and were effective^ free to choose their companions, it is highly improbable that they would choose the particular crew of; which they form part; it is practically certain that they would not choose it in its entirety. However, there they are, together, every day, every night, on a space of ground not perhaps more than twenty feet by twenty feet—often less. To find room to separate a little they live in layers, and it is the servant who is nearest heaven. That is how you must look at them.

Now it is, broadly speaking, a universal characteristic of this strange community that the members of it can depend upon each other in a crisis. They are what is called "loyal" to an extraordinary degree. Let one of them fall ill, and he can absolutely rely on tireless nursing.

Again, let one of them get into trouble, and his companions will stand by him, and if they cannot, or will not, help him materially, they will, at any rate, make sympathetic excuses for not doing so. Or let one of them sutler a loss, and he will instantly be surrounded by all the consolations that kindness can invent. Or let one of them be ill-spoken of, and every individual of the community will defend him, usually with heat, always with conviction.

But I have drawn only the foul-weather picture. We come to the fine-weather picture. Imagine a stranger from the moon, to whom I had quite truthfully described the great qualities of this strange community presided over by Mr. Smith—imagine him invisibly introduced into the said community!

You can fancy the lunatic's astonishment! Instead of heaven he would decidedly consider that he had strayed into an armed camp, or into a cage of porcupines. He would conclude, being a lunatic, that the members of the community either hated each other, or at best suffered the sight of each other only as a supreme act of toleration. He would hear surly voices, curt demands, impolite answers; and if he did not hear amazing silences it would be because you cannot physically hear a silence.

He would no doubt think that the truth was not in me. He would remonstrate: "But you told me—"

Then I should justify myself: "'In a crisis,' I said, my dear gentleman from the moon. I said nothing about ordinary daily life. Now you see this well-favoured girl who has been nagging at her brother all through tea because of some omission or commission—I can assure you that if, for instance, her brother had typhoid fever that girl would nurse him with the devotion of a saint. Similarly, if she lost her sweetheart by death or breach of promise, he would envelope her in brotherly affection."

"How often does he have typhoid fever?" the lunatic might ask. "Once a month?"

"Well," I should answer, "he hasn't had it yet. But if he had it—you see!"

"And does she frequently get thrown over?"

"Oh, no! Her young man worships her. She is to be married next spring. But if—"

"And so, while waiting for crises and disasters, they go on—like this?"

"Yes," I should defend my fellow-terrestrials. "But you must not jump to the conclusion that they are always like this. They can be just as nice as anybody. They are perfectly charming, really."

"Well, then," he might inquire, "how do they justify this behaviour to one another?"

"By the hazard of birth," I should reply, "or by the equally great hazard of marriage. With us, when you happen to have the same father and mother, or even the same uncle, or when you happen to be married, it is generally considered that you may abandon the forms of politeness and the expressions of sympathy, and that you have an unlimited right of criticism."

"I should have thought precisely the contrary," he would probably say, being a lunatic.

The lunatic having been allowed to depart, I should like to ask the Smiths—middle-aged Mr. Smith and Mrs. Smith—a question somewhat in these terms: "What is the uppermost, the most frequent feeling in your minds about this community which you call 'home'? You needn't tell me that you love it, that it is the dearest place on earth, that no other place could ever have quite the same, etc., etc. I know all about that. I admit it. Is not your uppermost, commonest feeling a feeling that it is rather a tedious, tiresome place, and that the human components of it are excellent persons, but... and that really you have had a great deal to put up with?"

In reply, do not be sentimental, be honest.. . .

Such being your impression of home (not your deepest, but your most obvious impression), can it fairly be stated that the home of the Smiths is a success?

There are two traits which have prevented the home of the Smiths from being a complete success, from being that success which both Mr. and Mrs. Smith fully intended to achieve when they started, and which young John and young Mary fully intend to achieve when they at length start without having decided precisely *how* they will do better than their elders. The first is British independence of action, which causes the owner of a British temperament to seek to combine the advantages of anarchical solitude with the advantages of a community:

273

impossible feat! In the home of the Smiths each room is a separate Norman fortress, sheltering an individuality that will be untrammelled or perish.

And the second is the unchangeable conviction at the bottom of every Briton's heart that formal politeness in intimacy is insincere. This is especially true of the Midlands and the North. When I left the Midlands and went South, I truly thought, for several days, that Southerners were a hypocritical lot, just because they said, "If you wouldn't mind moving," instead of "Now, then, out of it!" Gruffness and the malicious satisfaction of candid gratuitous criticism are the root of the evil in the home of the Smiths. And the consequences of them are very much more serious than the Smiths in their gruffness imagine.

III

SPENDING-AND GETTING VALUE

I now allude to those financial harassments which have been a marked feature of the home founded and managed by Mr. Smith, who has been eternally worried about money. The children have grown up in this atmosphere of fiscal anxiety, accustomed to the everlasting question whether ends will meet; accustomed to the everlasting debate whether a certain thing can be afforded. And nearly every house in the street where the Smiths live is in the same case.

Why is this? Is it that incomes are lower and commodities and taxes higher in England than in other large European countries? No; the contrary is the fact. In no large European country will money go so far as in England. Is it that the English race is deficient in financial skill? England is the only large European country which genuinely balances its national budget every year and regularly liquidates its debts.

I wish to hint to Mr. Smith that he differs in one very important respect from the Mr. Smith of France, and the Mr. Smith of Germany, his only serious rivals. In the matter of money, he always asks himself, not how little he can spend, but how much he can spend. At the end of a lifetime the result is apparent. Or when he has a daughter to marry off, the result is apparent. In England economy is a virtue. In France, for example, it is merely a habit.

* * * * *

Mr. Smith is extravagant. He has an extravagant way of looking at life. On his own plane Mr. Smith is a haughty nobleman of old days; he is royal; he is a born hangman of expense.

"What?" cries Mr. Smith, furiousi. "Me extravagant! Why, I have always been most careful! I have had to be, with my income!"

He may protest. But I am right. The very tone with which he says: "With my income!" gives Mr. Smith away. What is the matter with Mr. Smith's income? Has it been less than the average? Not at all. The only thing that is the matter with Mr. Smith's income is that he has never accepted it as a hard, prosaic fact. He has always pretended that it was a magic income, with which miracles could be performed. He has always been trying to pour two pints and a gill out of a quart pot. He has always hoped that luck would befall him. On a hundred and fifty a year he ever endeavoured to live as though he had two hundred. And so on, as his income increased.

When he married he began by taking the highest-rented house that he could possibly afford, instead of the cheapest that he could possibly do with, and he has been going on ever since in the same style—creating an effect, cutting a figure.

This system of living, the English system, has indubitable advantages. It encourages enterprise and prevents fossilisation. It gives dramatic interest to existence. And, after all, though at the age of 50 Mr. Smith possesses little beside a houseful of furniture and his insurance policy, he can say that he has had something for his money every year and every day of the year. He can truthfully say, when charged with having "eaten his cake," that a cake is a futile thing till it is eaten.

The French system has disadvantages. The French Mr. Smith does not try to make money, he tries merely to save it. He shrinks from the perils of enterprise. He does not want to create. He frequently becomes parsimonious, and he may postpone the attempt to get some fun out of life until he is past the capacity for fun.

On the other hand, the financial independence with which his habits endow him is a very precious thing. One finds it everywhere in France; it is instinctive in the attitude of the average man. That chronic tightness has often led Mr. Smith to make unpleasing compromises with his dignity; such compromises are rarer in France. Take a person into your employ in France, even the humblest, and you will soon find out how the habit of a margin affects the demeanour of the employed. Personally, I have often been inconvenienced by this in France. But I have liked it. After all, one prefers to be dealing with people who can call their souls their own.

Mr. Smith need not go to the extremes of the extremists in France, but he might advantageously go a long way towards them. Pie ought to reconcile himself definitely to his income. He ought to cease his constant attempt to perform miracles with his income. It is really not pleasant for him to be fixed as he is at the age of fifty, worried because he has to provide wedding presents for his son and his daughter. And how can he preach thrift to his son John? John knows his father.

There is another, and an even more ticklish, point. It being notorious that Mr. Smith spends too much money, let us ask whether Mr. Smith gets value for the money he spends. I must again compare with France, whose homes I know. Now, as regards solid, standing comfort, there is no comparison between Mr. Smith's home and the home of the French Mr. Smith. Our Mr. Smith wins. His standard is higher. He has more room, more rooms, more hygiene, and more general facilities for putting himself at his ease.

But these contrivances, once acquired, do not involve a regular outlay, except so far as they affect rent. And in the household budget rent is a less important item than food and cleansing. Now, the raw materials of the stuff necessary to keep a household healthily alive cost more in France than in England. And the French Mr. Smith's income is a little less than our Mr. Smith's. Yet the French Mr. Smith, while sitting on a less comfortable chair in a smaller room, most decidedly consumes better meals than our Mr. Smith. In other words, he lives better.

I have often asked myself, in observing the family life of Monsieur and Madame Smith: "How on earth do they do it?" Only one explanation is possible. They understand better how to run a house economically in France than we do in England.

Now Mrs. Smith in her turn cries: "Me extravagant?"

Yes, relatively, extravagant! It is a hard saying, but, I believe, a true one. Extravagance is in the air of England. A person always in a room where there is a slight escape of gas does not smell the gas—until he has been out for a walk and returned. So it is with us.

As for you, Mrs. Smith, I would not presume to say in what you are extravagant. But I guarantee that Madame Smith would "do it on less."

The enormous periodical literature now devoted largely to hints on household management shows that we, perhaps unconsciously, realise a defect. You don't find this literature in France. They don't seem to need it.

IV

THE PARENTS

Let us look at Mr. and Mrs. Smith one evening when they are by themselves, leaving the children entirely out of account. For in addition to being father and mother, they are husband and wife. Not that I wish to examine the whole institution of marriage—people who dare to do so deserve the Victoria Cross! My concern is simply with the effects of the organisation of the home—on marriage and other things.

Well, you see them together. Mr. Smith has done earning money for the day, and Mrs. Smith has done spending it. They are at leisure to enjoy this home of theirs. This is what Mr. Smith passes seven hours a day at business for. This is what he got married for. This is what he wanted when he decided to take Mrs. Smith, if he could get her. These hours ought to be the flower of their joint life. How are these hours affected by the organisation of the home?

I will tell you how Mrs. Smith is affected. Mrs. Smith is worried by it. And in addition she is conscious that her efforts are imperfectly appreciated, and her difficulties unrealised. As regards the directing and daily recreation of the home, Mr. Smith's attitude on this evening by the domestic hearth is at best one of armed neutrality. His criticism is seldom other than destructive. Mr. Smith is a strange man. If he went to a lot of trouble to get a small holding under the Small Holdings Act, and then left the cultivation of the ground to another person not scientifically trained to agriculture he would be looked upon as a ninny. When a man takes up a hobby, he ought surely

279

to be terrifically interested in it. What is Mr. Smith's home but his hobby?

He has put Mrs. Smith in to manage it. He himself, once a quarter, discharges the complicated and delicate function of paying the rent. All the rest, the little matters, such as victualling and brightening—trifles, nothings!—he leaves to Mrs. Smith. He is not satisfied with Mrs. Smith's activities, and he does not disguise the fact. He is convinced that Mrs. Smith spends too much, and that she is not businesslike. He is convinced that running a house is child's play compared to what *he* has to do. Now, as to Mrs. Smith being unbusinesslike, is Mr. Smith himself businesslike? If he is, he greatly differs from his companions in the second-class smoker. The average office and the average works are emphatically not run on business lines, except in theory. Daily experience proves this. The businesslikeness of the average business man is a vast and hollow pretence.

Besides, who could expect Mrs. Smith to be businesslike? She was never taught to be businesslike. Mr. Smith was apprenticed, or indentured, to his vocation. But Mrs. Smith wasn't. Mrs. Smith has to feed a family, and doesn't know the principles of diet. She has to keep children in health, and couldn't describe their organs to save her life. She has to make herself and the home agreeable to the eye, and knows nothing artistic about colour or form.

I am an ardent advocate of Mrs. Smith. The marvel is not that Mrs. Smith does so badly, but that she does so well. If women were not more conscientious than men in their duties Mr. Smith's home would be more amateurish than it is, and Mr. Smith's "moods" more frequent than they are. For Mrs. Smith is amateurish. Example: Mrs. Smith is bothered to death by the daily question, What can we have for dinner? She splits her head in two in order to avoid monotony. Mrs. Smith's *répertoire* probably consists of about 50 dishes, and if she could recall them all to her mind at once her task would be much simplified. But she can't think of them when she wants to think of them. Supposing that in Mrs. Smith's kitchen hung a card containing a list of all her dishes, she could run her eyes over it and choose instantly what dishes would suit that day's larder. Did you ever see such a list in Mrs. Smith's kitchen? No. The idea has not occurred to Mrs. Smith!

I say also that to spend money efficiently is quite as difficult as to earn it efficiently. Any fool can, somehow, earn a sovereign, but to get value for a sovereign in small purchases means skill and immense knowledge. Mr. Smith has never had experience of the difficulty of spending money efficiently. Most of Mr. Smith's payments are fixed and mechanical. Mrs. Smith is the spender. Mr. Smith chiefly exercises his skill as a spender in his clothes and in tobacco. Look at the result. Any showy necktie shop and furiously-advertised tobacco is capable of hood-winking Mr. Smith.

In further comparison of their respective "jobs" it has to be noted that Mrs. Smith's is rendered doubly difficult by the fact that she is always at close quarters with the caprices of human nature. Mrs. Smith is continually bumping up against human nature in various manifestations. The human butcher-boy may arrive late owing to marbles, and so the dinner must either be late or the meat undercooked; or Mr. Smith, through too much smoking, may have lost his appetite, and veal out of Paradise wouldn't please him! Mrs. Smith's job is transcendently delicate.

In fine, though Mrs. Smith's job is perhaps not quite so difficult as she fancies it to be, it is much more difficult than Mr. Smith fancies it to be. And if it is not as well done as she thinks, it is much better done than Mr. Smith thinks. But she will never persuade Mr. Smith that he is wrong until Mr. Smith condescends to know what he is talking about in the discussion of household matters. Mr. Smith's opportunities of criticism are far too ample; or, at any rate, he makes use of them unfairly, and not as a man of honour. Supposing that Mrs. Smith finished all her work at four o'clock, and was free to stroll into Mr. Smith's place of business and criticise there everything that did not please her! (It is true that she wouldn't know what she was talking about; but neither does Mr. Smith at home; at home Mr. Smith finds pride in not knowing what he is talking about.) Mr. Smith would have a bit of a "time" between four and six.

Mr. and Mrs. Smith are united by a genuine affection. But their secret attitudes on the subject of home management cause that affection, by a constant slight friction, to wear thin. It must be so. And it will be so until (a) Mr. Smith deigns to learn the business of his home; (b) Mr. Smith ceases to expect Mrs. Smith to perform miracles; (c) Mrs. Smith ceases to be an amateur in domestic economy—i. e., until domestic economy becomes the principal subject in the upper forms of the average girls' school.

At present the organisation of the home is an agency against the triumph of marriage as an institution.

V

HAMIT'S POINT OF VIEW

You may have forgotten young Harry Smith, whom I casually mentioned in my first section, the schoolboy of fifteen. I should not be surprised to hear that you had forgotten him. He is often forgotten in the home of the Smiths., Compared with Mr. Smith, the creator of the home, or with the lordly eldest son John, who earns his own living and is nearly engaged, or with Mary, who actually is engaged, young Harry is unimportant. Still, his case is very interesting, and his own personal impression of the home of the Smiths must be of value. .

Is Harry Smith happy in the home? Of course, one would not expect him to be perfectly happy. But is he as happy as circumstances in themselves allow? My firm answer is that he is not. I am entirely certain that on the whole Harry Smith regards home as a fag, a grind, and a bore. Mr. Smith, on reading these lines, is furious, and Mrs. Smith is hurt. What! Our dear Harry experiences tedium and disappointment with his dear parents? Nonsense!

The fact is, no parents will believe that their children are avoidably unhappy. It is universally agreed nowadays, that children in the eighteenth century, and in the first half of the nineteenth, had a pretty bad time under the sway of their elders. But the parent of those epochs would have been indignant at any accusation of ill-treatment. He would have called his sway beneficent and his affection doting. The same with Mr. and Mrs. Smith! Now, I do not mean, Mr. and Mrs. Smith, that you crudely ill-treat your son, tying him to posts, depriving him of sleep, or pulling chestnuts out of the fire with his fingers. (See reports of S.P.C.C.) A thousand times, no! You are softhearted. Mrs. Smith is occasionally somewhat too soft-hearted. Still, I maintain that you ill-treat Harry in a very subtle, moral way, by being fundamentally unjust to him in your own minds.

Just look at your Harry, my excellent and conscientious Mr. Smith. He is all alive there, a real human being, not a mechanical doll; he has feelings just like yours, only, perhaps, more sensitive. He finds himself in a world which—well, of which the less said the better. *You* know what the world is, Mr. Smith, and you have often said what you know. He is in this world, and he can't get out of it. You have started him on the dubious adventure, and he has got to go through with it. And what is the reason of his being here? Did you start him out of a desire to raise citizens for the greatest of empires? Did you imagine he would enjoy it hugely? Did you act from a sense of duty to the universe? None of these things, Mr. Smith! Your Harry is merely here because you thought that Mrs. Smith was somehow charmingly different from other girls. He is a consequence of your egotistic desire to enlarge your borders, of your determination to have what you wanted. Every time you cast eyes on him he ought to remind you what a self-seeking and consequence-scorning person you are, Mr. Smith. And not only is he from no choice or wish of his own in a world as to which the most powerful intellects are still arguing whether it is tragic or ridiculous; but he is unarmed for the perils of the business. He is very ignorant and very inexperienced, and he is continually passing through disconcerting modifications.

These are the facts, my dear sir. You cannot deny that you, for your own satisfaction, have got Harry into a rather fearful mess. Do you constantly make the effort to be sympathetic to this helpless victim of your egotism? You do not. And what is worse, to quiet your own consciences, both you and Mrs. Smith are for ever pouring into his ear a shocking—I won't call it "lie"—perversion of the truth. You are always absurdly trying to persuade him that the obligation is on his side. Not a day wears to night but Mrs. Smith expresses to Harry her conviction that by good behaviour he ought to prove his *gratitude* to you for being such a kind father.

And you talk to him in the same strain of Mrs. Smith. The sum of your teaching is an insinuation—often more than an insinuation—that you have conferred a favour on Harry, Supposing that some one pitched you into the Ship Canal—one of the salubrious reaches near Warrington, Mr. Smith—and then clumsily dragged you half-way out, and punctured his efforts by a reiterated statement that gratitude to him ought to fill your breast, how would you feel?

Things are better than they were, but the general attitude of the parent to the child is still fundamentally insincere, and it mars the success of the home, for it engenders in the child a sense of injustice. Do you fancy that Harry is for an instant deceived by the rhetoric of his parents? Not he! Children are very difficult to deceive, and they are horribly frank to themselves. It is quite bad enough for Harry to be compelled to go to school. Harry, however, has enough sense to perceive that he must go to school. But when his parents begin to yarn that he ought to be *glad* to go to school, that he ought to *enjoy* the privilege of solving quadratic equations and learning the specific gravities of elements, he is quite naturally alienated.

He does not fail to observe that in a hundred things the actions of his parents contradict their precepts. When, being a boy, he behaves like a hoy, and his parents affect astonishment and disgust, he knows it is an affectation. When his father, irritated by a superabundance of noise, frowns and instructs Harry to get away for he is tired of the sight of him, Harry is excusably affronted in his secret pride.

These are illustrations of the imperfect success of the Smiths' home as an organisation for making Harry happy. Useless for Mr. Smith to argue that it is "all for Harry's own good." He would simply be aggravating his offence. Discipline, the enforcement of regulations, is necessary for Harry. I strongly favour discipline.

But discipline can be practised with sympathy or without sympathy; with or without the accompaniment of hypocritical remarks that deceive no one; with or without odious assumptions of superiority and philanthropy.

I trust that young John and young Mary will take note, and that their attitude to *their* Harrys will be, not: "You ought to be glad you're alive," but: "We thoroughly sympathise with your difficulties. We quite agree that these rules and prohibitions and injunctions are a nuisance for you, but they will save you trouble later, and we will be as un-cast-iron as we can." Honesty is the best policy.

VI

_____

THE FUTURE

The cry is that the institution of the home is being undermined, and that, therefore, society is in the way of perishing. It is stated that the home is insidiously attacked, at one end of the scale, by the hotel and restaurant habit, and, at the other, by such innovations as the feeding-of-school-children habit. We are asked to contemplate the crowded and glittering dining-rooms of the Midland, the Carlton, the Adelphi, on, for instance, Christmas Night, when, of all nights, people ought! to be on their own hearths, and we are told: "It has come to this. This! is the result of the craze for pleasure! Where is the home now?"

To which my reply would be that the home remains just about where it was. The spectacular existence of a few great hotels has never mirrored the national life. Is the home of the Smiths, for example, being gradually overthrown by the restaurant habit? The restaurant habit will only strengthen the institution of the home. The most restaurant-loving people on the face of the earth are the French, and the French home is a far more powerful, more closely-knit organisation than our own. Why! Up to last year a Frenchman of sixty could not marry without the consent of his parents, if they happened to be alive. I wonder what the Smiths would say to that as an example of the disintegration of the home by the restaurant habit!

Most assuredly the modest, medium, average home founded by Mr. Smith has not been in the slightest degree affected either by the increase of luxury and leisure, or by any alleged meddlesomeness on the part of the State. The home founded by

287

Mr. Smith, with all its faults—and I have not spared them—is too convenient, too economical, too efficient, and, above all, too natural, to be overthrown, or even shaken, by either luxury or grandmotherliness. To change the metaphor and call it a ship, it remains absolutely right and tight. It is true that Mr. and Mrs. Smith assert sadly that young John and young Mary have much more liberty than *they* ever had, but Mr. and Mrs. Smith's parents asserted exactly the same thing of Mr. and Mrs. Smith, and their grandparents of their parents, and so on backwards doubtless up to Noah. That is only part of a process, a beneficent process.

Nevertheless, the home of the Smiths has a very real enemy, and that enemy is not outside, but inside. That enemy is Matilda. I have not hitherto discussed Matilda. She sleeps in the attic, and earns £18 a year, rising to £20. She doesn't count, and yet she is the factor which, more than any other, will modify the home of the Smiths.

Let me say no word against Matilda. She is a respectable and a passably industrious, and a passably obedient girl. I know her. She usually opens the door for me, and we converse "like anything"! "Good evening, Matilda," I say to her. "Good evening, sir," says she. And in her tone and mine is an implicit recognition of the fact that I have been very good-natured and sympathetic in greeting her as a human being. "Mr. Smith in?" I ask, smiling. "Yes, sir. Will you come this way?" says she. Then I forget her. A nice, pleasant girl! And she has a good place, too. The hygienic conditions are superior to those of a mill, and the labour less fatiguing. And both Mrs. Smith and Miss Mary, help her enormously in "little ways." She eats better food than she would eat at home, and she has a bedroom all to herself. You might say she was on velvet.

And yet, in the middle of one of those jolly, unaffected evenings that I occasionally spend with the Smiths, when the piano has been going, and I have helped Mrs. Smith to cheat herself at patience, and given Mr. Smith the impression that he can teach me a thing or two, and discussed cigarettes with John, and songs with Mary, and the sense of intimate fellowship and mutual comprehension is in the air, in comes Matilda suddenly with a tray of coffee—and makes me think furiously! She goes out as rapidly as she came in, for she is bound by an iron law not to stop an instant, and if she happened to remark in a friendly, human way: "You seem to be having a good time here!"

All the Smiths, and I too, would probably drop down dead from pained shock.

But though she is gone I continue to think furiously. Where had she been all the jolly evening? Where has she returned to? Well, to her beautiful hygienic kitchen, where she sits or works all by herself, on velvet. My thoughts follow her existence through the day, and I remember that from morn till onerous eve she must not, save on business, speak unless she is spoken to. Then I give up thinking about Matilda's case, because it annoys me. I recall a phrase of young John's; he is youthfully interested in social problems, and he wants a latch-key vote. Said John to me once, when another Matilda had left: "Of course, if one thought too much about Matilda's case, one wouldn't be able to sleep at nights."

When you visit the Smiths the home seems always to be in smooth working order. But ask Mrs. Smith! Ask Mary! Get beneath the surface. And you will glimpse the terrible trouble that lies concealed. Mrs. Smith began with Matilda the First. Are you aware that this is Matilda the Fortieth, and that between Matilda the Fortieth and Matilda the Forty-first there will probably be an interregnum? Mrs. Smith simply cannot get Matildas. And when by happy chance she does get a Matilda, the misguided girl won't see the velvet with which the kitchen and the attic are carpeted.

Mrs. Smith says the time will come when the race of Matildas will have disappeared. And Mrs. Smith is right. The "general servant" is bound to disappear utterly. In North America she has already almost disappeared. Think of that! Instead of her, in many parts of the American continent, there is an independent stranger who, if she came to the Smiths, would have the ineffable impudence to eat at the same table as the Smiths, just as though she was of the same clay, and who, when told to do something, would be quite equal to snapping out: "Do it yourself."

But you say that the inconvenience brought about by the disappearance of Matilda would be too awful to contemplate. I venture to predict that the disappearance of Matilda will not exhaust the resources of civilisation. The home will continue. But mechanical invention will have to be quickened in order to replace Matilda's red hands. And there will be those suburban restaurants! And I have a pleasing vision of young John, in the home which *he* builds, cleaning his own boots. Inconvenient, but it is coming!

STREETS, ROADS AND TRAINS

1907-1909

I

IN WATLING STREET

Upon an evening in early autumn, I, who had never owned an orchard before, stood in my orchard; behind me were a phalanx of some sixty trees bearing (miraculously, to my simplicity) a fine crop of apples and plums—my apples and plums, and a mead of some two acres, my mead, upon which I discerned possibilities of football and cricket; behind these was a double greenhouse containing three hundred pendent bunches of grapes of the dark and aristocratic variety which I thought I had seen in Piccadilly ticketed at four shillings a pound—my grapes; still further behind uprose the chimneys of a country-house, uncompromisingly plain and to some eyes perhaps ugly, but my country-house, the lease of which, stamped, was in my pocket. Immediately in front of me was a luxuriant hedge which, long unclipped, had attained a height of at least fifteen feet. Beyond the hedge the ground fell away sharply into a draining ditch, and on the other side of the ditch, through the interstices of the hedge, I perceived glimpses of a very straight and very white highway.

This highway was Watling Street, built of the Romans, and even now surviving as the most famous road in England. I had "learnt" it at school, and knew that it once ran from Dover to London, from London to Chester and from Chester to York. Just recently I had tracked it diligently on a series of county maps, and discovered that, though only vague fragments of it remained in Kent, Surrey, Shropshire, Cheshire, and Yorkshire, it still flourished and abounded exceedingly in my particular neighbourhood as a right line, austere, renowned, indispensable, clothed in its own immortal dust. I could see but patches of it in the twilight, but I was aware that it stretched fifteen miles southeast of me, and unnumbered miles northwest of me, with scarcely a curve to break the splendid inexorable monotony of its career. To me it was a wonderful road—more wonderful than the Great North Road, or the military road from Moscow to Vladivostock. And the most wonderful thing about it was that I lived on it. After all, few people can stamp the top of their notepaper, "Watling Street, England." It is not a residential thoroughfare.

Only persons of imagination can enter into my feelings at that moment. I had spent two-thirds of my life in a town (squalid, industrial) and the remaining third in Town. I thought I knew every creosoted block in Fleet Street, every bookstall in Shoreditch, every hosier's in Piccadilly. I certainly did know the order of stations on the Inner Circle, the various frowns of publishers, the strange hysteric, silly atmosphere of theatrical first-nights, and stars of the Empire and Alhambra (by sight), and the vicious odours of a thousand and one restaurants. And lo! burdened with all this accumulated knowledge, shackled by all these habits, associations, entrancements, I was yet moved by some mysterious and far-off atavism to pack up, harness the oxen, "trek," and go and live in "the country."

Of course I soon discovered that there is no such thing as "the country," just as there is no such thing as Herbert Spencer's "state."

"The country" is an entity which exists only in the brains

of an urban population, whose members ridiculously regard the terrene surface as a concatenation of towns surrounded by earthy space. There is England, and there are spots on England called towns: that is all. But at that time I too had the illusion of "the country," a district where one saw "trees," "flowers," and "birds." For me, a tree was not an oak or an ash or an elm or a birch or a chestnut; it was just a "tree." For me there were robins, sparrows, and crows; the rest of the winged fauna was merely "birds." I recognised roses, daisies, dandelions, forget-me-nots, chrysanthemums, and one or two more blossoms; all else was "flowers." Remember that all this happened before the advent of the nature-book and the sublime invention of week-ending, and conceive me plunging into this unknown, inscrutable, and recondite "country," as I might have plunged fully clothed and unable to swim into the sea. It was a prodigious adventure! When my friends asked me, with furtive glances at each other as in the presence of a lunatic, why I was going to live in the country, I could only reply: "Because I want to. I want to see what it's like." I might have attributed my action to the dearness of season-tickets on the Underground, to the slowness of omnibuses or the danger of cabs: my friends would have been just as wise, and I just as foolish, in their esteem. I admit that their attitude of benevolent contempt, of far-seeing sagacity, gave me to think. And although I was obstinate, it was with a pang of misgiving that I posted the notice of quitting my suburban residence; and the pang was more acute when I signed the contract for the removal of my furniture. I called on my friends before the sinister day of exodus.

"Good-bye," I said.

"Au revoir," they replied, with calm vaticinatory assurance, "we shall see you back again in a year."

Thus, outwardly braggart, inwardly quaking, I departed. The quaking had not ceased as I stood, in the autumn twilight, in my beautiful orchard, in front of my country-house. Toiling up the slope from the southward, I saw an enormous van with three horses: the last instalment of my chattels. As it turned lumberingly at right angles into my private road or boreen, I said aloud:

"I've done it."

I had. I felt like a statesman who has handed an ultimatum to a king's messenger. No withdrawal was now possible. From the reverie natural to this melancholy occasion I was aroused by a disconcerting sound of collision, the rattle of chains, and the oaths customary to drivers in a difficulty. I ran towards the house and down the weedy drive bordered by trees which a learned gardener had told me were of the variety, *cupressus lawsoniana*. In essaying the perilous manoeuvre of twisting round three horses and a long van on a space about twenty feet square, the driver had overset the brick pier upon which swung my garden-gate. The unicorn horse of the team was nosing at the cupressus lawsoniana and the van was scotched in the gateway. I thought, "This is an omen." I was, however, reassured by the sight of two butchers and two bakers each asseverating that nothing could afford him greater pleasure than to call every day for orders. A minute later the postman, in his own lordly equipage, arrived with my newspapers and his respects. I tore open a paper and read news of London. I convinced myself that London actually existed, though I were never to see it again. The smashing of the pier dwindled from a catastrophe to an episode.

The next morning very early I was in Watling Street. Since then

Full many a glorious morning have I seen
Flatter the mountain tops with sovereign eye,

but this was the first in the sequence of those Shaksperean mornings, and it was also, subjectively, the finest. I shall not describe it, since, objectively and in the quietude of hard fact, I now perceive that it could not have been in the least remarkable. The sun rose over the southward range which Bunyan took for the model of his Delectable Mountains, and forty or fifty square miles of diversified land was spread out in front of me. The road cut down for a couple of miles like a geometrician's rule, and disappeared in a slight S curve, the work of a modern generation afraid of gradients, on to the other side of the Delectable Mountains. I thought: "How magnificent were those Romans in their disregard of everything except direction!" And being a professional novelist I naturally began at once to consider the possibilities of exploiting Watling Street in fiction. Then I climbed to the brow of my own hill, whence, at the foot of the long northerly slope, I could descry the outposts of my village, a mile away; there was no habitation of mankind nearer to me than this picturesque and venerable hamlet, which seemed to lie inconsiderable on the great road like a piece of paper. The seventy-four telegraph wires which border the great road run above the roofs of Winghurst as if they were unaware of its existence. "And Winghurst," I reflected, "is henceforth my metropolis." No office! No memorising of time-tables! No daily struggle-for-lunch! Winghurst, with three hundred inhabitants, the centre of excitement, the fount of external life!

The course of these ordinary but inevitable thoughts was interrupted by my consciousness of a presence near me. A man coughed. He had approached me, in almost soleless boots, on the grassy footpath. For a brief second I regarded him with that peculiar fellow-feeling which a man who has risen extremely early is wont to exhibit towards another man who has risen extremely early. But finding no answering vanity in his undistinguished features I quickly put on an appearance of usualness, to indicate that I might be found on that spot at that hour every morning. The man looked shabby, and that Sherlock Holmes who lies concealed in each one of us decided for me that he must be a tailor out-of-work.

"Good morning, sir," he said.

"Good morning," I said.

"Do you want to buy a good recipe for a horse, sir?" he asked.

"A horse?" I repeated, wondering whether he was a lunatic, or a genius who had discovered a way to manufacture horses.

"Yes, sir," he said, "They often fall sick, sir, you know. The saying is, as I daresay you've heard, 'Never trust a woman's word or a horse's health.'"

I corrected his quotation.

"I've got one or two real good recipes," he resumed.

"But I've got no horse," I replied, and that seemed to finish the interview.

"No offence, I hope, sir," he said, and passed on towards the Delectable Mountains.

He was a mystery; his speech disclosed no marked local accent; he had certainly had some education; and he was hawking horse-remedies in Watling Street at sunrise. Here was the germ of my first lesson in rusticity. Except in towns, the "horsey" man does not necessarily look horsey. That particular man resembled a tailor, and by a curious coincidence the man most fearfully and wonderfully learned in equine lore that I have yet known is a tailor.

But horses! Six miles away to the West I could see the steam of expresses on the London and North Western Main line; four miles to the East I could see the steam of expresses on the Midland. And here was an individual offering stable-recipes as simply as though they had been muffins! I reflected on my empty stable, harness-room, coachhouse. I began to suspect that I was in a land where horses entered in the daily and hourly existence of the people. I had known for weeks that I must buy a horse; the nearest town and the nearest railway station were three miles off. But now, with apprehension, I saw that mysterious and dangerous mercantile operation to be dreadfully imminent: me, *coram publico*, buying a horse, me the dupe of copers, me a butt for the covert sarcasm of a village omniscient about horses and intolerant of ignorance on such a subject!

Down in the village, that early morning, I saw a pony and an evidently precarious trap standing in front of the principal shop. I had read about the "village-shop" in novels; I had even ventured to describe it in fiction of my own; and I was equally

296

surprised and delighted to find that the villageshop of fiction was also the village-shop of fact. It was the mere truth that one could buy everything in this diminutive emporium, that the multifariousness of its odours excelled that of the odours of Cologne, and that the proprietor, who had never seen me before, instantly knew me and all about me. Soon I, was in a fair way to know something of the proprietor. He was informing me that he had five little children, when one of the five, snuffling and in a critical mood, tumbled into the shop out of an obscure Beyond.

"And what's your name?" I enquired of the girl, with that fatuous, false blandness of tone which the inexpert always adopt toward children. I thought of the five maidens whose names were five sweet symphonies, and moreover I deemed it politic to establish friendly relations with my monopolist.

"She's a little shy," I remarked.

"It's a boy, sir," said the monopolist.

It occurred to me that Nature was singularly uninventive in devising new quandaries for the foolish.

"Tell the gentleman your name.'"

Thus admonished, the boy emitted one monosyllable: "Guy."

"We called him Guy because he was horn on the fifth of November," the monopolist was good enough to explain.

As I left the shop a man driving a pony drew up at the door with an immense and sudden flourish calculated to impress the simple. I noticed that the pony was the same animal which I had previously seen standing there.

"Want to buy a pony, sir?" The question was thrown at me like a missile that narrowly escaped my head; launched in a voice which must once have been extremely powerful, but which now, whether by abuse of shouting in the open air or by the deteriorating effect of gin on the vocal chords, was only a loud, passionate whisper: so that, though the man obviously bawled with all his might, the drum of one's ear was not shattered. I judged, partly from the cut of his coat and the size of the buttons on it, and partly from the creaminess of the shaggy, long-tailed pony, that my questioner was or had been connected with circuses. His very hand was against him; the turned-back podgy thumb showed acquisitiveness, and the enormous Gophir diamonds in brass rings argued a certain lack of really fine taste. His face had literally the brazen look, and that absolutely hard, impudent, glaring impassivity acquired only by those who earn more than enough to drink by continually bouncing the public.

"The finest pony in the county, sir." (It was an animal organism gingerly supported on four crooked legs; a quadruped and nothing more.) "The finest pony in the county!" he screamed, "Finest pony in England, sir! Not another like him! I took him to the Rothschild horse-show, but they wouldn't have him. Said I'd come too late to enter him for the first-clawss. They were afraid—afferaid! There was the water-jump. 'Stand aside, you blighters,' I said, 'and he'll jump that, the d——d gig and all,' But they were afferaid!"

I asked if the animal was quiet to drive.

"Quiet to drive, sir, did you say? I should *say* so. I says *Away*, and *off* he goes." Here the thin scream became a screech. "Then I says *Pull up, you blighter*, and he stops dead. A child could drive him. He don't want no driving. You could drive him with a silken thread." His voice melted, and with an exquisite tender cadence he repeated: "With a silk-en therredd!"

"Well," I said. "How much?"

"How much, did you say, sir? How much?" He made it appear that this question came upon him as an extraordinary surprise. I nodded.

He meditated on the startling problem, and then yelled: "Thirty guineas. It's giving him away."

"Make it shillings," I said. I was ingenuously satisfied with my retort, but the man somehow failed to appreciate it.

"Come here," he said, in a tone of intimate confidence. "Come here. Listen. I've had that pony's picture painted. Finest artist in England, sir. And frame! You never see such a frame! At thirty guineas I'll throw the picture in. Look ye! That picture cost me two quid, and here's the receipt." He pulled forth a grimy paper, and I accepted it from his villainous fingers. It proved, however, to be a receipt for four pounds, and for the portrait, not of a pony, but of a man.

"This is a receipt for your own portrait," I said.

"Now wasn't that a coorious mistake for me to make?" he asked, as if demanding information. "Wasn't that a coorious mistake?"

I was obliged to give him the answer he desired, and then he produced the correct receipt.

"Now," he said wooingly, "There! Is it a trade? I'll bring you the picture to-night. Finest frame you ever saw! What? No? Look here, buy him at thirty guineas—say pounds—and I'll chuck you both the blighted pictures in!"

"*Away!*" he screamed a minute later, and the cream pony, galvanised into frantic activity by that sound, and surely not controllable by a silken thread, scurried off towards the Delectable Mountains.

This was my first insight into horse dealing.

II

STREET TALKING

Few forms of amusement are more amusing and few forms of amusement cost less than to walk slowly along the crowded central thoroughfares of a great capital—London, Paris, or Timbuctoo—with ears open to catch fragments of conversation not specially intended for your personal consumption. It, perhaps, resembles slightly the justly blamed habit of listening at keyholes and the universally practised habit of reading other people's postcards; it is possibly not quite "nice." But, like both these habits, it is within the law, and the chances of it doing any one any harm are exceedingly remote. Moreover, it has in an amazing degree the excellent quality of taking you out of yourself—and putting you into some one else. Detectives employ it, and if it were forbidden where would novelists be? Where, for example, would Mr. Pett Ridge be? Once yielded to, it grows on you; it takes hold of you in its fell, insidious clutch, as does the habit of whisky, and becomes incurable. You then treat it seriously; you make of it a passkey to the seventy and seven riddles of the universe, with wards for each department of life. You judge national characteristics by it; by it alone you compare rival civilisations. And, incidentally, you somewhat increase your social value as a diner-out.

For a long time I practised it in the streets of Paris, the city of efficient chatter, the city in which wayfarers talk with more exuberance and more grammar than anywhere else. Here are a few phrases, fair samples from lists of hundreds, which I have gathered and stored, on the boulevards and in quieter streets, such as the Rue Blanche, where conversation grows intimate on mild nights:—

She is mad.

She lived on the fourth floor last year.

Yes, she is not bad, after all.

Thou knowest, my old one, that my wife is a little bizarre.

He has left her.

They say she is very jealous.

Anything except oysters.

Thou annoyest me terribly, my dear.

It is a question solely of the cache-corset.

With those feet!

He is a beau garçon, but—

He is the fourth in three years.

My big wolf!

Do not say that, my small rabbit.

She doesn't look it.

It is open to any one to assert that such phrases have no significance, or that, if they have significance, their significance must necessarily be hidden from the casual observer. But to me they are like the finest lines in the tragedies of John Ford.

Marlow was at his best in the pentameter, but Ford usually got his thrill in a chipped line of about three words—three words which, while they mean nothing, mean everything. All depends on what you "read into" them. And the true impassioned student of human nature will read into the overheard exclamations of the street a whole revealing philosophy. What! Two temperaments are separately born, by the agency of chance or the equally puzzling agency of design, they one day collide, become intimate, and run parallel for a space. You perceive them darkly afar off; they approach you; you are in utter ignorance of them; and then in the instant of passing you receive a blinding flash of illumination, and the next instant they are eternally hidden from you again. That blinding flash of illumination may consist of "My big wolf!" or it may consist of "It is solely a question of the cache-corset." But in any case it is and must be profoundly significant. In any case it is a gleam of light on a mysterious place. Even the matter of the height of the floor on which she lived is charged with an overwhelming effect for one who loves his fellow-man. And lives there the being stupid or audacious enough to maintain that the French national character does not emerge charmingly and with a curious coherence from the fragments of soul-communication which I have set down?

On New Year's Eve I was watching the phenomena of the universal scheme of things in Putney High-street. A man and a girl came down the footpath locked in the most intimate conversation. I could see that they were perfectly absorbed in each other. And I heard the man say:—

"Yes, Charlie is a very good judge of beer—Charlie is!"

And then they were out of hearing, vanished from the realm of my senses for ever more. And yet people complain that the suburbs are dull! As for me, when I grasped the fact that Charlie was a good judge of beer I knew for certain that I was back in England, the foundation of whose greatness we all know. I walked on a little farther and overtook two men, silently smoking pipes. The companionship seemed to be a taciturn communion of spirits, such as Carlyle and Tennyson are said to have enjoyed on a certain historic evening. But I was destined to hear strange messages that night. As I forged ahead of them, one murmured:—

"I done him down a fair treat!"

No more! I loitered to steal the other's answer. But there was no answer. Two intelligences that exist from everlasting to everlasting had momentarily joined the path of my intelligence, and the unique message was that some one had been done down a fair treat. They disappeared into the unknown of Werter-road, and I was left meditating upon the queer coincidence of the word "beer" preceding the word "treat." A disturbing coincidence, a caprice of hazard! And my mind flew back to a smoking-concert of my later youth, in which "Beer, beer, glorious beer" was followed, on the programme, by Handel's Largo.

In the early brightness of yesterday morning fate led me to Downing-street, which is assuredly the oddest street in the world (except Bow-street). Everything in Downing-street is significant, save the official residence of the Prime Minister, which, with its three electric bells and its absurdly inadequate area steps, is merely comic. The way in which the vast pile of the Home Office frowns down upon that devoted comic house is symbolic of the empire of the permanent official over the elected of the people. It might be thought that from his second-floor window the Prime Minister would keep a stern eye on the trembling permanent official. But experienced haunters of Downing-street know that the Hessian boot is on the other leg. Why does that dark and grim tunnel run from the side of No. 10, Downing-street, into the spacious trackless freedom of the Horse Guards Parade, if it is not to facilitate the escape of Prime Ministers fleeing from the chicane of conspiracies? And how is it that if you slip out of No. 10 in your slippers of a morning, and toddle across to the foot of the steps leading to St. James's Park, you have instantly a view (a) of Carlton House Terrace and (b) of the sinister inviting water of St. James's Park pond? I say that the mute significance of things is unsettling, in the highest degree. That morning a motor-brougham was seeking repose in Downing-street. By the motorbrougham stood a chauffeur, and by the chauffeur stood a girl under a feathered hat. They were exchanging confidences, these two. I strolled nonchalantly past. The girl was saying:—

"Look at this skirt as I've got on now. Me and her went 'alves in it. She was to have it one Sunday, and me the other. But do you suppose as I could get it when it come to my turn? Not me! Whenever I called for it she was always—" I heard no more. I could not decently wait. But I was glad the wearer had ultimately got the skirt. The fact was immensely significant.

III

ON THE ROAD

The reader may remember a contrivance called a bicycle on which people used to move from one place to another. The thing is still employed by postmen in remote parts. We discovered a couple in the stable, had them polished with the electroplate powder and went off on them. It seemed a strange freak. Equally strange was the freak of quitting Fontainebleau, even for three days. I had thought that no one ever willingly left Fontainebleau.

Everybody knows what the roads of France are. Smooth and straight perfection, bordered by double rows of trees. They were assuredly constructed with a prevision of automobiles. They run in an absolutely straight line for about five miles, then there is a slight bend and you are faced with another straight line of five miles. It is magnificent on a motor-car at a mile a minute. On a bicycle it is tedious; you never get anywhere, and the one fact you learn is that France consists of ten thousand million plane trees and a dust-cloud. We left the main road at the very first turn. As a rule, the bye-roads of France are as well kept as the main roads, often better, and they are far more amusing. But we soon got lost in a labyrinth of bad roads. We went back to the main roads, despite their lack of humour, and they were just as bad. All the roads of the department which we had invaded were criminal—as criminal as anything in industrial Yorkshire. A person who had travelled only on the roads of the Loiret would certainly say that French roads were the worst in Europe. This shows the folly of generalising. We held an inquisition as to these roads when we halted for lunch.

Fontainebleau

"What would you?" replied the landlady. "It is like that!" She was a stoic philosopher. She said the state of the roads was due to the heavy loads of beetroot that pass over them, the beetroot being used for sugar. This seemed to us a feeble excuse. She also said we should find that the roads got worse. She then proved that in addition to being a great philosopher she was a great tactician. We implored lunch, and it was only 11:15. She said, with the most charming politeness, that her regular clients— *ces messieurs*—arrived at twelve, and not before, but that as we were "pressed" she would prepare us a special lunch (founded on

305

an omelette) instantly. Meanwhile we could inspect her fowls, rabbits and guinea-pigs. Well, we inspected her fowls, rabbits and guinea-pigs till exactly five minutes past twelve, when *ces messieurs* began to arrive. The adorable creature had never had the least intention of serving us with a special lunch. Her one desire was not to hurt our sensitive, high-strung natures. The lunch consisted of mackerel, ham, cutlets, *fromage à la crème*, fruits and wine. I have been eating at French inns for years, and have not yet ceased to be astonished at the refined excellence of the repast which is offered in any little poky hole for a florin.

She was right about the roads. Emphatically they got worse. But we did not mind, for we had a strong wind at our hacks. The secret of happiness in such an excursion as ours is in the wind and in naught else. We bumped through some dozen villages, all exactly alike—it was a rolling pasture country—and then came to our first town, Puiseaux, whose church with its twisted spire must have been destined from its beginning to go on to a picture post card. And having taught the leading business house of Puiseaux how to brew tea, we took to the wind again, and were soon in England; that is to say, we might have been in England, judging by the hedges and ditches and the capriciousness of the road's direction, and the little occasional orchards, bridges and streams. This was not the hedgeless, severe landscape of Gaul—not a bit! Only the ancient farmhouses and the châteaux guarded by double pairs of round towers reminded us that we were not in Shropshire. The wind blew us in no time to within sight of the distant lofty spire of the great church of Pithiviers, and after staring at it during six kilomètres, we ran down into a green hollow and up into the masonry of Pithiviers, where the first spectacle we saw was a dog racing towards the church with a huge rat in his mouth. Pithiviers is one of the important towns of the department. It demands and receives respect. It has six cafés in its picturesque market square, and it specialises in lark patties. What on earth led Pithiviers to specialise in lark patties I cannot imagine. But it does. It is revered for its lark patties, which are on view everywhere. We are probably the only persons who have spent a night in Pithiviers without partaking of lark patties. We went into the hotel and at the end of the hall saw three maids sewing in the linen-room—a pleasing French sight— and, in a glass case, specimens of lark patties. We steadily and consistently refused lark patties. Still we did not starve. Not to mention lark patties, our two-and-tenpenny dinner comprised soup, boiled beef, carrots, turnips, *gnocchi*, fowl, beans, leg of mutton, cherries, strawberries and minor details. During this eternal meal, a man with a bag came vociferously into the *salle à manger*. He was selling the next day's morning paper! Chicago could not surpass that!

Largely owing to the propinquity and obstinacy of the striking clock of the great church I arose at 6 a. m. The market was already in progress. I spoke with! an official about the clock, but I could not make him see that I had got up in the middle of the night. In spite of my estimate of his clock, he good-naturedly promised me much better roads. And the promise was fulfilled. But we did not mind. For now the strong wind was against us. This altered all our relations with the universe, and transformed us into impolite, nagging pessimists; previously we had been truly delightful people.

All that day till tea-time we grumbled over a good road that wound its way through a gigantic wheat-field. True that sometimes the wheat was oats, or even a pine plantation; but, broadly speaking, the wheat was all wheat, and the vast heaving sea of it rolled up to the very sides of the road under our laggard wheels. And it was all right, and it was all being cut with two-horse McCormick reapers. We actually saw hundreds of McCormick reapers. Near and far, on all the horizons, we could detect the slow-revolving paddle of the McCormick reaper. And at least we reached Chateau Landon, against the walls of which huge waves of wheat were breaking. Chateau Landon was our destination. We meant to discover it and we did.

The little river Fusain

Château Landon is one of the most picturesque towns in France; but, as the landlady of the Red Hat said to us, "no one has yet known how to make come *messieurs*, the tourists." I should say that (except Carcassone, of course) Vezelay, in the Avalonnais, is perhaps *the* most picturesque town in all France. Chateau Landon comes near it, and is much easier to get at. On one side it rises straight up in a tremendous sheer escarpment out of the little river Fusain, in which the entire town washes its clothes. The view of the city from the wooded and murmurous valley is genuinely remarkable, and the most striking feature of the view is the feudal castle which soars with its terrific buttresses out of a thick mass of trees. Few more perfect relics of feudalism than this formidable building can exist anywhere. It will soon celebrate its thousandth birthday. In putting it to the uses of a home for the poor (Asile de St. Severin) the townsmen cannot be said to have dishonoured its old age. You climb up out of the river by granite steps cut into the escarpment and find yourself all of a sudden in the market square, which looks over a precipice. Everybody is waiting to relate to you the annals of the town since the beginning of history: how it had its own mint, and how the palace of the Mint still stands; how many an early Louis lived in the town, making laws and dispensing justice; how Louis le Gros put himself to the trouble of being buried in the cathedral there; and how the middlemen come from Fontainebleau to buy game at the market. We sought the tomb in the cathedral, but found nothing of interest there save a stout and merry priest instructing a class of young girls in the aisle. However, we did buy a pair of fowls in the market for 4s. and carried them at our saddles, all the way back to Fontainebleau. The landlady of the Red Hat asked us whether her city was not wondrous? We said it was. She asked us whether we should come again? We said we should. She asked us whether we could do anything to spread the fame of her wondrous town? We said we would do what we could.

To reach Fontainebleau it was necessary to pass through another ancient town which we have long loved, largely on account of Balzac, to wit, Nemours. After Chateau Landon, Nemours did not seem to be quite the exquisite survival that we had thought. It had almost a modern look. Thus on the afternoon of the third day we came to Fontainebleau again. And there was no wind at all. We had covered a prodigious number of miles, about as many as a fair automobile would swallow, up in two hours; in fact, eighty.

Asile De St. Séverin

IV

A TRAIN

At the present moment probably the dearest bed of its size in the world is that to be obtained on the Calais-Mediterranean express, which leaves Calais at 1.05 every afternoon and gets to Monte Carlo at 9.39 the next morning. This bed costs you between £4 and £5 if you take it from Calais, and between £3 and £4 if you take it from Paris (as I did), in addition to the first-class fare (no bagatelle that, either!), and, of course, in addition to your food. Why people should make such a terrific fuss about this train I don't know. It isn't the fastest train between Paris and Marseilles, because, though it beats almost every other train by nearly an hour, there is, in February, just one train that beats *it*—by one minute. [2] And after Marseilles it is slow. And as for comfort, well, Americans aver that it "don't cut much ice, anyway" (this is the sort of elegant diction you hear on it), seeing that it doesn't even comprise a drawingroom! car. Except when you are eating, you must remain boxed up in a compartment decidedly not as roomy as a plain, common, ordinary, decent Anglo-Saxon first-class compartment between Manchester and Liverpool.

However, it is the train of trains, outside the Siberian express, and the Chicago and Empire City Vestibule Flyer, Limited, and if decorations, silver, rare woods, plush, silk, satin, springs, cut-flowers, and white-gloved attendants will make a crack train, the International Sleeping Car Company (that bumptious but still useful association for the aggrandisement of railway directors)

---

2   In 1904.

has made one. You enter this train with awe, for you know that in entering you enrol yourself once and for ever among the élite. You know that nobody in Europe can go one better. For just as the whole of the Riviera coast has been finally specials ised into a winter playground for the rich idlers, dilettanti, hypochondriacs, and invalids of two or three continents, and into a field of manouvres for the always-accompanying gilded riff-raff and odalisques, so that train is a final instance of the specialisation of transit to suit the needs of the aforesaid plutocrats and adventurers. And whether you count yourself a plutocrat or an adventurer, you are correct, doing the correct thing, and proving every minute that money is no object, and thus realising the ideal of the age.

French railway platforms are so low that in the vast and resounding Gare de Lyon when the machine rolled magnificently in I was obliged to look up to it, whether I wanted to or not; and so I looked up reverently. The first human being that descended from it was an African; not a negro, but something nobler. He was a very big man, with a distinguished mien, and he wore the uniform, including the white gloves, of the dining-car staff. Now, I had learnt from previous excursions in this gipsy-van of the élite that the proper thing to do aboard! it is to display a keen interest in your stomach. So I approached the African and demanded the hour of dinner. He enveloped me in a glance of courteous but cold and distant disdain, and for quite five seconds, as he gazed silently down at me (I am 5ft.-8 3/4in.), he must have been saying to himself: "Here's another of 'em." I felt inclined to explain to him, as the reporter explained to the revivalist who inquired about his soul, that I was on the Press, and therefore not to be confused with the general élite. But I said nothing. I decided that if I told him that I worked as hard as he did he would probably take me for a liar as well as a plutocratic nincompoop.

Then the train went off, carrying its cargo of human parcels all wrapped up in pretty cloths and securely tied with tapes and things, and plunged with its glitter and meretricious flash down through the dark central quietudes of France. I must say that as I wandered about its shaking corridors, looking at faces and observing the deleterious effects of idleness, money, seasickness, lack of imagination, and other influences, I was impressed, nevertheless, by the bright gaudiness of the train's whole entity.

Château Landon

It isn't called a train *de luxe*; it is called a train *de grand luxe*; and though the artistic taste displayed throughout is uniformly deplorable, still it deserves the full epithet. As an example of ostentation, of an end aimed at and achieved, it will pass muster. And, lost in one of those profound meditations upon life and death and luxury which even the worst novelists must from time to time indulge in, I forgot everything save the idea of the significance of the train rushing, so complete and so self-contained, through unknown and uncared-for darkness. For me the train might have been whizzing at large through the world as the earth whizzes at large through space. Then that African came along and asserted with frigid politeness that dinner was ready.

And in the highly-decorated dining-car, where vines grew all up the walls, and the table-lamps were electric bulbs enshrined in the metallic curves of the *art nouveau*, and the fine cut flowers had probably been brought up from Grasse that morning, it happened that the African himself handed me the menu and waited on me. And when he arrived balancing the elaborate silver "contraption" containing ninety-nine varieties of *hors-d'oeuvres*, but not the particular variety I wanted, I determined that I would enter the lists with him. And, catching his eye, I said with frigid politeness: '*N'y a-t-il pas de sardines?*'

He restrained himself for his usual five seconds, and then he replied, with a politeness compared to which mine was sultry:

"*Non, monsieur.*"

And he went on to say (without speaking, but with his eyes, arms, legs, forehead, and spinal column): "Miserable European, parcel, poltroon, idler, degenerate, here I offer you ninety-and-nine *hors d'ouvres*, and you want the hundredth! You, living your unnatural and despicable existence! If I cared sufficiently I could kill every man on the train, but I don't care sufficiently! Have the goodness not to misinterpret my politeness, and take this Lyons sausage, and let me hear no more about sardines."

Hence I took the sausage and obediently ate it. I gave him best. Among the few men that I respected on that train were the engine-driver, out there in the nocturnal cold, with our lives in his pocket, and that African. He really could have killed any of us. I may never see him again. His circle of eternal energy just touched mine at the point where a tin of sardines ought to have been but was not. He was emphatically a man. He had the gestures and carriage of a monarch. Perhaps he was one, *de jure*, somewhere in the neighbourhood of Timbuctoo. For practical European, Riviera, plutocratic purposes he was a coloured waiter in the service of the International Sleeping Car Company.

V

ANOTHER TRAIN

After six hours' continuous sleep, I felt full of energy and joy. There were no servants to sadden by their incompetence; so I got up and made the tea and prepared the baths, and did many simple domestic things, the doing of which personally is the beginning of "the solution of the servant problem," so much talked about. Shall we catch the 9.25 fast or the 9.50 slow? Only my watch was going among all the clocks and watches in the flat. I looked at it from time to time, fighting against the instinct to hurry, the instinct to beat that one tiny watch in its struggle against me. Just when I was quite ready, I had to button a corsage with ten thousand buttons—toy buttons like sago, that must be persuaded into invisible nooses of thread. I turned off the gas at the meter and the electricity at the meter, and glanced 'round finally at the little museum of furniture, pictures, and prints that was nearly all I had to show in the way of spoils after forty years of living and twenty-five years of sharpshooting. I picked up the valise, and we went out on the staircase. I locked and double locked the door. (Instinct of property.) At the concierge's lodge a head stuck itself out and offered the "Mercure de France," which had just come. Strange how my pleasure in receiving new numbers never wanes! I shoved it into my left-hand pocket; in my right-hand pocket a new book was already reposing.

Out into the street, and though we had been up for an hour and a half, we were now for the first time in the light of day! Mist! It would probably be called "pearly" by some novelists; but it was like blue mousseline—diaphanous as a dancer's skirt. The damp air had the astringent, nipping quality that is so marked in November—like a friendly dog pretending to bite you. Pavements drying. The coal merchant's opposite was not yet open. The sight of his closed shutters pleased me; I owed him forty francs, and my pride might have forced me to pay him on the spot had I caught his eye. We met a cab instantly. The driver, a middle-aged parent, was in that state of waking up in which ideas have to push themselves into the brain. "Where?" he asked mechanically, after I had directed him, but before I could repeat the direction the idea had reached his brain, and he nodded. This driver was no ordinary man, for instead of taking the narrow, blocked streets, which form the shortest route, like the absurd 99 per cent. of drivers, he aimed straight for the grand boulevard, and was not delayed once by traffic in the whole journey. More pleasure in driving through the city as it woke! It was ugly, dirty—look at the dirty shirt of the waiter rubbing the door handles of the fashionable restaurant!—but it was refreshed. And the friendly dog kept on biting. Scarcely any motor-cars—all the chauffeurs were yet asleep—but the tram-cars were gliding in curves over the muddy wood, and the three horses in each omnibus had their early magnificent willingness of action, and the vegetable hawkers, old men and women, were earnestly pushing their barrows along in financial anxiety; their heads, as they pushed, were always much in advance of their feet. They moved forward with heedless fatalism; if we collided with them and spilled cauliflowers, so much the worse!

We reached the station, whose blue mousseline had evaporated as we approached it, half an hour too soon. A good horse, no stoppages, and the record had been lowered, and the driver had earned two francs in twenty-five minutes! Before the Revolution he would have had to pay a franc and a half of it in assorted taxes. Thirty minutes in a vast station, and nothing to do. We examined the platform signs. There was a train for Marseilles and Monte Carlo at 9.00 and another train for Marseilles at 9.15. Then ours at 9.25. Sometimes I go south by the "Cote d'Azur," so this morning I must inspect it, owning it. Very few people; a short, trying-to-be-proud train. The cook was busy in the kitchen of the restaurant-car—what filth and smell! Separated from him only by a partition were the flower-adorned white tables. On the platform the officials of the train, some in new uniforms, strolled and conversed. A young Frenchman dressed in the height of English fashion, with a fine-bred pink-under-white fox terrier, attracted my notice. He guessed it; became self-conscious, bridled, and called sportsmannishly to the dog. His recognition of his own vital existence had forced him into some action. He knew I was English, and that, therefore, I knew all about dogs. He made the dog jump into the car, but the animal hadn't enough sense to jump in without impatient and violent help from behind.

I never cared to have my dogs too well-bred, lest they should be as handsome and as silly as the scions of ancient families. This dog's master was really a beautiful example of perfect masculine dressing. His cap, the length of his trousers, the "roll" of the collar of his jacket—perfect! Yes, it is agreeable to see a faultless achievement. Not a woman on the train to compare to *him!* It is a fact that men are always at their sartorial best when travelling; they then put on gay colours, and give themselves a certain licence.. ... The train seemed to go off while no one was looking; no whistle, no waving of flags. It crept out. But to the minute.. ...

It is astounding the lively joy I find in staring at a railway bookstall. Men came up, threw down a sou, snatched a paper, and departed; scores of them; but I remained, staring, like a ploughman, vaguely.. ...

I was a quarter of an hour in buying the "Figaro." What decided me was the Saturday literary supplement. We mounted into our train before its toilette was finished. It smelt nice and damp. We had a compartment to ourselves. X. had one seat, I another, the "Mercure de France" a third, the "Figaro" a fourth, and the valise a fifth. Male travellers passed along the corridor and examined us with secret interest, but externally ferocious and damnatory.

Outside were two little Frenchmen of employés, palefaces, with short, straggly beards. One yawned suddenly, and then said something that the other smiled at. What diverts me is to detect the domestic man everywhere beneath the official, beneath the mere unit. I never see a porter without giving him a hearth and home, and worries, and a hasty breakfast. Then the train went, without warning, like the other, silently. I did not pick up my newspaper nor my magazine at once, nor take the new book out of my pocket. I felt so well, so full of potential energy.. . . and the friendly dog was still biting... I wanted to bathe deep in my consciousness of being alive. . . Then I read unpublished letters of de Maupassant, and a story by Matilde Serao and memoirs of Ernest Blum, and my new book. What pleasure! After all what joy I had in life! Is it not remarkable that so simple a mechanism as print, for the transmission of thought, can work so successfully!

At Melun there were teams of oxen, with the yoke on their foreheads, in the shunting-yard. Quaint, piquant, collusion of different centuries! And Melun, what a charming provincial town—to look at and pass on! I would not think of its hard narrowness, nor of its brewery.. . .

The landscape shed its mousseline, and day really began. Brilliant sunshine. We arrived. Suddenly I felt tired. I wished to sleep. I no longer tingled with the joy of life. I only remembered, rather sadly, that half an hour ago I had been a glorious and proud being.